READING MIXED SIGNALS

READING MIXED SIGNALS

Ambivalence in American Public Opinion about Government

Albert H. Cantril
and Susan Davis Cantril

Published by
WOODROW WILSON CENTER PRESS
Washington, D.C.

Distributed by
JOHNS HOPKINS UNIVERSITY PRESS
Baltimore and London

Editorial offices:
The Woodrow Wilson Center Press
One Woodrow Wilson Plaza
1300 Pennsylvania Avenue, NW
Washington, D.C. 20004-3027
Telephone 202-691-4010

Order from:
The Johns Hopkins University Press
P.O. Box 50370
Baltimore, Maryland 21211
Telephone 1-800-537-5487

2 4 6 8 9 7 5 3 1

Library of Congress Cataloging-in-Publication Data

Cantril, Albert Hadley, 1940–
    Reading mixed signals : ambivalence in American public opinion
about government / Albert H. Cantril and Susan Davis Cantril.
        p.   cm.
    Includes bibliographical references and index.
    ISBN 0-943875-92-7 (cloth : alk. paper).—ISBN 0-943875-91-9
(pbk. : alk. paper)
    1. Public opinion—United States.   2. United States—Politics and
government—Public opinion.   I. Cantril, Susan Davis.   II. Title.
HN90.P8 IN PROCESS
303.6'0973—dc21

99-16905
CIP

ABOUT THE CENTER

The Center is the living memorial of the United States of America to the nation's twenty-eighth president, Woodrow Wilson. Congress established the Woodrow Wilson Center in 1968 as an international institute for advanced study, "symbolizing and strengthening the fruitful relationship between the world of learning and the world of public affairs." The Center opened in 1970 under its own board of trustees.

In all its activities the Woodrow Wilson Center is a nonprofit, nonpartisan organization, supported financially by annual appropriations from the Congress, and by the contributions of foundations, corporations, and individuals. Conclusions or opinions expressed in Center publications and programs are those of the authors and speakers and do not necessarily reflect the views of the Center staff, fellows, trustees, advisory groups, or any individuals or organizations that provide financial support to the Center.

To the memory of
Barbara Glasier Davis

Contents

Tables and Figures

Foreword

Michael J. Lacey

The Wilson Center has published scholarly studies of many different kinds over the years, but *Reading Mixed Signals* marks its first venture into the scientific survey of American public opinion about government. Institutionally speaking this volume represents for the Center a foothold in the vast literature on the subject, and as thoughtful readers will discover, the work has a "benchmark" quality to it as well. The analysis has been carefully set within the historical context, and its questions flow from a deep knowledge of earlier research and writing in the field. Thus it engages a good deal more than the mood of the moment. It is rich in implications for those involved in the actual practice of American politics, and also for those who devote themselves to its study. Thanks are due to the Florence and John Schuman Foundation for its commitment to the long term value of the project, and especially to the authors of the work, Albert and Susan Cantril, for the imagination, insight, and painstaking effort that have gone into the job.

In an appendix to their celebrated study of relations between America's political culture and character, *Habits of the Heart: Individualism and Commitment in American Life,* Robert Bellah and his colleagues make the case that social science is not a disembodied cognitive enterprise. Rather it is a set of traditions, deeply rooted in the philosophical, humanistic, and religious history of civilization. It aims to contribute to social self understanding. When it does so successfully, it participates in the prevailing public philosophy of its time. "Social science as public philosophy," Bellah notes, "is public not just in the sense that its findings are publically available or useful to some group or institution outside the scholarly world. It is public in that it seeks to engage the public in dialogue." While it must for its integrity address the concerns of specialists and experts, it cannot stop there. It aims to transcend the boundaries of the specialist community and provide something useful to the shared concerns of an informed citizenry. Work on *Reading Mixed Signals* was undertaken in that spirit, and it is the hope of the Wilson Center as an institution devoted to knowledge in the public service that discussions of its findings will contribute to that tradition.

Michael J. Lacey is director, Division of United States Studies, Woodrow Wilson International Center for Scholars.

Preface

What should the place of government be in the life of the nation? If you turn to the public for an answer to this question, you confront a paradox in American public opinion:

> When people are asked what they think about government in general, many will say it does too many things people can do better for themselves and gets in the way of the market economy.

> But if you ask about specific activities of government, many of these *same* people will say that what government does in a host of areas should be continued, if not expanded.

If Americans who send such mixed signals about government represent a sizeable segment of the public, they could be key to any winning coalition whether at the ballot box or behind a major initiative. Whoever best captures their imagination gains an edge in the give-and-take between the Republican and Democratic Parties as well as within each party.

Signs of the apparent contradiction in public opinion have been with us for some time. Yet we have known little of what lies behind it.

Who is most likely to be ambivalent about government? And why do some express general views about government that appear to be at such odds with what they say they want government to do?

Are people ambivalent about government because of the way they size up the job it is doing? Does it have to do with their opinions about the workings of our economy, how the country should come to terms with some of its social problems, or whether the values and traditions of society are being respected? Is it because of some aspect of people's lives such as whether they are personally affected by what government does or how interested they are in what is going on in the news?

Beyond the politics are fundamental questions about public opinion itself and where it fits into our democratic process. Could ambivalence about government indicate that people lack the information they need as citizens or that they have not thought things through? In terms of the vitality of our system of government, it would be reassuring to find that being pulled in different directions in one's thinking about government is perfectly compatible with being an informed and involved citizen.

Ambivalence about government may prove to be as identifiable and per-sisting a feature of American public opinion as the gender gap or the influence of party preference on the decisions voters make. One sign pointing in this di-rection is that ambivalence about government appears to be linked to people's views on major issues more closely than many of the social and demographic characteristics often used to understand public opinion.

The seemingly conflicting sentiments expressed about government also serve as a red flag when it comes to the ways public opinion is described. They alert us to the difficulties of reporting what "the public" thinks. To say that "the public" is pro or con on an issue may slight, if not miss entirely, the fact that sometimes people are both.

Polls have been described as a snapshot at a point in time. In a sense this is correct, especially if the purpose is to gauge public reaction to an event or to track opinions on an unfolding issue.

But in another sense, a poll can be a good deal more. Individual questions in a single poll can be likened to pictures of the same subject taken simultane-ously but from different angles. If carefully designed and thoroughly analyzed, a poll can bring together the diverse perspectives that collectively make up public opinion.

This is especially the case when the topic at hand is as basic as attitudes about government. An underlying framework of public sensibility exists that has remained fairly constant over time even as issues of the day ebb and flow. Indeed, the paradox we explore here has probably been at work for more than three decades if not longer.

This study is based on 2,002 interviews conducted by telephone with a national cross section between August 22 and September 15, 1997. This period was not crowded with an international crisis, major political events, or an election campaign. It was also before the waters of public opinion were roiled by the controversy culminating in President Clinton's acquittal on the Articles of Impeachment brought against him.[1]

As the waters settle, the timing of these interviews will prove to be oppor-tune. It was a window with a clear view at what appears to be an enduring element of American public opinion about government.

---

[1] We should note there is little early evidence these events had much impact on the public's view of the institutions of government. *Washington Post* polls found public perceptions of gov-ernment after the acquittal virtually unchanged from what they were before news of the presi-dent's involvement with a White House intern. A poll in mid-February 1999 found 32 percent trust "the government in Washington" to do what is right "just about always" (3 percent) or "most of the time" (29 percent). These results are virtually unchanged from 31percent (4 per-cent + 27 percent) when the question was asked in January 1998. Similarly, approval of the job Congress is doing was at 47 percent in early 1999 compared to 46 percent in early 1998.

This book results from a set of circumstances that it was our good fortune to have come together in 1997. These acknowledgments are but a small expression of our gratitude.

Foremost is the interest of the Florence and John Schumann Foundation in the unanswered question of why so many Americans are ambivalent in their thinking about government. The Foundation's generous support has made possible the study reported here.

We are especially grateful to the Foundation's president, Bill Moyers, for the steadiness of his confidence in the project and his keen appreciation of what is involved in systematic inquiry into a complex topic. Thanks are due to Patricia McCarthy and her colleagues at the Foundation for their capable and cordial administration of the grant.

The project had a most congenial home in the Woodrow Wilson International Center for Scholars. The imagination and wide-ranging knowledge of Michael Lacey, director of the Center's Division of United States Studies, always prompted consideration of the larger issues the inquiry involved. The late Charles Blitzer, former director of the Wilson Center, was instrumental in the early stages of the study. Lee Hamilton, the Center's new director, has been very supportive of the endeavor. Susan Nugent has been at the ready with a willing and skilled hand at every turn. George Wagner's assist early on was much appreciated.

The study is much the richer for the wise counsel of Arthur H. Miller. Long a student of how Americans view their government, he alerted us to many nuances that helped sharpen the focus of the analyses. His thoughtful comments on drafts always pointed us in important directions.

The manuscript has benefited from the suggestions of Bernard Roshco. His comments helped us clarify several key points. The project also profited from early discussions with Larry Smith and toward the end from the good judgment of Calvin Kytle. We have very much valued the helpful comments of Nancy W. D. Archibald at crucial points and her encouragement from the outset.

Fieldwork for the study was carried out by Schulman, Ronca, and Bucuvalas, Inc. (SRBI), under the capable direction of John M. Boyle. Complexities in design of the study were handled with care and close attention to critical detail. In addition we appreciate the efforts of Patricia Vanderwolf, Andrew Evans, and SRBI's able interviewing staff.

We hasten to add that none of those who have been so helpful over the many months should be implicated for any of the deficiencies that remain. For those, we alone are responsible.

The conception for the project is in the tradition of two pioneers in the psychology of public opinion: Hadley Cantril, who wrote early of "general and specific attitudes," and Gordon W. Allport, whose attention to individual differences always tempered broad generalizations about the ways things come together in people's minds.

We had a superb publishing team at the Woodrow Wilson Center Press. The book came into being under the resourceful and discerning oversight of Joseph Brinley, director, and Carol Walker, senior editor. Derek Lawlor, production editor, was particularly diligent in wrestling with the many details a manuscript such as this involves. At the Johns Hopkins University Press, we commend the enterprise and interest of Henry Tom, MaryKatherine Callaway, and Mahinder Kingra.

Finally, this project would not have been possible without the 2,002 Americans who gave of their time and shared their thoughts. We hope we have reported faithfully what they collectively told us.

Albert H. Cantril
Susan Davis Cantril

Washington, D. C.

ONE

The Paradox

THE *NEW YORK TIMES*/CBS NEWS POLL REPORTED IN FEBRUARY 1996 that 60 percent of the American people thought "the government was doing things better left to businesses and individuals." It also found that, given the choice, 61 percent preferred having "a smaller government providing fewer services." Only 30 percent wanted "a bigger government providing more services."

One might conclude from these findings that the political thinking of Americans has a distinct "conservative" cast to it. But what is one to make of other findings from the same poll? These portray a public with strong "liberal" leanings.

Nearly two-thirds (64 percent) thought "the government in Washington should guarantee medical care for all people who don't have health insurance"; almost as many (63 percent) agreed "the federal government should see to it that every person who wants to work has a job"; and well over half (55 percent) thought the federal government should do more "when it comes to regulating the environment and safety practices of business."

What the poll registered were the mixed signals people often send when asked what they want from government. As a general matter, there is broad appeal to the argument that government is too big and does things better left to the private sector or to individuals themselves. Yet there is a widespread sense that what government does in concrete, specific areas is worthwhile.

We have seen these conflicting strands at work in American public opinion at decisive turns in our recent political life. Consider the following three examples.

In 1981 Ronald Reagan told the nation in his first inaugural address that "government is not the solution to our problem; government is the problem." Within weeks he presented Congress with his plans to scale back the scope of government. The foundations of what was to be called "Reaganomics" were soon put in place—without any serious challenge from congressional Democrats.

The Democrats were so cowed by Reagan's effectiveness as an advocate for reduced government that they never pressed issues to test just how much of a mandate the voters had bestowed a year earlier. Yet we know from polling at the time that the public was not fully on board with the kinds of reductions in government that were to take place.

The reason for Reagan's success with the public was that he framed his case in broad terms, stated it clearly, and repeated it often. Leaving the details of the agenda to his lieutenants (particularly in the Office of Management and Budget), he was free to roam rhetorically over the political landscape as he spoke of getting government "off our backs."

In 1991 then Governor Bill Clinton emerged on the national scene as a "new Democrat." In what would be a keynote to his administration, he spoke of people not caring "about the rhetoric of left and right and liberal and conservative. . . . They are real people, they have real problems, and they are crying desperately for someone who believes the purpose of government is to solve their problems and make progress."[1]

As the themes for his campaign for the presidency took form, Clinton made the case that major overhaul of government was necessary to make it more accountable and more efficient. Only then would it be able to address the problems of real people. He thus counteracted the Republican argument that government was the problem. Even after the defeat of his health care initiative, Clinton later would lay out a basically progressive agenda in his 1996 State of the Union address. But, in keeping with his theme of reinventing government, it was against the backdrop of his assurances that "the era of big government is over."

In 1994 congressional Republicans captured the imagination of many voters with their "Contract with America" and wrested control of the House of Representatives after four decades as the minority party. Yet, within a matter of a year after their impressive electoral gains, Republicans overplayed their hand by forcing a confrontation that shut down the federal government. The public balked when "closed" signs started appearing at government offices

---

[1] Address to the Democratic Leadership Council, Cleveland, May 6, 1991, as quoted in Stanley B. Greenberg, *Middle Class Dreams: The Politics and Power of the New American Majority* (New York: Times Books, 1995), 211. See also chapters 7 and 8 for Greenberg's account of how the message of the 1992 campaign came together.

across the country. Two wires had crossed in the circuitry of public opinion. The Republicans and the public were reminded that acting on an ideological antipathy toward government can have everyday consequences when popular services are put at risk.

These seemingly inconsistent messages in public opinion about government were picked up early on in a study just before the 1964 presidential election. The election will be remembered for bringing ideological divisions in American public opinion into sharper focus than many elections before or since. When Senator Barry Goldwater was nominated by the Republicans to oppose incumbent Lyndon Johnson, the line between "left" and "right" in American politics was clearly drawn.

Goldwater broke with the centrist Republicanism of Dwight Eisenhower and Richard Nixon. He was a fierce opponent of federal government involvement in matters of social policy, including racial integration. Most importantly, he framed his advocacy in essentially ideological terms as he popularized what it meant to be a "conservative." In contrast, Johnson's years in the Senate and White House showed him to be a pragmatic builder of coalitions. He went into the 1964 campaign having just secured congressional passage of the War on Poverty and the Civil Rights Act of 1964, evidence of the kind of activist government that Goldwater abhorred.

It was in this charged atmosphere that surveys conducted in September and October 1964 by Lloyd Free and Hadley Cantril revealed the mixed messages people were sending: one at the level of opinion about government *in general,* one at the level of opinion about *specific things* government actually does.

They asked whether people agreed or disagreed with a series of statements that picked up on the rhetoric of those arguing that the federal government should get out of areas seen as better handled closer to home or by the market economy. Answers to these questions were combined to create what Free and Cantril called the "ideological spectrum." They then asked whether people supported or opposed specific programs being run by the federal government or under consideration by the Congress. Answers to these questions were combined in what was called the "operational spectrum."[2]

They found that 50 percent of respondents could be described as "conservative" in general ideological terms, but 65 percent tended to be "liberal" when it came to specific government activities (table 1.1).

---

[2] Lloyd A. Free and Hadley Cantril, *The Political Beliefs of Americans* (New Brunswick: Rutgers University Press, 1967). See table A.1 in appendix A for questions asked in the 1964 study, the results, and how responses were combined for the "ideological spectrum" and "operational spectrum."

Table 1.1

Ideological and Operational Views about Government
(from Free-Cantril 1964 Study)

	Ideological spectrum		Operational spectrum	
Completely conservative	30%	} 50%	7%	} 14%
Predominantly conservative	20		7	
Middle of the road	34		21	
Predominantly liberal	12	} 16	21	} 65
Completely liberal	4		44	
	100%		100%	

What was especially striking about these results was that almost half
(46 percent) of those qualifying as "conservative" on the ideological spectrum
also qualified as "liberals" on the operational spectrum (table 1.2). These findings led Free and Cantril to conclude that a sizeable segment of the American
public could be described as "ideological conservatives" but also as "operational liberals."

THE NEED FOR A NEW LOOK

There has been little systematic exploration of this apparent paradox in
public opinion about government since the 1964 study in spite of its
potential significance in understanding our evolving political tradition.[3] Although the paradox has shown up in polls from time to time, trend lines have
not been kept to track it over the years.

To fill this void in our understanding it is necessary to focus on the different mixes of general and specific views people have about government.
When this is done it is possible to address many of the questions for which we
need answers:

• How many Americans are ambivalent when they think about
government? On the one hand, how many worry about government's

---

[3] An important exception is Stanley Feldman and John Zaller, "The Political Culture of
Ambivalence: Ideological Responses to the Welfare State," *American Journal of Political Science*
36 (February 1992): 268–307.

Table 1.2

Views of Government at Operational Level among Those Holding
Different Ideological Views (from Free-Cantril 1964 study)

	Ideological spectrum		
	Conservative	Middle of the road	Liberal
Operational spectrum			
Liberal	46%	78%	90%
Middle of the road	28	18	9
Conservative	26	4	1
	100%	100%	100%

Note: As in most tables in this report, percentages for different subgroups
appear in columns. Thus, in this table, 46% of those described as "conservative"
on the ideological spectrum qualify as "liberal" on the operational spectrum.

scope and power as a general matter *even as* they think many of its
specific activities should be continued or expanded? On the other
hand, how many are comfortable with government's scope and power
as a general matter *even as* they think some of what it does should be
scaled back?

• Who is most likely to be ambivalent in their thinking about government and who is least likely?

• What lies behind ambivalence?

Does it depend on views of how well government is handling things?

Do issues in public discussion affect whether or not people are ambivalent about government? Do their opinions about problems in their
own communities and beyond affect their views of when government
should pitch in and when it should stay out? Is ambivalence influenced
by worry about declining respect for values of personal responsibility or
the intensity of religious beliefs?

Are views about government affected by how well people feel they are
doing in their own lives or how much they think its activities bear on
them personally?

• What difference do ambivalent feelings about government make
in terms of how involved people get in political matters, both as voters
and as citizens between elections? Does ambivalence affect the intensity
with which opinions are held and expressed? Both considerations could

have a direct bearing on which voices get heard in our politics—and which do not.

Answers to these questions may tell us a lot about how events will unfold in the political life of the nation in coming months and early into the twenty-first century. Those with mixed minds about government will be at the center of the political arena as advocates for competing visions of government reach out for public support.

While the commitment of core constituencies cannot be taken for granted, the margins of victory in national elections usually come from persuading those in the middle. Much the same obtains between elections as coalitions come together on different sides of major issues facing the country.

As fundamental is competition among advocates *within* the right and *within* the left over future directions. For years the divisions were on the left. Diverse interests pursued their agendas regarding the environment, civil rights, the status of women, civil liberties, or gay rights. They often found it difficult to join forces behind a larger vision.

More recently, divisions have surfaced on the right as well. General agreement on matters of fiscal policy used to hold things together. Now comity within the ranks is often tested as concerns central to conservative Christians are pushed with extraordinary intensity and grassroots organizing. Added to that are tensions of reconciling a pro-business tradition with the populism of a Patrick Buchanan.

In addition to possible insight into forces that may shape our political life, listening closely to the conflicting messages people seem to send about government can help us better understand the nature of public opinion itself. We have an opportunity to build on earlier research and to extend our understanding on a number of critical issues.

Is ambivalence in thinking about government intrinsic to public opinion? Or, is it a reflection of something else, such as how much people know about politics and government, how closely they follow the news, or their personal experience with government?

Do ambivalent views about government help us understand the limits of broad concepts such as "conservative" and "liberal" in characterizing the state of American public opinion on specific issues? Similarly, what does ambivalence tell us about the difficulties of inferring a person's views on one issue from knowing their thinking on another issue?

In short, is ambivalence about government integral to the way many people view political matters?

OVERVIEW

Our inquiry into ambivalence begins in chapter 2 by describing ways in which opinions about what government should do often seem to be out of sync with more general opinions about government. We also estimate the proportions of the American people whose views reflect ambivalence about government. In addition we look at how closely descriptions people give of their own political views correspond to their opinions about when government should and should not be part of the picture.

Chapter 3 asks how the public's views about government performance bear on ambivalence. It explores whether ambivalence about government results primarily from assessments of how well government is seen to be handling things or whether we need to dig deeper for an explanation. The chapter also gauges how strongly people feel about the balance that should be struck between federal, state, and local government and whether, if at all, the issue relates to ambivalence about government.

Chapter 4 explores how ambivalence about government relates to ways people think about issues facing the country ranging from the workings of the market to matters such as race and poverty. We also touch upon worries that traditional norms regarding moral behavior are breaking down. In addition we look at public opinion on issues of particular concern to conservative Christians.

In chapter 5 we turn to aspects of everyday life that may affect views of government. We look at how people see things going in their own lives; their sense of their own personal financial security and views of society's equities and inequities; how much people feel they are affected personally by what government does; how closely they follow news and public affairs; how much they may know about the way government works; and the intensity of their religious beliefs and practices.

Chapter 6 examines how the many facets of opinion covered in preceding chapters come together in people's minds and weighs how much each contributes to ambivalence in thinking about government. Some considerations are especially important in explaining why some people are ambivalent. Other possible explanations for ambivalence turn out to be surprisingly unimportant.

What political consequences flow from ambivalence about government? Chapter 7 looks at how ambivalence affects the likelihood of voting, of supporting a political party, of being a political independent, and of casting ballots for candidates of different parties on election day. To conclude we return to the fact that, because of the paradox in public opinion, the nation's political debate seems to take place on two levels—one the rhetorical and symbolic, the other the concrete and specific.

NOTE ABOUT THE REPORTING OF RESULTS

A brief word is needed about the presentation of the findings of this study. In addition to the tables that appear in the chapters ahead, there are references from time to time to tables in appendix A. These supplementary tables expand on certain points, include findings that tell more of the story, and report related findings from other studies.

Critical to appreciating the results reported here is how matters were presented to respondents in the survey. The full questionnaire is included in appendix B. The numbers of the questions upon which tables are based are indicated in the tables.

In addition to reporting results regarding individual questions, there are times when responses to questions on a common topic have been combined in an overall measure (or "index"). By bringing together different aspects of opinion on an important issue, it is possible to increase the reliability with which opinion on that issue is gauged. Appendix C describes how these indices were built.

Once the several possible explanations of ambivalence are identified, the question becomes which are most important in accounting for ambivalence. Appendix D describes the multivariate analyses that make it possible to answer that question and close the circle.

TWO

Gauging the Public's Ambivalence about Government

T HE MIXED SIGNALS AMERICANS ARE SENDING WHEN THEY SPEAK about government reflect a tension inherent in our political tradition. In one form or another, the question animating our politics from the early days of the republic has been whether government is encroaching on individual liberties or is needed to safeguard those liberties.

To ensure that major themes of this debate were reflected in this study, we turned to the rich literature that places today's public discussion in the framework of our evolving political traditions.[1] We also drew extensively on sources such as news accounts of competing budgetary and related priorities of the White House, congressional Republicans, and congressional Democrats and speeches and columns of those promoting various points of view.

---

[1] Especially helpful have been: Samuel H. Beer, "In Search of a New Public Philosophy," in Anthony King, ed., *The New American Political System* (Washington, D.C.: American Enterprise Institute, 1978): 5–44; Samuel H. Beer, *To Make a Nation: The Rediscovery of American Federalism* (Cambridge, Mass.: Harvard University Press, 1993); E. J. Dionne Jr., *They Only Look Dead: Why Progressives Will Dominate the Next Political Era* (New York: Simon & Schuster, 1996); Jeff Faux, *The Party's Not Over: A New Vision for the Democrats* (New York: Basic Books, 1996); Alonzo L. Hamby, "The Democratic Moment: FDR to LBJ," in Peter B. Kovler, ed., *Democrats and the American Idea* (Washington, D.C.: Center for National Policy Press, 1992): 247–84; William Kristol, "The Politics of Liberty, the Sociology of Virtue," in Lamar Alexander and Chester E. Finn Jr., eds., *The New Promise of American Life* (Indianapolis, Ind.: Hudson Institute, 1995); James Leach and William P. McKenzie, *A Newer World: The Progressive Republican Vision of America* (Lanham, Md.: Madison Books, 1988); Paul E. Peterson, *The Price of Federalism* (Washington, D.C.: Brookings Institution Press, 1995, A Twentieth Century Fund Book); and William A. Schambra, "The Roots of the American Public Philosophy," in Robert B. Hawkins Jr., ed., *American Federalism: A New Partnership for the Republic* (San Francisco, Calif.: Institute for Contemporary Studies, 1982).

9

A brief word at the outset is needed about "ambivalence," a term that appears throughout this book. As used here, it refers to the situation in which a person simultaneously holds what seem to be conflicting sentiments about something. This does not mean that the individual is unable to make choices or express sensible opinions on issues.

Ambivalence suggests that more is involved than whether a person's views are "consistent" or "inconsistent." Those terms may suggest the presence or absence of a logical connection among opinions that should somehow be self-evident. Yet we know from earlier research that what seems consistent for one person may appear inconsistent to another.[2] We also know that the ways people work things through in their minds can vary from subject to subject, can be influenced by the extent to which values may be in conflict, and can be affected by assumptions that have been built up through past experience.[3]

MIXED SIGNALS: A FIRST LOOK AT THE FINDINGS

The paradox we are addressing in this study has to do with public opinion about what the place of government should be in the nation's life. We are dealing with three fundamental matters: the appropriate scope of what the government does; the amount of power it should have; and the balance that should be struck between the public and private sectors.

When asked about these matters in *general* terms, those interviewed in this study are reserved in their endorsement of the power and scope of government:

- A plurality of 45 percent think government "does too many things people could do better for themselves."[4]
- About as many think the federal government has too much power (42 percent) as think it has the right amount of power (46 percent). Seven percent say government does not have enough power; 5 percent are not sure or choose not to answer.

---

[2] The field of opinion research has learned much from social psychology, which wrestled with this problem in the 1950s and 1960s. An overview of this work is found in Robert P. Abelson, E. Aronson, W. J. McGuire, T. M. Newcomb, M. J. Rosenberg, and P. H. Tannenbaum, eds., *Theories of Cognitive Consistency: A Sourcebook* (Chicago: Rand McNally, 1968).

[3] See Herbert McClosky and John Zaller, *The American Ethos: Public Attitudes Toward Capitalism and Democracy* (Cambridge, Mass.: Harvard University Press, 1984); Paul M. Sniderman, Richard A. Brody, and Philip E. Tetlock, et al., *Reasoning and Choice: Explorations in Political Psychology* (New York: Cambridge University Press, 1991); and Albert H. Cantril, ed., *Psychology, Humanism, and Scientific Inquiry: The Selected Essays of Hadley Cantril* (New Brunswick, N.J.: Transaction Books, 1988).

[4] This quote, part of the question asked of respondents, is from one of the "principles" in the preamble to the 1996 Republican platform.

• While a majority of 56 percent think government ought to step in to make sure corporations act responsibly, a sizeable minority of 35 percent say there is too much regulation (table 2.1).

Asked about government in more *specific* terms, however, Americans want the government involved in a variety of areas. This is shown by the overwhelming proportions who think specific activities of government should be funded at current levels or that spending should be increased.[5]

The mix of activities included in the survey attempted to satisfy four criteria. First, the activities had to cover diverse public concerns such as health, education, employment, and the environment. Second, to the extent possible, they had to be part of the current debate, either as major bills before Congress or as key initiatives of the Clinton administration. Third, the mix had to include activities that might bear on the lives of low-, moderate-, and upper-income households. And fourth, each activity had to represent a substantial national commitment in addressing a major issue facing the country.

Ten activities were selected. For each, we describe how it was presented to respondents (material in quotes) and summarize briefly political debate surrounding it.

• *"Enforcing standards for clean air."* At the time of interviewing, the immediate question was whether the Environmental Protection Agency (EPA) should issue more stringent guidelines regarding air quality. EPA was vigorously opposed by Republicans and business groups, which claimed the costs of compliance would outweigh any benefit to the environment.

• *"Job training for low-income people who want to work and need skills."* Congressional Republicans wanted to consolidate job training programs. They had voted for a reduction in spending in 1995 and called for cuts in funding for summer jobs in 1996. Meanwhile, job training was part of the struggle over welfare reform. More than one presidential adviser on welfare policy ultimately resigned in part because they felt job training had been slighted in the bill that President Clinton signed.

---

[5] Respondents were asked whether they thought the amount of money the federal government spends "should be increased, kept at the present level, decreased, or ended altogether." The sequence of the questions was rotated to avoid possible bias from always starting with the same activity.

Table 2.1

Views about Government in General

Question: When it comes to the federal government, do you think it does too many things people could do better for themselves, it should do more given the problems the country faces, or that the government has struck about the right balance in what it is doing?

Does too many things	45%
Struck the right balance	21
Should do more	23
Depends	1
Don't know	11
	100%

Question: All things considered, when it comes to what is best for the country, do you think the federal government has about the right amount of power, too much power, or not enough?[a]

About right amount	46%
Too much	42
Not enough	7
Don't know	5
	100%

Question: Which statement do you agree with most?

Government regulation of business is needed to make sure corporations act responsibly.	56%[b]
Feel very strongly	38%
Feel not too strongly	18
In general, there is too much government regulation of business in this country.	35%
Feel very strongly	27%
Feel not too strongly	8
Depends	2
Don't know	7
	100%

[a] Two versions of this question were used to protect against bias being introduced by the order in which alternatives were presented. A slight difference was produced by the two versions of the question, but not sufficient to preclude combining results from the two forms in these percentages (see appendix B, Q.19).

[b] This subtotal indicates the sum of those feeling "very strongly" and "not too strongly."

[Q.9b;12;19]

- *"Keeping dangerous consumer products off the market."* The Consumer Product Safety Commission, though less visible than some regulatory bodies, is always part of the give-and-take regarding how to balance government and market forces in determining what is in the public's interest.
- *"Health care for low-income families through the Medicaid program."* Medicaid became contentious immediately after the 1994 election when Republicans in the House passed a budget for 1995 that called for cuts. Meanwhile the Clinton administration pushed for more funding. Revision of eligibility standards for Medicaid was also part of the argument over welfare reform. (This debate was distinct from that over Medicare.)
- *"Head Start, a program for preschool children from low-income families."* Reductions in spending (below then current levels) were part of the 1995 Republican agenda and vigorously resisted by the White House and congressional Democrats.
- *"Medical research on such things as cancer, AIDS, and heart disease."* While federal science programs have enjoyed considerable bipartisan support over the years, the 1996 Republican platform gave voice to two desired changes in the way the system works: de-emphasizing governmental involvement in favor of the private sector and using the tax code to foster research.
- *"Programs to help finance college education."* As Baby Boomers face tuition bills for their children, this is an issue that increasingly consumes the attention of politicians. Republicans and Democrats have been divided over whether to increase or decrease funding for Pell grants that provide scholarships to low-income students. They also have been divided on how loans should be provided to students and how to handle tax credits for education.
- *"Helping low-income families afford low-rent apartments."* The issues here were the level of funding and possible tax incentives that would make housing available to low-income families unable to pay for even low-rent apartments. Republicans wanted to reduce funding and limit tax incentives while the Clinton budget sought increases.
- *"Financial assistance to help poor school districts pay teachers' salaries."* Cuts in this area were agreed to by the White House and the GOP in 1996, even as the Clinton administration stressed the importance of education.
- *"Making sure working conditions in factories and plants are safe."* Cutting back on regulatory activities of the Occupational Safety and

Table 2.2

Support for Specific Activities of the Federal Government

	Increase	Keep at present level	Decrease	End	Don't know	Total
Job training for low-income people	68%	23%	4%	2%	2%	99%
Medical research	67	27	3	1	2	100
Teachers' salaries in poor school districts	61	26	6	4	4	101
Financing college education	59	30	6	3	2	100
Clean air standards	50	37	8	2	3	100
Head Start	50	36	5	5	3	99
Safe working conditions	45	43	6	2	4	100
Consumer product safety	45	37	8	5	4	99
Medicaid	40	40	11	4	5	100
Housing assistance for low-income families	34	42	14	5	5	100

Note: Unlike most tables in this report, this table should be read across. Percentages may add to other than 100 percent due to rounding.

[Q.4a–j]

Health Administration was a Republican priority in 1996 and was vigorously opposed by the White House and the congressional Democrats.

More than three out of four of those polled think each of these ten activities should receive continued or increased funding. At least half think spending should be increased for six of the activities. Most consistently popular with the public are job training and medical research (table 2.2).

What is particularly striking in these percentages is that the highest level of opposition to any of these activities amounts to only one in five: the 19 percent who think housing assistance for low-income families should be either cut back or ended. A larger proportion actually supports an increase.

SORTING OUT THE SIGNALS

To understand the ambivalence in public opinion revealed in these findings, we needed ways to summarize the pattern of responses. Accordingly we constructed an index of attitudes toward government in general that took into account responses to the three questions about governmental scope and power appearing in table 2.1. A similar index was built that took into account opinions about the ten specific governmental activities.[6]

Attitudes toward Government in General

Depending upon the mix of the attitudes expressed, respondents are counted as being "critical" or "supportive" of government as follows:

Question content	"Critical"	"Supportive"
What federal government does	Does things people could do better for themselves	Should do more or has struck the right balance
Power of federal government	Has too much power	Has right amount of power or should have more
Regulation of business	Too much government regulation of business	Regulation needed to ensure corporations act responsibly

Based on their responses to the three questions, each respondent fell into one of three categories:

Mostly critical: Critical of government in two or three of the
questions   38%
Mostly supportive: Support government in two or three of the
questions   51%
Neither critical nor supportive: Voice conflicting views in two
questions and have no opinion in the third; or have no opinion
in two or three questions   11%
     100%

This division of opinion differs from that found in the Free-Cantril 1964 survey in which 50 percent were characterized as ideological conservatives, 34 percent as middle of the road, and 16 percent as ideological liberals. One

---

[6] See appendix C for further discussion of these and other indices.

reason for the differences is that the approaches taken in framing questions were not the same. The 1964 study presented a series of statements with which respondents could agree or disagree. This study, in contrast, presented two contending statements and asked people which of the two came closer to their own view.

We chose this balanced-alternative approach because some people can be reluctant to disagree with an interviewer who has put forward a single idea without an opposing point of view. We wanted respondents to face alternatives that are, in the words of Herbert McClosky and Alida Brill, "fundamental and divergent" but also "equally plausible and socially acceptable."[7] In addition spelling out two alternatives gives the respondent more cues as to what a question is really asking.

The 38 percent emerging in this study as "mostly critical" is in line with a trend found in the biennial National Election Study. The proportion thinking "the government in Washington is getting too powerful for the good of the country" has fluctuated from 30 percent in 1964 to a high of 50 percent in 1976. It was 40 percent in the last sounding in 1992 (see table A.2 in appendix A).

We should note that questions asked here regarding "general attitudes toward government" are distinct from questions about trust in government. Much has been written about declining public trust in government.[8] Measures pollsters often use regarding trust deal with concerns such as whether government can be counted on to do what is right, whether those who work for government are honest, and whether government wastes taxpayers' money.

While questions about trust in government can be useful for many purposes, they are less suited for purposes of this study. This is because the "general attitudes" toward government pertinent to ambivalence deal with the issue of what government should do. Questions about trust, on the other hand, focus less on government's scope and size than matters such as its honesty and frugality.

---

[7] Herbert McClosky and Alida Brill, *Dimensions of Tolerance: What Americans Believe about Civil Liberties* (New York: Russell Sage, 1983), 26–27. We should also note that questions in the 1964 study contained provocative phrases such as "governmental welfare programs" and "if the government would only keep its hands off."

[8] Public trust in government took a dramatic downturn in the late 1960s and early 1970s. For a discussion of what lies behind these trends, see Arthur H. Miller, "Political Issues and Trust in Government: 1964–1970," *American Political Science Review* 68 (1974): 951–72; and Arthur H. Miller and Stephen A. Borrelli, "Confidence in Government during the 1980s," *American Politics Quarterly* 19 (April 1991): 147–73; and Arthur H. Miller, "Is Confidence Rebounding?" *Public Opinion* 6 (1983): 16–20.

Table 2.3

Number of Specific Activities of the Federal Government for Which Funding
Should Be Continued at Present Level or Increased

Number of specific activities	Percent	Cumulative percent
10 of 10	45%	45%
9 of 10	22	67
8 of 10	13	80
7 of 10	7	87
6 of 10	5	92
5 of 10	3	95
4 of 10	1	96
3 of 10	2	98
2 of 10	1	99
1 of 10	*a	99
None of 10	1	100
	100%	

[a] Designates less than half a percent.

Opinion about Specific Activities of Government

The index regarding opinion about specific activities of government was built
by counting the number of times a respondent said "the amount of money the
federal government spends" for an activity should be continued at the present
level or increased. Scores ranged from 10 for the person wanting to continue
or expand all ten activities to zero for those wanting spending for all ten activities either decreased or ended altogether.

Forty-five percent of those questioned want to see all ten activities continued at their current level or increased. Another 22 percent want nine of the
ten activities continued. Few disagree: 92 percent of the sample express support for half or more of the ten activities (table 2.3).

Views of Government: General versus Specific

We start with people who are "mostly critical" of government in general terms
and determine how they differ in the number of specific activities they think
should be continued or not. This provides a measure of ambivalence in the
criticism of government. Those critics who back fewer activities show *less* ambivalence about government since their specific views are mirroring their gen-

Figure 2.1

General versus Specific Views among Those "Mostly Critical"

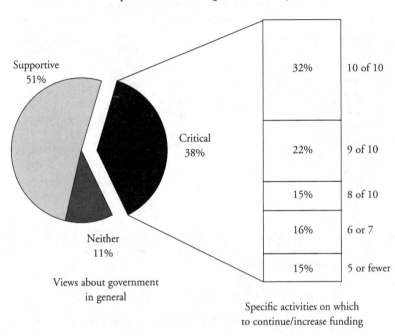

Views about government
in general

Specific activities on which
to continue/increase funding

eral views. Critics who approve of more activities express *greater* ambivalence since their specific views are more at odds with their general views.

We find 32 percent of those "mostly critical" want to see spending continued or increased for all ten specific activities about which they were asked. Another 22 percent endorse nine of the ten. Only 15 percent back half or fewer of the activities (figure 2.1).

Ambivalence among those "mostly supportive" of government can also be gauged by the number of specific activities of government they want continued or not continued. The more activities they back, the *less* their specific views are out of line with their general attitudes about government. The fewer activities they back, the *greater* their ambivalence.

Fifty-six percent of those "mostly supportive" of government in general terms also want continuation or expansion of all ten activities. Another 21 percent back nine of the ten (figure 2.2).

For many of the tables and analyses reported in this book, we have summarized findings in terms of five ways of thinking about government. We start with the distinction in general terms between respondents who are "mostly critical" and "mostly supportive." We then differentiate those backing nine or

Figure 2.2

General versus Specific Views among Those "Mostly Supportive"

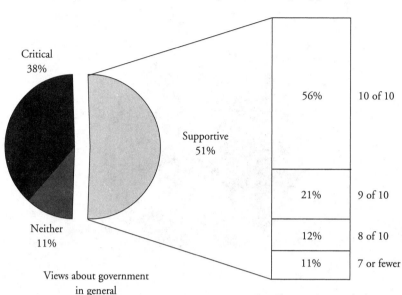

Views about government
in general

Specific activities on which
to continue/increase funding

ten specific activities from those approving eight or fewer.[9] When these two steps are taken, most respondents fall into one of four groups as follows:

	General view of government	Specific activities of government backed
"Steady Critic"	Mostly critical	8 or fewer
"Ambivalent Critic"	Mostly critical	9 or 10
"Ambivalent Supporter"	Mostly supportive	8 or fewer
"Steady Supporter"	Mostly supportive	9 or 10

A fifth group includes respondents whose general views about government have not come together one way or the other. Thus they cannot be described

---

[9] The distinction between those backing nine or ten and eight or fewer activities takes into account the distribution of respondents in terms of the number of specific activities they think should be continued or expanded. We considered alternative ways of differentiating among respondents and concluded this was the most reasonable approach. See appendix C for further discussion.

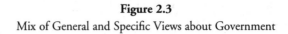

Figure 2.3
Mix of General and Specific Views about Government

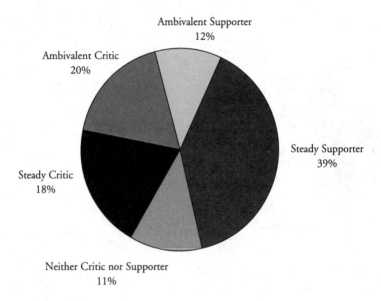

as "mostly critical" or "mostly supportive." Not being able to determine their general views about government, it is not possible to compare their views with their level of support for specific activities as a measure of their ambivalence. As a consequence this "neither critic nor supporter" group (11 percent of those interviewed) is excluded from most analyses of ambivalence that follow. We look at the 89 percent of respondents who are "steady" or "ambivalent" as critics or supporters of government.

The profile of the public that results appears in figure 2.3. We see that:

• Critics of government are split about evenly between those who are "steady" (18 percent) and "ambivalent" (20 percent).
• Supporters of government are less divided in their views than critics. Steady Supporters outnumber Ambivalent Supporters by more than three to one (39 percent versus 12 percent).
• Overall, about one-third (32 percent) of respondents may be considered "ambivalent" in their views about government one way or the other compared to more than half (57 percent) who are "steady" in their criticism or their support.

WHO IS AMBIVALENT ABOUT GOVERNMENT?
WHO IS NOT?

There are modest differences between men and women in the mix of their views about government. The most notable is that men are somewhat more likely to be Steady Critics than women.

Most striking in the diversity of public opinion about government, however, are differences by age. A higher proportion of Steady Critics is found among those over 60 than in any other age group. Conversely, half of those under 30 are Steady Supporters. Put another way, the average (mean) age of Steady Critics is 50 but for Steady Supporters is 41.

The relationship between age and views about government is potentially important for several reasons. First, the correspondence is direct: the older the respondent, the greater the chance of finding a Steady Critic; the younger the respondent, the greater the chance of finding a Steady Supporter. Note that the trend is unbroken. Had one or more of the intermediate age categories varied from the pattern, it would indicate that the effect of age had been weakened by some other social or demographic factor that has a bearing on how people think about government (table 2.4).

Second, views about government vary more by age *within* the sexes than they do *between* the sexes:

• Among women there are marked differences by age. Sixty-one percent of women under 30 are in the Steady Supporter column, compared to 43 percent of women from 30 to 39 and 39 percent of women from 40 to 59. Only 25 percent of women 60 and over are Steady Supporters. Conversely, a higher proportion of Steady Critics is found among older women than younger.
• Age differences among men are less pronounced, although younger men are more likely to be Steady Supporters and less likely to be Steady Critics (see table A.3 in appendix A).

Third, there is the possibility that these differences by age portend a shift in the center of political gravity in the country. Over time public opinion about government can change for many reasons. Events, issues of national security, and the state of the economy can all leave their mark. So, too, can one generation that may lean one way on the big issues succeeding an older generation in which a different view of things prevails. While it is true that younger people have yet to be tested in many of life's trials, there is little evidence that

Table 2.4

Mix of General and Specific Views about Government by Different Social and Demographic Groups

	Mostly critical		Mostly supportive			
	Steady Critic	Ambivalent Critic	Ambivalent Supporter	Steady Supporter	Neither critic nor supporter	Total
ALL	18%	20%	12%	39%	11%	100%
By sex						
Men	22	21	12	37	7	99
Women	13	19	12	41	14	99
By age						
18 to 29	10	23	11	50	6	100
30 to 39	14	18	13	42	13	100
40 to 59	21	20	11	37	11	99
60 and over	25	22	11	29	13	100
By region						
Northeast/ Mid-Atlantic	14	22	9	45	10	100
South	19	21	13	36	11	100
Midwest	16	23	13	35	13	100
Southwest/ Mountain	26	17	11	37	9	100
Far west	15	16	14	44	11	100
By size of locality						
Large city	13	16	13	44	14	100
Suburb	14	21	13	44	9	101
Small city/town	19	20	11	39	11	100
Rural area	23	25	10	31	11	100
By household income						
Under $30,000	14	20	11	42	13	100
$30,000–$49,999	19	22	12	37	11	101
$50,000–$74,999	20	21	12	41	6	100
$75,000 and over	22	20	13	42	4	101
By education						
Less than high school	12	20	15	35	18	100
High school graduate/GED/ technical	18	22	13	39	9	101
Some college	20	21	9	39	11	100
College graduate and beyond	20	18	12	44	7	101
By union member in household	12	17	13	48	10	100
By race[a]						
White	20	22	12	36	10	100
Black	3	13	5	67	13	101
By ethnicity						
Latino/Hispanic	8	13	15	50	14	100

Note: Percentages here should be read across. For example, 22 percent of men are Steady Critics, 21 percent are Ambivalent Critics, etc.

[a] Not enough cases of other races for reliable percentages.

there is something intrinsic to aging that leads people to become more conservative or more liberal as they grow older.[10]

Important differences emerge among regions of the country. There is a bicoastal cast to those who are Steady Supporters of government in contrast to a higher proportion of Steady Critics in the southwest and mountain states.[11] As the population becomes more dense, people are more likely to be supporters, and especially Steady Supporters. A higher proportion of critics, steady and ambivalent, is found in less densely populated areas (table 2.4).

The mix of views about government seems little affected by household income. A difference worth noting is that the less affluent are unlikely to be Steady Critics, although they are not much more likely than others to be Steady Supporters. Also noteworthy is the high proportion of Steady Supporters among respondents in households with a member of a labor union.

Two-thirds (67 percent) of African Americans are Steady Supporters as are half (50 percent) of Latinos.

In chapter 5 we look closely at the effect formal education and knowledge about the governmental process may have on views about government. We preview some of that discussion by noting that the greatest difference among educational groups is that those with less than a high school education are more likely than others to be neither supporters nor critics of government.

AMBIVALENCE AND SELF-DESCRIBED POLITICAL PHILOSOPHY

Political analysts have pointed to a trend toward "conservatism" on the part of the American public. There is evidence in the National Election Study that increasing numbers are calling themselves "conservatives." Yet, the trend from 1972 through 1996 indicates this increase has not been accompanied by a corresponding drop in the percent calling themselves "liberals." Conservative gains appear to have come mostly as fewer people have called themselves middle of the road or said they had not thought that much about it.[12]

In this study, when people were asked to describe their "views on most political matters," they divided as follows:[13]

---

[10] For a thorough examination of these issues, see William Mayer, *The Changing American Mind: How and Why American Public Opinion Changed between 1960 and 1988* (Ann Arbor: University of Michigan Press, 1992), 141–89.

[11] See appendix E for the states included in each region.

[12] See table A.4 in appendix A for trends in the National Election Study from 1972 to 1996.

[13] As a check on possible bias from the order of response categories, two forms of the question were used. Half of the sample was presented a continuum running from "very conservative" to "very liberal." For the other half the continuum ran from "very liberal" to "very conservative." The figures here are the combined percentages from both forms (see appendix B).

Very conservative	11%	39%
Moderately conservative	28	
Middle of the road	39	
Moderately liberal	14	17
Very liberal	3	
Not sure	4	
	99%	

While most respondents describe themselves as conservative, middle of the road, or liberal, it is difficult to infer too much about the direction of their thinking about government. Earlier research counsels caution in drawing hard and fast conclusions from such self-descriptions.[14]

Consider the following:

• Thirty-three percent of those who call themselves conservatives think that the federal government "should do more given the problems the country faces" or that "government has struck about the right balance in what it is doing." On the other hand, 34 percent of self-described liberals think the federal government "does too many things people could do better for themselves."

• Asked about the power of the federal government, 40 percent of conservatives think it has about the right amount or not enough power. Conversely, 27 percent of liberals think it has too much.

• On the matter of government's regulation of business, 42 percent of conservatives think "regulation is needed to make sure corporations act responsibly." On the other hand, 21 percent of liberals think there is "too much government regulation in this country."

Furthermore, in terms of the mix of general and specific attitudes toward government, there is often little correspondence between the terms people use to describe their views and what they think about government:

• Thirty-four percent of those who call themselves "very conservative" are mostly supportive of government (23 percent being Steady Supporters and 11 percent Ambivalent Supporters). Another 23 per-

---

[14] Studies have shown that many people are unable to say which is the "conservative" or "liberal" side of an issue. See Theresa E. Levitin and Warren E. Miller, "Ideological Interpretations of Presidential Elections," *American Political Science Review* 73 (1979): 751–71.

cent of these "very conservative" people are critics of government, but ambivalent in their criticism.

• While 26 percent of "moderate conservatives" are Steady Critics, just as many (27 percent) are Steady Supporters.

• "Middle of the road" respondents are most likely to be Steady Supporters (59 percent), but nearly one in three (31 percent) are critical of government in some way.

• While 71 percent of "liberals" are supportive of government, 23 percent are critical in some degree (table 2.5).

Putting it another way, the term "conservative" fails to capture the general attitudes toward government of about one-third of those who use it to describe their political views. The term "liberal" does not convey the views of government of about a quarter of those who identify with it.

These findings are consistent with considerable evidence that shows many people do not organize their views on political matters in ways easily described by the conservative-liberal continuum.[15] It cannot be assumed that because people may be for one idea that sounds "conservative" they will necessarily be against an idea that has a "liberal" cast to it and vice versa.[16] Moreover, the values and concepts people often associate with the two labels are so disparate that, at least in public opinion terms, the debate between "conservatism" and "liberalism" is not even about a common set of questions. That is, in terms of the content of what the labels convey for many people, conservatism and liberalism in public opinion are not two sides of the same coin.[17]

In short, to understand people's thinking about government, one needs to know a lot more than the way they describe their own political philosophy.

---

[15] W. Kerr was an early proponent of the idea that conservatism and liberalism in public opinion should be measured separately. See Kerr's "Untangling the Liberalism-Conservatism Continuum," *Journal of Social Psychology* 35 (1952): 111–25. Later Norman Luttbeg also concluded that for most people there is not an abstract continuum between left and right on political matters. See Luttbeg's "The Structure of Beliefs among Leaders and the Public," *Public Opinion Quarterly* 32 (1968): 398–409.

[16] Fred N. Kerlinger questioned a "bi-polar" approach to measuring political attitudes: to be "for" one thing does not require a person to be "against" another. Thus, in many respects, Kerlinger argued conservatism and liberalism should not be thought of as a continuum in public thinking. See Fred N. Kerlinger, *Liberalism and Conservatism: The Nature and Structure of Social Attitudes* (Hillsdale, N.J.: Erlbaum Associates, 1984).

[17] Research by Pamela Johnston Conover and Stanley Feldman demonstrated that the two points of view are, for most people, organized around different sets of ideas. See Conover and Feldman, "The Origins and Meaning of Liberal/Conservative Self-Identifications," *American Journal of Political Science* 25 (1981): 617–45.

Table 2.5

Mix of General and Specific Views about Government among Those with Differing Self-Described Political Philosophies

	All	Very conservative	Moderately conservative	Middle of the road	Very and moderately liberal[a]
Mostly critical					
Steady Critic	18%	35%	26%	12%	6%
Ambivalent Critic	20	23	25	19	17
	38%	58%	51%	31%	23%
Mostly supportive					
Ambivalent Supporter	12	11	9	14	11
Steady Supporter	39	23	27	45	60
	51	34	36	59	71
Neither supporter nor critic	11	8	12	10	6
	100%	100%	99%	100%	100%

[a] "Very" and "moderately" liberal are combined given the small number of respondents describing themselves as "very liberal."

[Q.44]

THREE

Government Performance and Ambivalence about Government

N O DOUBT THERE ARE MANY REASONS PEOPLE MAY FEEL AMBIVA-
lent about government. The challenge here is to identify possible
reasons and then sort out their relative importance. Major issues
before the country or one's own personal situation may be possible
explanations. But the first step is to find out how opinions about *what* government should do are affected by views of *how well* government is doing its job.

It is possible that some who are "mostly critical" of government as a general matter also support its specific activities because they think government is
performing well. And others who are "mostly supportive" in general terms may
have doubts about some specific activities because they rate government's performance negatively.

We explore these possibilities by looking at how much ambivalence about
government is affected by (a) views of how well it is doing its job; (b) opinions
on how important it is to improve the workings of government; and (c) ideas
about the appropriate mix of responsibilities among federal, state, and local
government in dealing with important issues.

THE PERFORMANCE OF GOVERNMENT

It is always a challenge to measure public opinion about different aspects of
a complex subject because they are often quite closely related to one another.
For example, if questions about two different aspects of a topic are not written
carefully, they may end up measuring basically the same sentiment. If this happens, it is not possible to determine whether there really are two distinct aspects of opinion on the issue and what relationship may exist between them.

27

Table 3.1

How the Public Rates Different Levels of Government

	Federal		State		Local	
Excellent	2%	} 53%	4%	} 61%	6%	} 60%
Pretty good	51		57		54	
Not so good	35	} 45	27	} 35	27	} 37
Very poor	10		8		10	
Don't know	2		4		3	
	100%		100%		100%	

[Q.16–18]

It is for this reason that measures used here relating to government's performance focus explicitly on its effectiveness. This is to avoid having questions about how government is handling things overlap with questions gauging what we call "general attitudes" toward government that relate to the power of government, the scope of its activities, and the desired balance between it and the private sector.

Accordingly we asked how respondents would "rate the job the federal government is doing when it comes to handling problems facing the country." Comparable questions were also asked about state and local government.

We then looked separately at the executive and legislative branches. While the principal interest was opinion about the federal government, questions were also asked about the performance of the executive and legislative branches at the state level.

Job Rating of Government

When asked to rate the job government is doing, 53 percent say the federal government is doing an "excellent" or "pretty good" job. Comparable figures for state and local government are somewhat higher, 61 percent and 60 percent, respectively (table 3.1).

Looked at in terms of ambivalence about government, some important differences in perspective become apparent. As expected, those who are "mostly critical" of government give decidedly lower ratings to the federal government than they do to state or local government. In contrast, those who are "mostly supportive" give all levels of government similarly favorable ratings (table 3.2).

Table 3.2

Favorable Ratings (Excellent/Pretty Good) of Different Levels of Government by
Mix of General and Specific Views about Government

		Mostly critical		Mostly supportive	
	All	Steady Critic	Ambivalent Critic	Ambivalent Supporter	Steady Supporter
Federal government	53%	30%	42%	67%	66%
State government	61	58	64	62	65
Local government	60	57	66	60	60

[Q.16–18]

Even though critics are not inclined to give the federal government high marks, what is surprising is that opinion among critics is quite divided. Ambivalent Critics are considerably more positive than Steady Critics. Forty-two percent of Ambivalent Critics rate the federal government favorably compared to only 30 percent of Steady Critics.

The cumulative effect of differences of view among those "mostly critical" of government is apparent when ratings for all three levels of government are considered together. Only 49 percent of Steady Critics give favorable ratings to at least two levels of government, whereas the proportion is 61 percent among Ambivalent Critics. In fact, half of Steady Critics rate only one or none of the levels favorably (table A.5 in appendix A).

Confidence in the Executive and Legislative Branches

We also sought separate public evaluations of the executive and legislative branches at both the federal and state levels. With respect to the executive branch, we asked how much confidence people have in "the quality of work done by career workers in the agencies." With respect to the legislative branch, we asked how much confidence the public has that "the interests of all the people" are being served "not just the interests of those with special influence."[1] Parallel questions were asked about the federal and state government.

---

[1] While these questions about the executive and legislative branches are not literally identical, it is reasonable to compare results to them since they focus respondents' attention on basic functions of each branch. Given the constraints of interview length, confidence measures were not obtained for the judicial branch.

Table 3.3

Confidence in Executive and Legislative Branches

	Federal government		State government	
	Executive agencies	U.S. Congress	Executive agencies	State legislature
Great deal	5% ⎫ 55%	7% ⎫ 35%	5% ⎫ 63%	5% ⎫ 50%
Fair amount	50 ⎭	28 ⎭	58 ⎭	45 ⎭
Not very much	31 ⎫ 37	45 ⎫ 63	26 ⎫ 31	36 ⎫ 46
None at all	6 ⎭	18 ⎭	5 ⎭	10 ⎭
Don't know	8	2	6	4
	100%	100%	100%	100%

Questions about executive agencies asked: "How much confidence do you have in the quality of work done by career workers in the agencies of [the federal/your state] government. . . ?" [Q.30–31]

Questions about legislatures asked: "How much confidence do you have that the members of the [U. S. Congress/legislature in your state] serve the interests of all [the people/residents of your state], not just the interests of those with special influence. . . ?" [Q.28–29]

At both the federal and state levels, the executive branch is looked upon more favorably than the legislative. A substantial majority (55 percent) of those asked express a "great deal" or "fair amount" of confidence in the quality of work done by agencies of the federal government. By contrast, only 35 percent have comparable confidence that members of Congress are serving the interests of all people not just those with special influence. A similar picture is seen at the state level: executive agencies are more highly regarded than the legislature[2] (table 3.3).

The disparity between confidence in the executive and legislative branches is greater regarding the federal government than state government. The magnitude of the disparity between the branches of the federal government could be the subject of an entire study of its own. A reason for this disparity could

---

[2] The tilt toward the executive branch in these assessments is comparable to findings in a nearly contemporaneous study in 1997 by Peter Hart and Robert Teeter for the Council on Excellence in Government. When asked "which is the bigger problem with the federal government," 50 percent said "politics has prevented government from serving the people well" as opposed to 35 percent who said "government programs have gotten too big, expensive, and intrusive." Thirteen percent volunteered "both" and 2 percent had no opinion.

Table 3.4

Percent Having "Great Deal" or "Fair Amount" of Confidence in Executive and
Legislative Branches by Mix of General and Specific Views of Government

		Mostly critical		Mostly supportive	
	All	Steady Critic	Ambivalent Critic	Ambivalent Supporter	Steady Supporter
Federal government					
Executive agencies	55%	37%	55%	60%	65%
U.S. Congress	35	29	29	34	41
State government					
Executive agencies	63	50	68	63	69
State legislature	50	52	51	47	53

[Q.28–31]

be the lingering aftermath of the government shutdown in 1995. Were this the case, however, we would expect to find Democrats significantly more critical of Congress than Republicans. Yet no such difference emerges in the survey. In fact, confidence in the Congress lags confidence in federal executive agencies by the same amount with both Republicans and Democrats (see table A.6 in appendix A).

What do these results tell us about ambivalence toward government? First, we gain considerable insight from the differences of perspective regarding the work of the executive agencies of the federal government:

- Most striking is the difference in confidence expressed by Ambivalent Critics (55 percent) and Steady Critics (37 percent).
- Ambivalent Critics do not differ dramatically from either Ambivalent Supporters or Steady Supporters in their level of confidence.
- It is the Steady Critics who see things differently from others (table 3.4).

Second, opinions about the executive agencies of state government vary among critics and supporters in about the same way they do regarding the federal agencies. The differences of perspective, however, are not so pronounced.

Third, there are no important differences between Ambivalent Supporters and Steady Supporters in their view of executive agencies at either the federal or state levels.

Fourth, views of the legislative branch are not a source of significant difference among either government's critics or its supporters. Confidence in the U.S. Congress is considerably lower across-the-board than confidence in the state legislatures.

The major impression left by these findings is that it is the Steady Critics who stand apart from others as having a fundamentally different view of the work of the executive agencies of the federal government. Those who are ambivalent in their criticism of government express a level of confidence in the federal agencies that is closer to that of government's supporters than to that of the Steady Critics.[3]

THE PERFORMANCE OF GOVERNMENT AS A PRIORITY

Measures of government performance tell only part of the story. Also significant is the degree of urgency people attach to improving government performance: where it stands as a priority for the country; what progress, if any, people sense the country is making; and how sanguine people are that changes can be made.

The question sequence probing these issues started by asking about the importance of "improving the way government works." Its relative standing was anchored by asking about other issues of recurring prominence in the public discussion.

Improving government performance is regarded as one of the "very most important things" for the good of the country by 65 percent of Americans. Twenty-one percent say it is "quite important," 10 percent "only somewhat important," and 1 percent "not very important."

A higher proportion of respondents attaches great importance to "teaching the values of personal responsibility and moral character" (79 percent) and "getting through to young people about the dangers of drug abuse" (77 percent). Even so, nearly two-thirds assign comparable importance to improving government's performance (table 3.5).

Also interesting in these rankings is the finding that government performance is seen as a significantly greater challenge for the country than "having national leaders who go beyond short-term solutions to put bold new ideas before the country."

---

[3] It will be noted that differences between Steady Critics and Ambivalent Critics are more pronounced regarding confidence in the executive agencies of the federal government than their ratings of the federal government as a whole. This suggests the confidence and job rating questions were drawing out somewhat different sentiments. See appendix C for further discussion.

Table 3.5

Importance of Matters for the Good of the Country
and Amount of Progress Country Is Making

	Consider matter as one of "very most important"	How much progess the country is making in each area				
		Making progress	Standing still	Losing ground	Don't know	Total
Teaching young people the values of personal responsibility and moral character	79%	16%	28%	54%	2%	100%
Getting through to young people about the dangers of drug abuse	77	37	32	28	3	100
Improving the way government works	65	20	43	32	5	100
Pulling together as a nation to get beyond divisions of class, race, and cultural heritage	57	29	45	25	2	101
Equal opportunities and pay for women in the workplace	50	58	34	5	3	100
Having leaders who go beyond short-term solutions to put bold ideas before country	42	18	43	29	9	99

[Q.7a–f;8a–f]

On the matter of how the country is doing in each area, 20 percent think the country is making progress in the way government works, 43 percent see us standing still, and 32 percent think we are losing ground (see table 3.5). Views on leadership ideas are quite similar. Where greatest progress is seen is in "providing equal opportunities and pay for women in the workplace." Least forward motion is seen in the teaching of personal responsibility, a subject that we return to later.

We get some insight into ambivalence about government from these questions, especially among critics of government:

• Ambivalent Critics and Steady Critics attach comparable importance to improving the way government works (75 percent versus
71 percent seeing the matter as one of the "very most important").
• Critics differ, however, on the importance assigned to the issue of
leadership. Leadership with bold ideas is significantly more important
to Ambivalent Critics (48 percent) than Steady Critics (35 percent).
• Consistent with the findings already reported regarding government performance, Steady Critics are more inclined than Ambivalent
Critics to see the country losing ground on both scores.
• Ambivalent Supporters (30 percent) are more likely than Steady
Supporters (23 percent) to see the country losing ground in leaders
going beyond short-term solutions. This difference of perspective is
small, but still large enough not to have occurred by chance in the
sampling process (see table 3.6).

As to the possibility that improvements can be made in the way government works, we asked which of three statements came closest to the respondent's view about "how much can be done to make government work better."

It is possible to make major changes that will really improve things.	39%
Minor changes are possible but they won't improve things all that much.	46
There is not much chance things can be changed for the better.	12
Don't know	3
	100%

What is intriguing about these results is that the proportion who think major
changes will bring real improvement does *not* vary in significant ways by how
well people think the federal government is handling its job or by their level of
confidence in the work of the federal executive agencies or confidence in the
U.S. Congress. It does not even vary by whether people think the nation is
making progress or losing ground in improving the way government works
(table 3.7).[4]

---

[4] There are some differences relating to the other two response alternatives: "minor changes
are possible but they won't improve things all that much" and "there is not much chance
things can be changed for the better." But because of the potential ambiguity to respondents of
the two alternatives, those differences are difficult to interpret. The wording does not present
respondents with a sharp enough distinction to conclude that one category is actually more
negative than the other. Were a question along these lines to be used in a subsequent survey, it
would need to be more clearly drafted.

Table 3.6

Percent Who Think Matter Is One of "Very Most Important"
and Whether the Country Is Making Progress or Losing Ground
by Mix of General and Specific Views about Government

	All	Steady Critic	Ambivalent Critic	Ambivalent Supporter	Steady Supporter
Improving the way government works					
One of "very most important"	65%	71%	75%	55%	61%
Country is					
Making progress	20%	12%	16%	25%	25%
Standing still	43	34	41	42	47
Losing ground	32	52	39	27	23
Not sure	5	2	4	6	4
	100%	100%	100%	100%	99%
Leaders who go beyond short-term solutions to put bold ideas before country					
One of "very most important"	42%	35%	48%	41%	45%
Country is					
Making progress	18%	11%	16%	17%	21%
Standing still	43	35	44	43	46
Losing ground	29	44	36	30	23
Not sure	9	10	4	10	7
	99%	100%	100%	100%	100%

[Q.7d,e; 8d,e]

How is it that people believe that "major changes . . . will really improve things," even though they give the federal government a poor job rating or lack confidence in its agencies or in the U.S. Congress? A likely answer is that, while they may be unhappy with the current lay of the land in Washington, they think change is possible down the road. In other words, even though these individuals are unhappy with the current state of affairs, they have not given up on the system.

Evidence consistent with this conjecture comes from looking at partisan differences on these questions. Republicans give the federal government a substantially lower job rating (39 percent) than do Democrats (67 percent). Republicans are also much more inclined to think the country is losing ground in making government work better (41 percent) than Democrats (28 percent).

Table 3.7

Possibility of Changes to Make Government Work Better
by Related Views of Government

	Major changes possible	Minor changes possible	Not much chance for change	Don't know	Total
ALL	39%	46%	12%	3%	100%
By overall rating of the federal government					
Excellent and pretty good	38	52	7	3	100
Not so good and very poor	41	39	18	2	100
By confidence in work of executive agencies of the federal government					
Great and fair amount	39	49	9	2	99
Not much and none at all	41	41	16	3	101
By confidence in the U.S. Congress serving all					
Great and fair amount	39	50	9	2	100
Not much and none at all	40	44	14	2	100
By progress in improving way government works					
Making progress	41	48	8	3	100
Standing still	37	50	11	3	101
Losing ground	42	39	18	1	100

Note: This table should be read across.

[Q.55]

But Republicans are about as likely as Democrats to think major changes can be made in government (40 percent versus 42 percent) (see table A.7 in appendix A).

LEVELS OF GOVERNMENT

Arguments about the competing authority of national and state government are as old as the republic. Today's debates have their roots in two theories of federalism.

The "compact" theory of federalism holds that the national government is a compact of the states, not the people of all the states. According to this theory, overlap is not contemplated between spheres of authority of the national and state governments. At least for early advocates, such as Thomas Jefferson and the Anti-Federalists, it would be the states, as representatives of the distinct interests of their citizens, which wrangle over issues facing the nation. The resourcefulness of individuals and communities would remain insulated from interventions by the national government.

In contrast, the "national" theory of federalism does not reject the idea of a national community of all the people and the institutions needed to serve those within it. Politics was to be competition of myriad interests that reach across state boundaries. As promoted by James Madison and Alexander Hamilton, only a national government could protect the rights of individuals from the excesses of powerful local interests as well as deal with the scale of the new country.[5]

The tension between these visions of federalism has persisted because neither has been fully responsive to the way Americans live their lives. As Michael J. Lacey writes, "Whatever the intention of the founders, a glance into the history of the national government makes it plain that the federal design was an ideal arrangement of governmental powers for a people unable to make up its mind whether to be one community or many, and apparently determined to be both."[6]

The dispute remains at the heart of many issues aired today, but it often gets confusing. Those who seek a national (federal) policy on matters such as eligibility for Medicaid are called "liberals." Yet, those who want a national (federal) policy on such things as the definition of what constitutes a marriage are called "conservatives."

Measuring Public Preferences

Clear and abiding preferences are hard to find in public opinion regarding which level of government should take the lead in dealing with different issues. Questions along these lines have been included in polls for years and frequently have produced widely varying results. Consider two sets of disparate results regarding the environment and civil rights:

---

[5] For a discussion of the evolution of the "compact" and "national" theories of federalism, see Samuel H. Beer, *To Make a Nation*, especially chapters 1 and 8.

[6] Michael J. Lacey, "Federalism and National Planning: The Nineteenth Century Legacy," in Robert Fishman, ed., *The American Planning Tradition: Culture and Policy* (Washington, D.C.: Woodrow Wilson Center Press; Baltimore: Johns Hopkins University Press, forthcoming).

• *Environment:* A survey in 1995 by Peter Hart and Robert Teeter found that 35 percent thought the federal government should be "most responsible for paying for protecting the environment," while 40 percent looked to state government and 22 percent to local. Yet, a survey by James Davison Hunter and Carl Bowman in 1996 found that 65 percent thought "air and water quality control" should be "mainly the responsibility" of the federal government compared to 20 percent who turned to state government and 7 percent to local.

• *Civil rights:* Hart and Teeter found that 35 percent thought the federal government should be "most responsible for paying" for "improving opportunities for racial and ethnic minorities" with the remainder turning to state or local government. In contrast, the Hunter and Bowman finding was that 67 percent thought "ensuring fair treatment of women and minorities" should be "mainly the responsibility" of the federal government.[7]

Such disparate results usually occur because poll questions differ in the aspects of a subject they highlight. Slight differences in the way a question is framed matter because most respondents pay close attention to exactly what they are being asked. It can be difficult, therefore, to conclude from results such as these that the public has strong views one way or the other regarding which level of government is appropriate for a broad area of public policy.

Findings in this survey carry the point a bit further. It turns out that people make quite nuanced distinctions in assigning responsibilities among levels of government even *within* one area of public policy.

We looked for an issue that is close to people's everyday lives where distinctions among levels of government are not just an abstract matter. Public education was an obvious candidate. Three tasks were identified: running the schools day-to-day, certifying that teachers are qualified, and providing financial assistance to schools in low-income areas. Questions about each task asked whether it should be handled "mostly at the local or county level, state level, or federal level."

Respondents make clear distinctions that would have been lost had we asked simply about "public education." Most of those interviewed look to local government to run schools day-to-day (59 percent), to state government for certification of teachers (54 percent), and jointly to state (47 percent) and fed-

---

7 Survey by Peter D. Hart and Robert Teeter for the Council on Excellence in Government, 1995; and James Davison Hunter and Carl Bowman, *The State of Disunion: 1996 Survey of American Political Culture* (Ivy, Va.: In Media Res Education Foundation, 1996).

Table 3.8

Levels of Government Relevant to Aspects of Public Education

	Running the schools day-to-day	Certifying that teachers are qualified	Providing financial assistance to schools in low-income areas
Local or county	59%	22%	16%
State	27	54	47
Federal	9	20	29
More than one level (volunteered)	1	1	4
Don't know	4	2	4
	100%	99%	100%

[Q.40a–c]

eral government (29 percent) in providing financial assistance for schools in low-income areas (table 3.8).

Only one in four (24 percent) of those polled hold out for just one level of government (whether local, state, or federal) handling all three aspects of public education. Most respondents (61 percent) think the tasks should be divided between some mix of two levels of government. This leaves 15 percent who envision each of the three levels of government as principally responsible for a facet of public education.

In some respects, even this formulation of the problem is artificial since in reality more than one level of government is involved in most areas of public policy. In fact, some argue that overlapping responsibilities among levels of government serve as a check on an increase in governmental power of any one level.[8]

As we find here, respondents' views about which level of government should take the lead depend upon the aspect of "public education" about which they are asked. It is likely that the same would hold if they were asked about other matters such as the environment or providing health care. If respondents are asked only about broad areas of public policy, there appear to be limits to what can be learned about public opinion regarding the levels of government appropriate to address problems.

---

[8] See Stephen L. Schechter, "The State of American Federalism," in Robert B. Hawkins Jr., *American Federalism: A New Partnership for America* (San Francisco: Institute for Contemporary Studies, 1982), 66–67.

Government Closest to Home

An additional element in the level-of-government debate revolves around the presumption that people have more ties with and feel closer to smaller units of government than larger. One of the principles appearing at the outset of the 1996 Republican platform, for example, called for "pushing power away from official Washington and returning it to the people in their communities and states." The counter argument is that this is a romantic view that slights the size and complexity of most state governments—at least from the vantage point of the average citizen.[9] Nor does it address the Madisonian question of how to ensure that competition among locally powerful factions does not restrict the range of choices available to those with less power.

Our approach to the issue was to ask: "When it comes to knowing what they stand for, would you say you know more about the views of the people who represent you in your state legislature or the people who represent you in the U.S. Congress, or don't you have a chance to follow it all that closely?"

For most people things are not as clear-cut as they are among those debating the pros and cons of devolution of power to the states. In fact, almost three times as many do not follow the matter closely (60 percent) as say they have a sense of what either their representatives in the Congress (16 percent) or state legislature stand for (21 percent).

Only Steady Critics differ from this pattern. They are significantly more likely than others to know what their representative in the U.S. Congress stands for. Their familiarity with what is going on in the state legislature is virtually the same as among others. But when awareness of both legislatures is taken into account, almost six out of ten (59 percent) Steady Critics stay in touch compared to about four out of ten among other respondents (table 3.9).

PERFORMANCE OF GOVERNMENT AND AMBIVALENCE: A RECAP

To summarize briefly what has been learned about government performance as a possible explanation for ambivalence in the thinking of some Americans:

- Critics of government judge the performance of the federal government more harshly than do its supporters. This comes as no surprise. What is new are two other findings:

[9] See Kathleen M. Sullivan, "The Contemporary Relevance of *The Federalist*," in Alan Brinkley, Nelson W. Polsby, and Kathleen M. Sullivan, *New Federalist Papers: Essays in Defense of the Constitution* (New York: W. W. Norton, 1997; A Twentieth Century Fund Book), 7–14.

Table 3.9

Know More about Representative in U.S. Congress or State Legislature
by Mix of General and Specific Views about Government

	All	Steady Critic	Ambivalent Critic	Ambivalent Supporter	Steady Supporter
State legislature	21%	24%	24%	22%	20%
U.S. Congress	16	27	13	16	15
About even (volunteered)	3	8	1	4	2
Don't follow closely enough	60	41	61	58	63
	100%	100%	99%	100%	100%

Ambivalent Critics are not nearly as negative in their opinions as Steady Critics.

Critics are more divided among themselves in the amount of confidence they have in the work of the federal agencies than in the rating they give the federal government as a whole.

The conclusion: ambivalence in the thinking of critics of government is distinctly related to views of how well government is performing, and greatest insight comes from gauging confidence in the work of the agencies.

• Steady and Ambivalent Supporters tend to rate the job the federal government is doing in much the same way and hold comparable views of the work of its executive agencies.

• Confidence in the U.S. Congress is considerably lower across-the-board than confidence in federal executive agencies. This is true whether people are ambivalent or steady in their criticism or support of government. That confidence in the Congress is less related to the mix of general and specific views of government than confidence in federal executive agencies suggests people are not as likely to have Congress in mind as the executive branch when asked about "government."[10]

• There are few notable differences in the level of confidence expressed in either the executive agencies of state government or state legislatures.

• Steady Critics see the country losing more ground than Ambivalent Critics in improving the way government works.

[10] Some support for this conclusion is that the job rating people give the federal government as a whole is more highly correlated with their confidence in its executive agencies (r=.31) than with their confidence in the U.S. Congress (r=.21).

• Steady Critics also see the country losing more ground than Ambivalent Critics in leadership with ideas, although they do not attach as much importance to leaders who go beyond short-term solutions as do Ambivalent Critics.

• Even those who are most unhappy about the way government is working and rate it poorly are as likely as others to think that "major changes" can be made. They may be discontented with the current situation, but they have not given up on the system.

• People make careful distinctions regarding different aspects of public education, when asked which level of government should have the lead responsibility for them. If this is true for public education, there is little reason to suspect it is not also true for other areas of public policy.

FOUR

Issues and Ambivalence about Government

M ANY TOPICS THAT ARE DEBATED HEATEDLY TODAY ARE CON-
temporary expressions of long-standing questions about the appropriate role of government in the country. What balance
should be struck between the unfettered operation of the marketplace and government oversight sufficient to ensure competition? Where
does government fit in when it comes to matters such as poverty, crime, race
relations, immigration? When and how should public institutions play a part
in passing along society's norms and traditions while maintaining separation
of church and state?

The way people approach some of these issues may go some distance in
explaining the ambivalence in their thinking about government. In contrast,
other issues may have little to do with the mix of their general and specific
views about government.

Our interest here is less the absolute division of opinion on an issue than
identifying the differing frames of reference through which people see the world.
Like so much else in gauging public opinion, we have to remember that these issues may be more clearly differentiated in the minds of those who live and breathe
politics than they are in the experience of many Americans. Thus the point is not
to read the results that follow as a referendum up or down on issues. Rather, it is
to see how sharply defined issues are in people's minds and whether those issues
shed light on the amount of ambivalence expressed about government.

INDIVIDUAL INITIATIVE AND THE MARKETPLACE

E conomic individualism is central to the credo of both the right and left in
our politics. The virtues of getting ahead and benefiting from the rewards
of enterprise are values about which right and left do not disagree. But there

43

are differences. The priority for the right is decreasing the chances that re-
straints may be put upon those values. The priority of the left is increasing the
chances anyone can experience them.

These competing conceptions of economic individualism surface in many
ways. Closest to home they have to do with people confronting the odds in
their everyday lives. But they also extend to corporations looking for competitive advantage in the global economy.

Accordingly we took two approaches to the matter by presenting respondents with pairs of statements. One pair of statements focused on individual
initiative; the other pair addressed the larger marketplace. People were asked
which statement in each pair was closest to their own view:

Individual initiative:
Anyone in the United States can get ahead
    if they are willing to work hard enough.   55%
Hard work is often not enough to overcome
    the barriers some people face in our society.   42
Qualified or don't know   3
                                              100%

The larger marketplace:
The federal government should keep an eye on
    our free enterprise system and step in if
    corporations get so powerful they crowd out
    competition.   50%
The federal government should stay out of
    our free enterprise system and let the market
    decide who gets ahead.   40
Qualified or don't know   10
                                              100%

That critics and supporters of government would have diverging perspectives
on these facets of economic individualism is not unexpected. But what is surprising is the size of the difference in view between Steady Critics and Ambivalent Critics. Seventy-one percent of Steady Critics think anyone can get
ahead if they work hard enough. The comparable proportion among Ambivalent Critics is only 57 percent. Equally disparate opinions are expressed regarding the marketplace: 68 percent of Steady Critics believe the government

should stay out of the picture entirely compared to 47 percent of Ambivalent Critics having the same view (table 4.1).

On the supporter side of the ledger, differences between Steady Supporters and Ambivalent Supporters are much less pronounced. In fact, when sampling tolerances are taken into account, there is no difference in opinion between Steady and Ambivalent Supporters on whether the government should keep an eye on things to ensure market competition. It should also be noted that almost half of Steady Supporters subscribe to the idea that anyone can get ahead if they work hard enough at it.

If we combine the responses to these two questions, we can get a rough sense of the two meanings of economic individualism that are at work in public opinion. Laissez-faire individualism is captured by a person thinking that anyone can get ahead in the United States *and* that government should stay out of the marketplace. An alternative conception affirms the importance of enterprise *but* sees a need to ensure a competitive marketplace.

Steady Critics lean to the laissez-faire conception of individualism by three to one (51 percent to 17 percent), whereas Ambivalent Critics are more evenly divided (30 percent to 23 percent). Whether they are ambivalent or not, supporters of government incline toward a conception of individualism in which government is involved enough to preserve the opportunity for competition (see table 4.1).

Kind of economic individualism aside, the main finding here is that differences in opinion on matters of initiative and the market are much greater among those "mostly critical" of government than among those who are "mostly supportive."

It is interesting that there are no major differences on these issues among those living in more and less affluent households. Perspectives on individual initiative and the operation of the marketplace have their roots elsewhere than how well-off people are financially (see table A.8 in appendix A).

DEALING WITH SOCIAL PROBLEMS

Just as economic individualism can be found in the credo of the right and left, so can the idea of community. The struggle is over its many meanings. From the conservative vantage point, it calls for, among other things, appreciation of a unifying set of values and preservation of the social order. From the liberal perspective, it means, among other things, drawing strength from diversity and looking out for the vulnerable in society. We explore these differing visions in three areas: crime and justice, race and diversity, and poverty.

Table 4.1
Views of Opportunity and the Marketplace by Mix of General and Specific Views about Government

	All	Mostly critical		Mostly supportive	
		Steady Critic	Ambivalent Critic	Ambivalent Supporter	Steady Supporter
Individual initiative					
Anyone can get ahead with hard work	55%	71%	57%	56%	49%
Hard work often not enough	42	27	40	42	49
Qualified/don't know	3	2	3	2	2
	100%	100%	100%	100%	100%
The larger marketplace					
Government should keep an eye on things; step in if needed	50%	27%	44%	63%	60%
Government should stay out; let the market decide	40	68	47	29	31
Qualified/don't know	10	5	9	8	9
	100%	100%	100%	100%	100%
Combined:					
Anyone can get ahead *and* Government should keep an eye on things; step in if needed	24%	17%	23%	29%	27%
Government should stay out; let market decide	26	51	30	22	18
Hard work often not enough *and* Government should keep an eye on things; step in if needed	25	9	20	32	32
Government should stay out; let market decide	13	16	6	7	12
Qualified/don't know	12	7	11	10	11
	100%	100%	100%	100%	100%

[Q.9a,c]

Crime and Justice

As with many subjects covered in this survey, issues relating to crime and justice could fill an entire questionnaire. The facet of opinion most pertinent for a survey of attitudes about government was the urgency people attach to decisive law enforcement when set against competing values. We took two tacks. We started by asking what balance should be struck between stiffer penalties for breaking the law and efforts to prevent crime from happening. We then sought out the public's view on the Fourth Amendment issue of what constitutes reasonable search.

The first dimension was addressed in the framework of "two ways of dealing with juvenile crime." People were asked to think of $100 they could allocate between two approaches: "getting tougher on young offenders to make clear there is a price to pay for breaking the law," or "finding ways to help young people stay out of trouble in the first place."[1] Respondents divided the $100 between the two approaches as follows:

Spend on getting tougher	*and*	*Spend on helping stay out of trouble*		
$100		Nothing	11%	⎫ 23%
$51 to $99		$1 to $49	12	⎭
$50		$50	29	
$1 to $49		$51 to $99	23	⎫ 46
Nothing		$100	23	⎭
	Not sure		2	
			100%	

The prevention option draws twice as much support from respondents as getting tough: 46 percent allocating more than $50 to it compared with 23 percent allocating more than $50 to getting tougher. Twenty-nine percent of respondents would allocate equal amounts on the two approaches.

The second dimension was posed in terms of the "Taking Back Our Streets Act of 1994" passed by the Congress as part of the Contract with America of House Republicans. The act held that evidence gathered by police without a search warrant could not be dismissed if the search "was carried out in circumstances justifying an objectively reasonable belief that it was in conformity with the Fourth Amendment."

---

[1] The order of these options was altered randomly to minimize bias that might have resulted if one option was always mentioned first.

The survey question asked which of two statements was closest to the respondent's view:

> If the police suspect a person is hiding something, they should be able to search that person's home without a search warrant from the court if they believe they are acting legally.

> A search warrant should be required because it is up to the courts, not just the police, to determine if there is a good enough reason to search a person's home.

Opinion is decidedly against the idea of a search without a warrant—even if there are grounds for suspicion and the police think they are acting lawfully. Almost nine in ten (86 percent) feel a warrant should be required. Only one in ten (11 percent) approve of a search without a warrant.

Opposition to the idea of giving police discretion over the presumed legality of a search is so strong and pervasive, in fact, that it holds up regardless of the mix of a person's general and specific views about government (table 4.2).

The same cannot be said of opinion on dealing with juvenile crime. There is a distinct difference of view among critics of government: Steady Critics are much more inclined to get tougher on young offenders than are Ambivalent Critics. A plurality of 39 percent of Steady Critics would put most or all of their $100 into tougher measures compared to only 21 percent of Ambivalent Critics.

Significant differences of opinion exist among government's supporters. Whereas 52 percent of Steady Supporters allocate more money to prevention, only 43 percent of Ambivalent Supporters would do likewise. Even with this difference of opinion, however, the prevailing view among all supporters is that most or all money should be spent on prevention.

Race and Immigration

Efforts to measure public attitudes on matters of race and ethnic diversity present one of the trickiest challenges facing pollsters. Our interest here was in getting beyond expressions of support for the broad goal of equality and closer to sentiments that are at work in everyday life.[2]

---

[2] It has been demonstrated, for example, that whites have become more accepting of the principle of racial integration over the years, even as they have remained resistant to steps to implement those principles. See Howard Schuman, Charlotte Steeh, and Lawrence Bobo, *Racial Attitudes in America: Trends and Interpretations* (Cambridge, Mass.: Harvard University Press, 1985), 103–4.

Table 4.2

Views on Criminal Justice Issues by Mix of General
and Specific Views about Government

	All	Mostly critical		Mostly supportive	
		Steady Critic	Ambivalent Critic	Ambivalent Supporter	Steady Supporter
Allocation of spending for juvenile crime					
All on getting tough	11%	18% ⎱ 39%	11% ⎱ 21%	14% ⎱ 27%	8% ⎱ 18%
Most on getting tough	12	21 ⎰	10 ⎰	13 ⎰	10 ⎰
Split evenly	29	25	33	27	29
Most on preventing	23	15 ⎱ 31	22 ⎱ 45	23 ⎱ 43	28 ⎱ 52
All on preventing	23	16 ⎰	23 ⎰	20 ⎰	24 ⎰
Don't know	2	5	2	3	1
	100%	99%	101%	100%	101%
Police search					
If police think legal	11%	13%	13%	16%	8%
Need warrant	86	83	84	80	90
Qualified/don't know	3	4	2	4	2
	100%	100%	99%	100%	100%

[Q.11;23]

Our approach was to assert the validity of the principle of racial equality in two statements and then to draw people out on how much of an effort the nation should make in living up to the principle:

> In light of how far we have come, we don't need to push quite so hard now as in the past in dealing with the issue of race.

> We still have a long way to go and now is no time to let up working for true equality.

Seventy-five percent of those polled select the statement "now is no time to let up" as closest to their own view. Twenty percent say we no longer "need to push quite so hard." The remaining 5 percent give a qualified response or express no opinion.

Table 4.3

Views on How to Deal with Issues of Race and Immigration
by Mix of General and Specific Views about Government

	All	Steady Critic	Ambivalent Critic	Ambivalent Supporter	Steady Supporter
Issue of race					
Don't need to push so hard	20%	40%	21%	23%	12%
No time to let up	75	53	76	73	85
Qualified/don't know	5	7	3	4	3
	100%	100%	100%	100%	100%
Immigrants to U.S.					
Should try to fit in	54%	62%	55%	56%	51%
Live by own traditions	38	29	39	38	43
Qualified/don't know	8	9	6	6	6
	100%	100%	100%	100%	100%

[Q.9d;10]

In spite of so broad a consensus, a sharp division of opinion exists between Steady Critics and Ambivalent Critics on how to deal with the subject. Forty percent of Steady Critics think we do not need "to push quite so hard" compared to only 21 percent of Ambivalent Critics (table 4.3).

The issue of race is not as strongly related to ambivalence among those generally supportive of government as among critics of government. Ambivalent Supporters are somewhat more likely than Steady Supporters to think we need not push so hard in dealing with the matter but by a smaller margin than that between Steady Critics and Ambivalent Critics.

Something is at work on the matter of race among critics of government. The proportion of Steady Critics who think we need not push quite so hard (40 percent) is substantially higher than that found among any major social or demographic subgroup within the population. It is also higher than that found among any grouping of respondents by party supported or political philosophy (see table A.9 in appendix A).

Turning to immigration and the matter of ethnic and cultural diversity, we again presented two statements. One statement made the case that those new to our shores should attempt to assimilate into the American mainstream. The other statement expressed the value of cultural pluralism. Respondents were reminded that "people from all over the world become U.S. citizens" and then asked which statement was closest to their view:

People who come to the United States from other countries really become "Americans" only if they make an effort to fit into the mainstream of American society.

So long as they support the values of a free society, people coming to the United States from other countries can be just as "American" if they continue to live by their own traditions.

Fifty-four percent think that immigrants should try to fit in while 38 percent hold the view that distinct traditions should be encouraged.

Even though responses to this question vary among social and demographic groups, there is only a slight link between opinions expressed and the mix of general and specific views about government. In fact, taking into account sample size considerations, the difference between Steady and Ambivalent Critics is barely significant and there is no significant difference among supporters (table 4.3).

Poverty

Public opinion about poverty is more multifaceted than one might conclude from the way the issue is often debated in political circles. Poll results vary widely depending on the questions that are asked. This demonstrates that people are quite attentive to the content of poll questions. It also indicates that the matter of poverty touches the many, and sometimes conflicting, values people have.

If the question is whether the government should help those who cannot fend for themselves, people tend to respond positively. If the question is about "welfare" or the "welfare system," the public often responds negatively. If questions ask about support for such things as job training or Head Start, people are most often favorably disposed. If questions suggest any possibility of dependence, people are opposed.[3]

Our approach was to explore how those with different mixes of general and specific views about government perceive the matter of poverty. We fo-

---

[3] For a useful summary of poll findings on poverty and welfare, see R. Kent Weaver, Robert Y. Shapiro, and Lawrence R. Jacobs, "Poll Trends: Welfare," *Public Opinion Quarterly* 59 (Winter 1995): 606–27.

cused on two aspects of their thinking: their judgments about the amount of attention government pays to "the concerns of low-income people" and their sense of what causes poverty.

On the matter of government's attention to the poor, 52 percent of the American people think government is paying too little attention to the concerns of low-income households. Eighteen percent think government is paying too much attention, and 28 percent think it pays about the right amount of attention.

Behind these national percentages, however, are some strong differences of opinion. Critics of government are divided in their view: 48 percent of Steady Critics think the government is paying too much attention to those of limited means in sharp contrast to only 11 percent of Ambivalent Critics. Supporters are also divided with Steady Supporters more persuaded than Ambivalent Supporters that government is paying too little attention to the concerns of low-income people (see table 4.4).

Such diverging perspectives on government's attention to the poor suggest people may also have different understandings of the causes of poverty. To explore this, respondents were asked the extent to which each of four reasons "has to do with why some people are poor."[4] The percentages of the overall sample citing each reason as having "a lot" to do with poverty are:

A lack of skills needed to get a steady job	51%
People not trying hard enough to make it on their own	44
Poor schools in low-income areas	35
Not being able to hold a job because of family circumstances, such as young children or a dependent parent or spouse	24

Here again differing perspectives show up when we compare the views of those "steady" and "ambivalent" in their criticism or support of government. Several significant points emerge.

Critics of government are clearly divided in how much weight to give to "not trying hard enough" as a reason for poverty. Fifty-nine percent of Steady Critics see it as the most compelling reason, in contrast to only 36 percent of Ambivalent Critics. For Ambivalent Critics the main reason some people are poor is a lack of job skills (48 percent) (table 4.4).

----

[4] The reasons were presented to respondents in random order to reduce possible bias that might result from the sequence in which questions were asked. These questions were asked of half the sample. Therefore the sample size considerations that have been taken into account require greater differences among groups to be sure they did not occur by chance.

Table 4.4

Amount of Attention Government Pays to Low-Income People and Reasons Why Some People Are Poor by Mix of General and Specific Views about Government

		Mostly critical		Mostly supportive	
	All	Steady Critic	Ambivalent Critic	Ambivalent Supporter	Steady Supporter
Amount of attention government is paying to low-income people					
Too much	18%	48%	11%	25%	7%
About right	28	24	33	31	28
Too little	52	26	55	41	63
Qualified/don't know	2	2	1	3	1
	100%	100%	100%	100%	99%
Percent who say each reason has "a lot" to do with poverty[a]					
Lack of job skills	51%	42%	48%	46%	59%
Not trying hard enough	44	59	36	53	38
Poor schools	35	26	37	27	41
Family circumstances	24	13	22	23	28

[a]Percentages for response alternatives for each reason other than "a lot" not shown.

[Q.25b;27a–d]

Supporters are also of different minds. Greatest divergence is on whether poverty results from not trying hard enough: mentioned by only 38 percent of Steady Supporters in contrast to 53 percent of Ambivalent Supporters. Another area of difference is lack of job skills, which is cited by 59 percent of Steady Supporters compared to 46 percent of Ambivalent Supporters. Poor schools are mentioned more often by Steady Supporters (41 percent) than Ambivalent Supporters (27 percent).

These findings suggest two major conclusions regarding the possible influence of views about poverty on ambivalence in thinking about government:

• The amount of attention government is seen as paying to the concerns of low-income Americans is a major point of difference between Steady Critics and Ambivalent Critics. Nearly half of Steady Critics (48 percent) think government pays too much attention, and more than half of Ambivalent Critics (55 percent) think it pays too little. Government's supporters are also divided on the matter, but not nearly as much as critics.

• As to reasons for poverty, critics of government divide primarily on whether people are trying hard enough. Government's supporters differ on how much to emphasize not trying hard enough. But they also differ in the greater significance Steady Supporters attach to factors less under the individual's control such as lack of job skills and poor schools.[5]

TRADITIONS AND SOCIAL NORMS

In addition to the differing conceptions of economic individualism and community just discussed, there are differences between conservatives and liberals regarding the balance they strike between standards and values that are external to the individual and those that are acquired through individual experience.

The conservative perspective tends to emphasize traditions and values that have withstood the test of time. Without dismissing the potential of learning through doing, this point of view sees personal experience as most worthwhile if it is linked in important ways to the great ideas that have survived the fads of the moment.

The liberal perspective tends to emphasize the contribution of individual experience. Without dismissing the importance of tradition or knowledge that has built up over time, this point of view sees personal experience as most worthwhile if it gives expression to ideas that originate within the individual.

These diverging notions are long-standing. What is new is that they are now an explicit part of the nation's public discussion. They are important for purposes of this study because they bear on opinions about what government should do—or not do—in many areas. How should values be taught in public schools? What is the place of faith-based institutions in the delivery of publicly funded services? When should divorce be allowed? Should rights be written into law regarding gays and lesbians? How should sex education be handled in the schools?

---

[5] These findings pertain to differences between those who are "steady" and "ambivalent" in their thinking. Setting aside for a moment the issue of ambivalence, an interesting finding emerges when comparing the views of those with different general views about government ("mostly critical" versus "mostly supportive"). It turns out that critics and supporters may agree on the issue of how much attention government is paying to the poor. What is of interest is that they come to that conclusion for quite different reasons. See appendix D for further discussion.

Table 4.5

Teaching Personal Responsibility and Moral Character:
Percent Who Think Important for Good of Country and
Percent Who Think Country Is Losing Ground by Party
and Self-described Political Views

	One of very most important	Losing ground
ALL	79%	54%
By party loyalty		
Republican	83	67
Democratic	77	47
Don't support a party	77	50
By views of political matters (self-described)		
Conservative	84	61
Middle of the road	77	51
Liberal	72	48

[Q.7a;44;47–50;54a]

Personal Responsibility

We begin our account of the public's sense of these issues by noting the concern reported earlier about "teaching young people the values of personal responsibility and moral character." It is regarded as one of the "very most important" matters for the good of the country by 79 percent of respondents and is seen by 54 percent as an area in which the country is losing ground.

A remarkable consensus exists on the importance of the issue. There are few significant differences of opinion among diverse social and demographic groups across the country, whether they are defined by age, education, household income, sex, or race (see table A.10 in appendix A).

There are some differences among subgroups in the perception of how well the country is doing on this front. But these differences are eclipsed by diverging assessments of those with opposing political points of view. Sixty-seven percent of Republicans think the country is losing ground on the matter of personal responsibility compared to 47 percent of Democrats. Opinions are almost as sharply divided when looked at in terms of how people describe their political views: 61 percent of conservatives see a loss of ground compared to 51 percent of those calling themselves "middle of the road" and 48 percent of liberals (table 4.5).

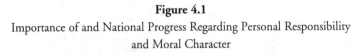

Figure 4.1

Importance of and National Progress Regarding Personal Responsibility
and Moral Character

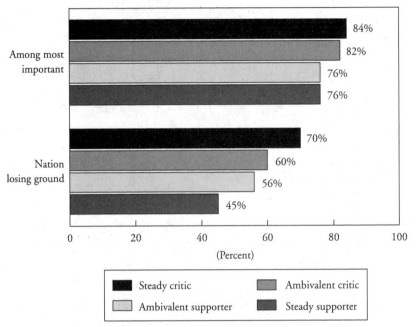

An even sharper difference of perspective on teaching personal responsibility and moral character appears when general and specific views of government are taken into account. Critics and supporters of government share a sense of the importance of the issue, but they differ markedly on whether the country is losing ground. Over two-thirds (70 percent) of Steady Critics think things are getting worse compared to fewer than half (45 percent) of Steady Supporters (figure 4.1). The importance of these differing evaluations is highlighted by the fact that the proportion of Steady Critics who see a downward trend (70 percent) is higher than that of any social or demographic group (see table A.10 in appendix A).

Respect for Norms and Traditions

Voice has been given to these concerns by conservative commentator William Bennett and others. Bennett writes that we are "living in an era in which it has become unfashionable to make judgments on a whole range of behaviors and attitudes." The consequence, he argues, is the removal of social sanctions in the name of 'tolerance' and 'openmindedness' and the devaluing of the idea of personal responsibility."[6]

We picked up on these concerns by presenting respondents with a pair of statements. One attempted to capture the spirit of Bennett's sentiment. The aim of the other was to reflect an idea at the heart of civil liberties: with freedom of expression comes the freedom to be unconventional. The statements were:

> Too many people are trying to do their own thing these days without showing respect for the values of self-control and discipline that have made this country great.

> What has made this country great is that people can act freely and express themselves, even if others may not approve.

Public opinion as a whole is evenly divided on this formulation of the issue: 46 percent say the "self-control" statement is closest to their way of thinking and 47 percent select the "freedom of expression" statement. Seven percent have a qualified response or no opinion.

But there are contrasting opinions on the issue depending upon the mix of general and specific views of government a person happens to hold. Steady Critics are more inclined than others to worry about loss of respect for the value of self-restraint. For their part, Ambivalent Critics are much more likely than Steady Critics to disagree with Bennett and affirm the importance of acting freely and self-expression. Among supporters, Steady Supporters place greater emphasis on self-expression than do Ambivalent Supporters (table 4.6).

In another tack on the same issue we asked respondents which of two statements came closer to their idea of what children should learn about getting along in life. Fifty-four percent choose the idea that children should learn "to be themselves and not pay too much attention to what other children are doing, even if it means they go it alone later in life." The alternative, selected by 37 percent, urged that children "be encouraged to fit in with what other children are doing because it will help them adjust to life later as an adult." Nine percent give a qualified response or have no opinion.

In contrast to the matter of self-restraint and expression, views about how children should deal with their peers have little to do with general and specific views about government. It is true that Ambivalent Critics place greater importance on children going out on their own than do Steady Critics. But other differences are not large (see table 4.6).

---

[6] William Bennett, "What to Do about the Children," *Commentary* (March 1995): 24–25.

Table 4.6

Views on Teaching Personal Responsibility, Respect for Self-Control versus
Self-Expression and What Children Should Learn by Mix of General
and Specific Views about Government

	All	Steady Critic	Ambivalent Critic	Ambivalent Supporter	Steady Supporter
Teaching respect for values of personal responsibility and moral character					
One of "very most important"	79%	84%	82%	76%	76%
Country is					
Making progress	16%	6%	13%	17%	23%
Standing still	28	24	27	25	30
Losing ground	54	70	60	56	45
Not sure	2	1	*a	2	2
	100%	101%	100%	100%	100%
Self-control versus self-expression					
Loss of respect for value of self-control	46%	56%	45%	46%	42%
Self-expression even if others may not approve	47	36	51	45	53
Qualified/don't know	7	8	5	9	5
	100%	100%	101%	100%	100%
What children should learn					
To be themselves	54%	50%	58%	52%	55%
To fit in	37	41	36	36	37
Qualified/don't know	9	10	6	13	8
	100%	101%	100%	101%	100%

aDesignates less than half a percent. [Q.13b;14]

Challenges Facing American Families

Foremost among institutions responsible for passing along values and traditions is the family. Some of the most valued currency in American politics
since the 1980s has been minted in the name of the American family, and spent
advancing quite diverging agendas.

In the survey we asked about a number of reasons that have been suggested
for difficulties families are experiencing.[7] The number one concern for every-

---

[7] The sequence in which these issues were presented to respondents was randomized to reduce bias from question order.

Table 4.7

Percent Who Say Reasons Have "Great Deal" to Do with Problems of Families
by Mix of General and Specific Views about Government

	All	Steady Critic	Ambivalent Critic	Ambivalent Supporter	Steady Supporter
Parents working long hours	70%	73%	69%	63%	71%
Too much sex and violence in television and movies	56	66	54	51	53
Not enough after-school activities	38	30	35	35	41
Schools do not spend enough time teaching right from wrong	33	40	33	32	31

[Q.20a–d]

one is that "many parents have to work such long hours that they do not get enough time to spend with their children." More than two-thirds of those questioned (70 percent) see this as having "a great deal" to do with problems of families (as opposed to "a fair amount," "not very much," or "nothing at all").

A solid majority (56 percent) express a great deal of concern about "young people [seeing] too much sex and violence on television and in the movies." There is less comparable concern (38 percent) about a direct link between family problems and the view that "there are not enough after school activities where young people can keep busy and out of trouble." And, 33 percent of Americans think the failure of public schools to "spend enough time teaching children right from wrong" has a great deal to do with family problems.

Whether critics or supporters of government are ambivalent or not has little to do with how they diagnose the problems facing American families[8] (table 4.7). Thus even though views about government appear related to perceived trends in the matter of personal responsibility and moral character, they do not have much to do with conclusions people draw about what is troubling American families.

---

[8] These questions were asked of half the sample. Thus, taking into account sizes of the subsamples, differences need to be nine to ten percentage points to be sure they did not occur by chance in the sampling process. The one difference worth noting is that Steady Critics feel more strongly than others that sex and violence portrayed in the media is a serious problem for families.

CONSERVATIVE CHRISTIAN ORGANIZATIONS:
ISSUES AND ACTIVITIES

From the standpoint of those pressing for a faith-based vision of a moral society, social norms and institutions are threatened by the corrosive influence of "secular humanism." Given the intensity with which these concerns are
voiced in the political arena, the public's impression of the issues and activities
of conservative Christian organizations is crucial to an understanding of how
Americans see government.

We start with opinions on major elements of the conservative Christian
agenda. We then look at the public's sense of whether conservative Christian
groups are good for the country and the degree to which people identify with
the movement itself.

Issues of Concern

While many facets of modern life are in jeopardy from the perspective of conservative Christians, none is in greater danger than the traditional family,
which is seen to be threatened by lifestyles and values inimical to Christian
teachings. Of particular concern are three issues: homosexuality, the conditions under which divorce should be permitted, and the content of sex education for young people.

First, with respect to homosexuality, respondents were presented with two
statements and asked whether they agreed or disagreed with each.

> • Fifty-one percent of those polled agree that "homosexuality threat-
> ens the values of the American family." Forty-four percent disagree and
> 5 percent have no opinion.
> • Seventy-two percent agree that "a homosexual relationship be-
> tween consenting adults is their own private matter." Twenty-four per-
> cent disagree and 4 percent have no opinion.

At the outset these findings appear to be in conflict. But when taken together, they tell us that many who think homosexuality is a threat to the family *also* think it is a private matter. This is seen in figure 4.2. The pie on the
left displays the agree/disagree percentages regarding the first statement. The
bar to the right focuses just on the views of those who feel homosexuality is a
threat. Among these people, well over half (57 percent) consider homosexuality to be a private matter.

Figure 4.2
Whether Homosexuality Threatens Values and Is a Private Matter

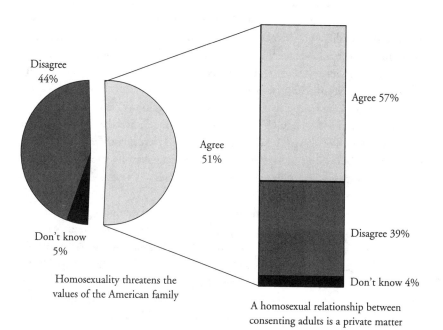

Disagree
44%

Agree
51%

Don't know
5%

Homosexuality threatens the
values of the American family

Agree 57%

Disagree 39%

Don't know 4%

A homosexual relationship between
consenting adults is a private matter

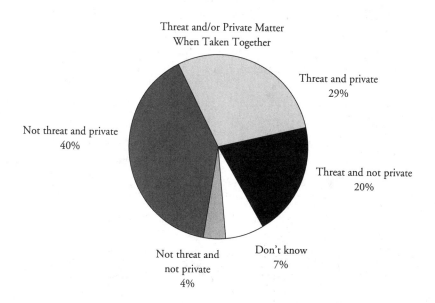

Threat and/or Private Matter
When Taken Together

Threat and private
29%

Not threat and private
40%

Threat and not private
20%

Not threat and
not private
4%

Don't know
7%

Taking reactions to both statements into account, the prevailing view (40 percent) is that homosexuality does not present a threat and is a private matter. Twenty-nine percent see homosexuality as a threat *but also* as a private matter. Twenty percent see it as a threat *but not* private. Four percent disagree that homosexuality is a threat and disagree that is it a private matter. The remaining 7 percent have no opinion on one or both questions.

As for the relevance of these results to the public's general and specific views about government, critics of government do not speak with one voice. Forty-three percent of Ambivalent Critics do not see homosexuality as a threat. Only 28 percent of Steady Critics concur. Moreover, Steady Critics (33 percent) are more likely than Ambivalent Critics (20 percent) to view homosexuality as both a threat and a matter that is not private. Among supporters of government the prevailing view is that homosexuality is not a threat and is a private matter (see table 4.8).

While there are some variations among social and demographic groups on the issue, the sharpest divisions of opinion are with respect to whether homosexuality is a threat and fall along partisan lines. Seventy-two percent of Republicans regard homosexuality as a threat compared to only 38 percent of Democrats. In other words, differences by party exceed differences associated with being ambivalent about government (see table A.11 in appendix A).

A second issue of concern to conservative Christian organizations is that marriage is, to quote the Reverend Pat Robertson, "for keeps." Contemporary society is seen as failing to impress upon young people the permanence of the marital commitments they make.[9]

Among those questioned, support for limiting divorce to situations involving adultery, abuse, or desertion appears to be modest at best. We asked:

> There has been talk about trying to reduce the number of divorces in the country. Some people think divorce should be allowed only for adultery, abuse, or desertion as a way of getting couples to think more seriously about what marriage involves. Others think that most couples make serious commitments when they get married but that, if they drift apart, divorce may be the best way to deal with an unhappy situation. How do you feel?

---

[9] "The basic rule is that divorce and remarriage are not permitted, except for adultery or desertion," writes the Rev. Pat Robertson in his "Teaching Sheet on Divorce and Remarriage" (1996). This philosophy was extended into law in 1997 when the state of Louisiana enacted a "covenant" option for couples getting married. In a related vein are calls for an end to "no-fault" divorces by groups such as Empower America.

Table 4.8

Opinion on Issues of Concern to Conservative Christian Organizations
by Mix of General and Specific Views about Government

		Mostly critical		Mostly supportive	
	All	Steady Critic	Ambivalent Critic	Ambivalent Supporter	Steady Supporter
Homosexuality threatens values of the family					
Agree	51%	69%	54%	47%	41%
Disagree	44	28	43	47	54
No opinion	5	2	3	6	5
	100%	99%	100%	100%	100%
Homosexual relationship between consenting adults is a private matter					
Agree	72%	61%	73%	68%	80%
Disagree	24	36	26	29	17
No opinion	4	3	2	3	3
	100%	100%	101%	100%	100%
Homosexuality: as threat and as private (combined)					
Threat and private	29%	34%	33%	22%	27%
Threat and not private	20	33	20	24	13
Not threat and private	40	26	37	43	50
Not threat and not private	4	2	6	4	3
Don't know	7	5	4	6	6
	100%	100%	100%	99%	99%
Divorce allowed for					
Adultery/abuse only	28%	37%	33%	27%	21%
Other reasons as well	66	58	63	64	73
Qualified/don't know	6	5	4	9	5
	100%	100%	100%	100%	99%
Sex education					
Abstain completely	29%	47%	29%	26%	21%
Need to know choices	65	45	66	67	74
Qualified/don't know	6	7	5	7	5
	100%	99%	100%	100%	100%

[Q.21;22;24a,b]

By more than two to one, people think divorce should be allowed under circumstances other than adultery or abuse. Only 28 percent hold the view that divorce should be limited to these circumstances compared to 66 percent who say divorce should be allowed for other reasons as well. Even among those who consider themselves "born again" Christians, only 38 percent are inclined to a restrictive view of when divorce is permissible. (This and other detailed tabulations are in table A.11 in appendix A).

Unlike the issue of homosexuality, divorce does not elicit much division of opinion among those with differing mixes of general and specific views about government. The across the board consensus is that there are times when divorce is the only way out of certain situations in a marriage. While it is true that Steady Critics are more likely than others to take a restrictive view on the matter, well over half are nonetheless open to the idea of divorce for reasons other than abuse or adultery (table 4.8).

A third feature prominent in the advocacy of conservative Christian organizations is that sex education that fails to stress abstinence has the effect of encouraging promiscuity. Accordingly we asked:

> People have different ideas about sex education for young people. Some think
> it should aim at getting young people to abstain from sex completely until
> they are married. Others think you have to be realistic and that young people
> need to know about birth control choices if they are to protect themselves.
> Which view comes closer to your own?

The prevailing opinion of nearly two-thirds (65 percent) is that young people should have the information they may need. Less than one-third (29 percent) think sex education should be limited to counseling complete abstinence.

This division of opinion holds fairly constant across groups having different general and specific views about government with an important exception. Steady Critics diverge from others by coming down mostly on the side of abstinence. By more than two to one, all others think that sex education should include information about birth control (table 4.8).

To summarize, sex education is the issue of concern to conservative Christians on which critics of government are most divided. Differences of opinion among critics are somewhat less pronounced regarding the issue of homosexuality. Least divisive is the matter of divorce. Majorities of both Steady Critics and Ambivalent Critics think divorce should be allowed for reasons other than abuse or adultery. Differences among supporters of government on all of these issues are not significant.

Good for the Country?

Conservative Christian organizations are forthright regarding their objective: to mobilize citizens for the kind of political action that will bring their understanding of Christian values into the decisions of government. This reassures some while for others it raises serious First Amendment questions about the separation of church and state.[10]

We explored the public's sense of the tension between these competing perspectives as follows:

> There has been talk about conservative Christian groups that organize in their communities, taking part in politics, distributing voter guides, and working to promote Christian values at all levels of government.

> Some people think this is good for the country because it is the only way to make sure government is run by Christian principles. Others feel this is not good for the country because they believe in the separation of church and state, and think religion should be kept out of government. Which view is closest to yours?

Opinion is divided fairly evenly with a narrow plurality of 48 percent holding that these activities are not good for the country compared to 43 percent who say the opposite. The remainder give a qualified response or do not state an opinion.

With respect to views on government, it is critics of government who are divided. Over half (55 percent) of Steady Critics think conservative Christian groups are good for the country. In contrast, almost half (49 percent) of Ambivalent Critics have their doubts. There is virtually no difference in opinion between Steady Supporters and Ambivalent Supporters, both of whom doubt that the activities of these groups are in the best interests of the country (table 4.9).

Identification with the Conservative Christian Movement

When asked whether "you think of yourself as part of the conservative Christian movement that is active in politics," only 13 percent answer in the affir-

---

[10] Illustrative of this concern is theologian Harvey Cox's account of the centrality of "dominion theology" to the beliefs of the Rev. Pat Robertson. This theology asserts that only those who believe in Judeo-Christian values should be at the seat of power until Christ comes again. See Harvey Cox, "The Warring Visions of the Religious Right," *Atlantic Monthly* (November 1995): 66.

Table 4.9

View of Conservative Christian Organizations
and Identification with the Conservative Christian Movement
by Mix of General and Specific Views about Government

		Mostly critical		Mostly supportive	
	All	Steady Critic	Ambivalent Critic	Ambivalent Supporter	Steady Supporter
Political activities of conservative Christian groups are					
Good for country	43%	55%	41%	38%	39%
Not good for country	48	35	49	55	55
Qualified/don't know	9	10	10	7	6
	100%	100%	100%	100%	100%
Consider self part of conservative Christian movement?					
Yes	13%	17%	13%	12%	11%
No	83	79	82	81	87
Qualified/don't know	4	4	5	7	1
	100%	100%	100%	100%	99%

[Q.41;60]

mative.[11] Those who do identify with the movement more often than others
are blacks, Republicans, and self-described political conservatives. A sense of
affinity with the movement varies only slightly by where people live. It is somewhat higher in the South and somewhat lower on the east and west coasts
(table A.11 in appendix A).

Whereas Steady Critics are much more likely to think conservative Christian organizations are good for the country than Ambivalent Critics, they are
not more likely than Ambivalent Critics to identify with it. Seventeen percent
of Steady Critics consider themselves part of the movement compared to
13 percent of Ambivalent Critics, a difference that is not statistically significant
(table 4.9). In fact only 26 percent of Steady Critics who think the movement
is a good thing also think of themselves as part of it.

---

[11] Pollsters have taken different approaches to asking this question. For a discussion of the
rationale for our approach, see appendix C.

This raises the interesting question of how much people identify with the conservative Christian movement when their opinions on related matters might suggest particular affinity. We found the following:

Percent identifying with the conservative Christian movement among . . .
All respondents   13%
Those describing their views on political matters
    as "conservative"   20
Those calling themselves "born again"   24
Those thinking the activities of conservative
    Christian groups are good for the country   25

We will return to these findings in chapter 5 where the intensity of a person's religious beliefs and practices are weighed against other considerations as possible explanations for ambivalent feelings about government.

ISSUES AND AMBIVALENCE ABOUT GOVERNMENT: A RECAP

We have been gauging the relationship between opinions on issues and ambivalence about government. We have been comparing the views of Steady Critics and Ambivalent Critics, on the one hand, and the views of Steady Supporters and Ambivalent Supporters, on the other. The greater the differences of opinion on an issue, the greater the chance that issue may help us understand why some have mixed feelings about government and others do not.[12]

The evidence is that some issues are particularly associated with the ambivalence found among critics of government. Other issues relate to ambivalence among both critics and supporters. Still other issues appear to have no bearing on either kind of ambivalence.

Among those Critical of Government

With respect to those who are "mostly critical" in their general views about government, differences of opinion are especially noteworthy on six issues (table 4.10).

---

[12] The differences reported here are with respect to the *direction* of opinion. But what about the *intensity* of the opinions? It turns out there is nothing inherent to being "ambivalent" as a critic or supporter that makes respondents feel less intensely about these issues (see appendix C).

Table 4.10

Summary of Differences of Opinion on Issues Between Steady
and Ambivalent Critics and Between Steady and Ambivalent Supporters

	Size of difference between Steady Critics and Ambivalent Critics	Size of difference between Steady Supporters and Ambivalent Supporters
Performance of government		
Favorable rating of job done by:		
Federal government	Medium[a]	n.s.
State government	n.s.	n.s.
Local government	Small	n.s.
Express confidence in:		
Quality of work in federal agencies	Large	n.s.
U.S. Congress serving all	n.s.	n.s.
Quality of work in state agencies	Large	n.s.
State legislature serving all	n.s.	n.s.
Improving way government works:		
One of very most important matters	n.s.	n.s.
Amount of progress: losing ground	Medium	n.s.
Leaders who go beyond short-term solutions:		
One of very most important matters	Medium	n.s.
Amount of progress: losing ground	Small	Small
Marketplace and opportunity		
Getting ahead: anyone can versus barriers	Large	n.s.
Market: govenment keep eye on versus stay out	Large	n.s.
Social problems		
Juvenile crime: get tough versus prevent	Large	Small
Police search: without versus with warrant	n.s.	Small
Dealing with race: not push versus no let up	Large	Medium
Immigrants: fit in versus own traditions	Small	n.s.
Low-income: too much/little government attention	Large	Large
Poverty is due to:		
Lack of job skills	n.s.	Medium
People not trying hard enough to make it	Large	Medium
Poor schools in low-income areas	Medium	Medium
Unable to work (family circumstances)	Small	n.s.
Traditions and social norms		
Personal responsibility:		
One of very most important problems	n.s.	n.s.
Amount of progress: losing ground	Small	Medium
Family problems have to do with:		
Parents working long hours	n.s.	Small

Table 4.10   Continued

	Size of difference between Steady Critics and Ambivalent Critics	Size of difference between Steady Supporters and Ambivalent Supporters
Too much sex/violence on TV and in media	Medium	n.s.
Not enough after school activities	n.s.	n.s.
Schools not teaching right from wrong	Small	n.s.
Conduct: self-control versus self-expression	Medium	Small
Children: learn to fit in versus be selves	Small	n.s.
Concerns of conservative Christian organizations		
Homosexuality threatens values of family	Medium	n.s.
Divorce for: adultery/abuse or other reasons	n.s.	Small
Sex education: abstain versus information	Large	n.s.
Christian groups good/bad for country	Medium	n.s.
Consider self part of movement or not	n.s.	n.s.

Note: This display is based on data reported in tables 3.2, 3.4, 3.6, 4.1–4.4, 4.6–4.9. For a summary of those data and the differences between groups, see table A.12 in appendix A.

[a]Differences of 16 percentage points or more are considered "large"; differences from 11 to 15 points are "medium"; and differences less than 10 points are "small" if they are statistically significant. Differences that are not statistically significant are designated "n.s." Differences regarding reasons for poverty and family difficulties need to be larger since the questions were asked of half the sample.

• Most Ambivalent Critics think the government is paying too little attention to the concerns of low-income people. Steady Critics, in contrast, are likely to think government is paying too much attention.

• Ambivalent Critics see poverty resulting most often from people lacking the skills needed to get a steady job. Steady Critics are much more likely to think people are poor because they are not trying hard enough to make it on their own.

• The overwhelming majority of Ambivalent Critics think now is no time to let up in pushing for racial equality. Steady Critics, on the other hand, are divided on the matter with a sizeable minority who think the country does not need to push so hard in light of the gains that have been made.

• Ambivalent Critics are more willing to have government keep an eye on things to ensure fair competition than are Steady Critics who are strongly of the opinion government should stay out and let the market decide who gets ahead.

• Ambivalent Critics are much more convinced that sex education should provide young people with the information they may need, whereas Steady Critics tend to believe that complete abstinence is what should be taught.
• Ambivalent Critics come down decisively on the strategy of trying to prevent juvenile crime, while Steady Critics lean toward getting tougher with young offenders.

A second tier of issues separates Ambivalent Critics from Steady Critics but not by the margins of the issues above.

• Ambivalent Critics are less likely to see homosexuality as a threat to the American family than Steady Critics.
• Ambivalent Critics are divided in their view of whether anyone can get ahead if they work hard enough or whether hard work is not enough to overcome some barriers. For Steady Critics, there is no such division of opinion: hard work is what it takes.
• A plurality of Ambivalent Critics think conservative Christian groups are not good for the country in contrast to a majority of Steady Critics who feel the opposite.
• Ambivalent Critics worry less than Steady Critics about declining respect for the values of discipline and self-restraint.

Among those Supportive of Government

There are few differences of opinion among those who are "mostly supportive" in their general views of government. Unlike those who are "mostly critical" of government, supporters see things pretty much eye to eye (table 4.10).

Only one of the differences between Steady Supporters and Ambivalent Supporters is large. While the prevailing view among both groups is that government is paying too little attention to low-income households, Ambivalent Supporters are noticeably less united in that view than are Steady Supporters.

Modest divergence in opinion does occur in three other areas:

• Ambivalent Supporters are more likely than Steady Supporters to think poverty is due to a lack of effort and less likely to see it resulting from poor schools and a shortage of job skills.
• Ambivalent Supporters are slightly more inclined than Steady Supporters to think we need not push so hard on race, although the

overwhelming view of both groups is that now is not the time to let up working for racial equality.

• Ambivalent Supporters are somewhat more concerned than Steady Supporters that the country is losing ground in teaching personal responsibility and moral character.

But again, the principal conclusion here is that Ambivalent Supporters and Steady Supporters agree on more issues than they disagree.

Issues Not Linked to Ambivalence about Government

The issues and aspects of opinion covered in this survey were included because they plausibly might help explain ambivalence about government. Consequently we should take note when differences of opinion do *not* occur between those who are "steady" and "ambivalent" as critics or as supporters in their thinking about government.

Several matters discussed in this chapter seem to provide little insight into the ambivalence of either government's critics or its supporters. Accordingly they can be dropped as candidates for possible explanations of ambivalence. Two have to do with social policy:

• Opposition to police searches without a warrant is so widespread that it is expressed by critics and supporters alike regardless of how ambivalent they may be.

• The issue of immigration elicits only slight variation of opinion among critics and none among supporters.

Three issues deal with passing values and traditions on to future generations:

• Critics and supporters of government tend to see many of the same sources for the difficulties many American families are facing. It is only with respect to violence and sex in the media that critics have a modest difference of emphasis.

• The issue of how much attention children should pay to their peers does not divide critics or supporters.

• Views about the circumstances under which divorce should be permitted do not separate Steady Critics from Ambivalent Critics or Ambivalent Supporters from Steady Supporters.

FIVE

Personal Situation and Ambivalence about Government

W E HAVE TAKEN SEVERAL STEPS IN TRYING TO UNDERSTAND
what might account for the ambivalence many Americans
feel about government. We have looked at ways in which it
may be connected to views about the government's performance and opinions on a wide range of issues. We turn here to another possible source of ambivalence about government: the differing personal situations in which people find themselves. Our interest here is whether
ambivalence about government is explained by differences among people in
matters such as their sense of personal financial security or their knowledge
about or experience with government.

SENSE OF PERSONAL WELL-BEING

"How are you?" Few questions are asked more often by more people
around the world. Answers may reflect the ups and downs of the moment, but they are always rooted in the balance of hopes and fears making up
a person's sense of well-being.

Answers people give to that question may bear on how they think about
government. For some, government's involvement in their life may be a source
of reassurance. For others, it may be an irritant. And still others may feel cut
off from or unaffected by what government does.

To gauge the sense of personal well-being we asked respondents to think
of a ladder with the top rung (step 10) representing "the best possible life you
could think of for yourself" and the bottom rung (step 0) representing "the
worst possible life you could think of for yourself." People were then asked on
which step of the ladder they felt they stood at the present time. They were

also asked where they stood five years ago and where they think they will be five years from now.[1]

The average (mean) ratings of personal well-being in this survey:

Mean ratings
Past	5.6
Present	6.8
Future	8.0

Shifts in ratings
Past to present	+1.2
Present to future	+1.2
Overall: past to future	+2.4

Most significant in these ratings are the shifts from past to present and present to future. A present ladder rating that is higher than the past can be taken as indicating a person has a sense of personal accomplishment over the past five years. The larger the shift, the greater the sense of progress. Conversely, a sense of sliding backwards is picked up when the present rating is lower than the past. Similarly, feelings of optimism and pessimism can be picked up when present and future ratings are compared.

These ladder-rating shifts tell many stories when looked at in terms of different social and economic groups. One of the most striking is the contrast between the optimism of youth and the less buoyant approach of older people (see table A.13 in appendix A).

A host of considerations may lie behind differences in the shifts in these personal ladder ratings. In order to understand what is really at work we need a way of gauging the relative importance of different possible explanations for rating shifts. This can be accomplished by taking one explanation at a time and

---

[1] This approach, the "self-anchoring striving scale," was developed by Hadley Cantril in connection with an international study of human aspirations. The ladder ratings are "anchored" in the unique experience of each individual. Thus they provide a way of comparing the perspectives of people in disparate situations. For example, a forty-year-old person who has just been laid off might give the same present rating as a seventy-year-old person who is worried about the health of a spouse. The two ratings would be equivalent in psychological terms even though the concerns of the two individuals are worlds apart. It is interesting that the mean ladder ratings Americans give their personal lives have remained fairly stable over the years. In fact the ratings in this survey are almost the same as those given by the public when the ladder question sequence was first used in 1959. Then, the past rating was 5.9; present was 6.6; and the future was 7.8. See Hadley Cantril, *The Pattern of Human Concerns* (New Brunswick, N.J.: Rutgers University Press, 1965).

determining the strength of its relationship to the ladder ratings while *at the same time* taking into account other possible explanations.[2]

Such an analysis shows that age is the most important consideration in explaining shifts in personal ratings. It is followed in importance by a person's sense of being financially secure. Both age and financial security (to which we turn in the next section) have more to do with both feelings of progress from the past and optimism about the future than such things as education, household income, the respondent's sex, or ratings of the performance of the federal government.

What does perceived personal well-being tell us about ambivalence toward government? The only effect the personal ladder ratings appear to have on the mix of views about government is among government's critics. Steady Critics are less optimistic about where they will be in five years. This is explained in part by the larger number of older persons among Steady Critics who are less hopeful about the future than others. Among supporters of government, ladder ratings are virtually the same, regardless of ambivalence expressed about government (table 5.1).

We sought an additional indication of respondents' overall feelings of accomplishment or frustration in the achievement of their personal goals. After giving ladder ratings for the past, present, and future, people were asked: "You said you thought you were at [present ladder rating] on the ladder at the present time. As you look back on things, is this about where you thought you would be now, or have you done better, or have you done worse than you thought you might?"

Forty-five percent say they have done better, 29 percent are about where they thought they would be, 21 percent have done worse, and 5 percent are not sure. A kind of irrepressible "can do" attitude is reflected in these figures. It is underscored by the fact that those who say they have done worse than they expected are most optimistic about the future (see table A.13 in appendix A). This corroborates one of the major conclusions of the original "striving scale" studies: "Human beings are creatures of hope and are not genetically designed to resign themselves."[3]

When looked at in terms of ambivalence about government, there are no substantial differences among critics or supporters. Accomplishments relative to expectations are virtually the same for Steady Critics and Ambivalent Critics. Compared to Ambivalent Supporters, Steady Supporters are slightly more inclined to think they have done better than they expected (table 5.1).

---

[2] These multivariate analyses relied on multiple regression as described in appendix D, especially table D.2.

[3] Cantril, *Pattern of Human Concerns*, 317.

Table 5.1

Personal Ladder Ratings and Shifts by Mix of General and
Specific Views about Government

	All	Steady Critic	Ambivalent Critic	Ambivalent Supporter	Steady Supporter
Average (mean) ratings[a]					
Past	5.6	6.1	5.6	5.5	5.4
Present	6.8	7.2	6.8	6.6	6.6
Future	8.0	7.7	8.1	8.0	8.2
Rating shifts					
Past to Present	1.2	1.1	1.2	1.1	1.2
Present to Future	1.2	0.5	1.3	1.4	1.6
Overall: Past to Future	2.4	1.6	2.5	2.5	2.8
Present ladder rating compared to where expected would be now					
Have done better	44%	45%	47%	39%	46%
Where thought would be	29	32	30	35	28
Have done worse	21	20	20	19	22
Not sure	6	3	3	7	4
	100%	100%	100%	100%	100%

[a]We can be 95 percent sure that differences of 0.4 or more between ratings of the critic/supporter groups are significant, that is did not occur by chance in the sampling process.

[Q.2a–d]

For most Americans there is not a strong link between their attitudes toward government and how they feel they are doing overall in their personal lives. The exception is among Steady Critics, who tend to be somewhat older than others and less upbeat about the future.

On balance, other than respondents' age, it is difficult to infer much about a person's thinking about government from such a broad-gauged measure of personal well-being as the ladder ratings. The ladder-rating questions take in many personal concerns, some of which may pertain to government and others that may not.

PERSONAL FINANCIAL SECURITY, PERCEIVED EQUITIES, AND AMBIVALENCE

We have seen that financial security is second only to age as a foundation of a sense of personal well-being. Such security, however, involves more than income. It is the feeling of being able to weather a variety of uncertainties that can affect even those who may seem to be doing well.

The financial insecurity of many middle-income households is put at center stage in accounts of the politics of the 1980s and early 1990s. This insecurity is said to have dislodged the confidence people had during those years that government had struck the right balance in the attention it pays to different groups and fueled uneasiness about its inattention to the concerns of middle-income households.

It was on this terrain that Ronald Reagan made inroads among Democrats in 1984, especially in the industrial midwest. As described by Stanley Greenberg, these were traditional Democrats who "were disillusioned, angry voters, but they were not Republicans. They spoke of a broken contract, not a new vision. Their way of life was . . . threatened by profound economic changes beyond their control, yet their leaders, who were supposed to look out for them, were preoccupied with other groups and other issues."[4]

When Democrats attempted to respond to these signals of insecurity, fissures within the party were exposed. Those affiliated with the Democratic Leadership Council rejected "liberal fundamentalism," which they saw as "a coalition increasingly dominated by minority groups and white elites—a coalition viewed by the middle class as unsympathetic to its interests and values."[5] Those aligned more closely with the party's traditional base called for a "liberal nationalism" that would affirm "the mutual obligation of Americans to Americans" and do so by focusing on the inner city, public education, and the environment.[6]

Now, even in relatively good times, there are reasons to be nervous on the financial front: employee benefits are being trimmed; some are having to finance their own retirement; new skills are required to be competitive in the job market; and corporations downsize in the name of productivity.

To determine how much, if at all, financial insecurity bears on attitudes toward government, we need to consider three things. First, we need a sense of how secure people really feel. Second, we need to know what effect feelings of insecurity may have on evaluations of government's fairness in addressing the concerns of different income groups. Third, we need to find out whether these judgments influence the mix of general and specific views about government.

Financial Security

Questions to assess feelings of financial security asked about five areas "that make some people uneasy when they think about their personal situation." Re-

---

[4] Greenberg, *Middle Class Dreams*, 34.

[5] William Galston and Elaine Ciulla Kamarck, *The Politics of Evasion: Democrats and the Presidency* (Washington, D.C.: Progressive Policy Institute, September 1989), 3.

[6] Jeff Faux, *The Party's Not Over*, 171–232.

spondents express considerable uncertainty regarding each of the five items. The proportions who say they are worried "a great deal" about these matters are:

> Social Security not being able to pay the benefits people expect   44%
> Not having adequate health care or health insurance when you or
>   someone in your family really need it   40
> Not having enough to live on when you are retired   38
> Not being able to pay the bills at some point in the next few years   34
> You or someone in your household not having a job or losing a job   30

We created an index of financial security based on responses to these questions. The index ranged from very insecure through moderately insecure and moderately secure to very secure.[7]

People in all income brackets experience financial insecurity in one way or another. Almost two-thirds (63 percent) of those in households with incomes under $30,000 feel very or moderately insecure. It is also the case that nearly one-third (31 percent) of those in households with incomes in excess of $75,000 feel insecure (see table A.14 in appendix A).

Financial Security and Perceived Equities

We get a window into perceived equities and inequities by looking at how much attention people think government is paying to different income groups. The prevailing view is that all but the affluent are receiving too little attention from government (table 5.2).

Of particular interest is that those who think government is paying too little attention to middle-income households are also *most likely* to think that the poor are receiving too little of government's attention. Similar views are seen among those who think "people like you" are not getting enough attention (see table A.15 in appendix A).

The relationship between financial insecurity and these perceived equities is seen by looking at those who think different groups receive too little attention from government:

> • Seventy percent of respondents who feel very insecure think government is paying too little attention to "people like you." Yet only

---

[7] The index took into account responses to three questions asked of the full sample: having enough to live on in retirement; being able to pay the bills; and not losing a job. Questions about Social Security and health care were asked of only half the sample. The three-question index was nearly as reliable as a five-question index (see appendix C for details).

Table 5.2

Amount of Attention Government Is Paying to Different Income Groups

	People like you	Middle income	Low income	Upper income
Too much	6%	5%	18%	63%
About right	38	28	28	22
Too little	52	64	52	11
Don't know	4	3	2	4
	100%	100%	100%	100%

[Q.25a–d]

half as many (36 percent) among those who feel very secure think they are being neglected by government.

• Less striking but still significant is the difference regarding the view that middle-income people are receiving too little attention. Of those feeling most financially stressed, 70 percent think government pays too little attention to middle-income people. Fewer but still a majority (52 percent) of those who feel very secure share that view.

• When it comes to the poor, 66 percent of those who feel very insecure think government is paying too little attention compared to 40 percent of those who feel very secure.

• Feelings of financial security have little to do with opinions about government's attention to those with higher incomes: even a solid majority (59 percent) of the most secure think there is too much government attention to those who are better off (table 5.3).

The relationship between insecurity and views about government's attention to "people like you" and to low-income people deserves an additional comment. In both cases, the relationship holds up *regardless* of the respondent's household income. The more insecure people feel, the more they think government is paying too little attention to people in their situation or to the poor, whether they themselves are from more or less affluent households.

To underscore the point, let us consider people in households with incomes of $50,000 or more. Those who feel insecure are much more likely than the more secure to think government is inattentive to the concerns of "people like you." When it comes to concerns of the poor, 53 percent of those in more affluent households who feel insecure think government is paying too little attention. Yet among the more secure within this income group, only 39 percent see

Table 5.3

Amount of Attention Government Is Seen as Paying to Different Income Groups by Level of Financial Security and Mix of General and Specific Views about Government

	All	By level of financial security				By mix of views about government			
		Very secure	Moderately secure	Moderately insecure	Very insecure	Steady Critic	Ambivalent Critic	Ambivalent Supporter	Steady Supporter
Attention paid to low-income people									
Too much	18%	20%	21%	18%	13%	48%	11%	25%	7%
About right	28	37	32	26	18	24	33	31	28
Too little	52	40	46	54	66	26	55	41	64
Don't know	2	4	1	2	2	2	1	3	1
	100%	99%	101%	99%	101%	100%	100%	100%	100%
Attention paid to middle-income people									
Too much	5%	7%	4%	5%	4%	7%	7%	4%	4%
About right	28	36	27	27	22	22	26	30	34
Too little	64	52	65	67	70	67	66	62	61
Don't know	3	5	3	1	4	3	1	3	2
	100%	100%	99%	100%	100%	99%	100%	99%	101%
Attention paid to upper-income people									
Too much	63%	59%	64%	62%	69%	63%	64%	61%	63%
About right	22	26	26	23	15	23	23	23	24
Too little	11	10	7	13	12	10	11	14	11
Don't know	4	5	3	2	4	5	2	3	2
	100%	100%	100%	100%	100%	101%	100%	101%	100%
Attention paid to people like you									
Too much	6%	9%	5%	6%	3%	14%	6%	4%	3%
About right	38	51	45	36	23	31	38	42	45
Too little	52	36	47	55	70	52	54	51	50
Don't know	4	4	3	3	4	4	2	2	2
	100%	100%	100%	100%	100%	101%	100%	99%	100%

[O.25a-d:33a-e]

government's attention as too little. The same pattern is seen among respondents in households in other income brackets (see table A.16 in appendix A).

These findings suggest three conclusions regarding public attitudes, especially toward those at the bottom of the income scale.

- Those who think middle-income people are receiving too little attention from government are more likely than others to think it is also paying too little attention to the poor.
- Whatever the reason, it is the least secure who think government is paying *too little* attention to lower-income households. The connection between feelings of financial insecurity and government's perceived fairness is just the opposite of what we would find if insecurity were a seedbed of feelings that government was tilting unfairly to the poor. Perhaps this is a reflection of better economic times for many.
- The relationship between feelings of insecurity and governmental fairness cannot be accounted for simply by looking at household income.

Closely related is the finding that most people do not seem to buy the argument that the benefits of economic growth are dispersed widely throughout the society. We asked the question: "When you hear that the U.S. economy has been growing, do you think it is more likely to mean that all Americans are gaining or that the gap between the rich and the poor is getting bigger?"

Seventy-seven percent of those polled share the view that growth in the economy means the gap between the rich and poor gets bigger. Only 17 percent see all Americans gaining.

This consensus is strong among diverse groups. A sense the rich-poor gap only gets larger with economic growth is shared by more than two-thirds of those who: (a) feel financially secure; (b) live in households with incomes over $100,000; and (c) think anyone can get ahead in this country if they work hard enough (see table A.17 in appendix A).

Perceived Equities and Ambivalence about Government

For purposes of this study, the crucial question is whether these questions of fairness influence the mix of general and specific views about government.

On three fronts, perceived fairness appears to have no major bearing on whether critics or supporters of government are ambivalent in their thinking: government's attention to "people like you," those in the middle, and those in the upper income brackets (table 5.3).

But on the fourth front, noted earlier, government's attention to the poor, perceived equities have a major influence on what people think about government.

- Forty-eight percent of Steady Critics think government is paying too much attention to low-income people. In contrast, most Ambivalent Critics (55 percent) think government is paying too little attention.
- Ambivalent Supporters are significantly less inclined to think government pays too little attention to low-income households than Steady Supporters. Even so, a plurality of 41 percent of Ambivalent Supporters think government does not pay enough attention.

Further indication of differing perspectives between Steady Critics and Ambivalent Critics is the matter of who is seen to gain when the economy grows. Steady Critics are twice as likely as Ambivalent Critics to think all benefit with growth in the economy. This is consistent with findings reported in the last chapter where it was shown that Steady Critics are significantly more confident than Ambivalent Critics that anyone can get ahead with hard work and that the government has no role in ensuring competitiveness in the marketplace.

Nonetheless, the prevailing view among Steady Critics is that the effect of economic growth is to widen the gap between rich and poor. This suggests that the case for the benefits of "growing the economy" faces a kind of populist skepticism even among those who might be expected to be most responsive (table 5.4).[8]

These are findings that we will return to in chapter 6 as we weigh the relative contribution of different components of public opinion in helping us understand ambivalence toward government.

Class

Much of the politics of financial insecurity has been played out in recent years in terms of social class. Phrases such as "middle-class values" and "working-class issues" serve many agendas. More specifically, the belief appears wide-

---

[8] We do not know how much the current state of the economy accounts for the relationships discussed among feelings of insecurity, perceived equities, and views of government. It is beyond the scope of this study to anchor these findings in historical trends regarding the economic life of the nation. This would require showing plausible long-term relationships among the way people view government, their own financial situation, and ups and downs in the larger economy, including changes in the distribution of income and wealth.

Table 5.4

Whether Economic Growth Means All Gain or Gap Between Rich and Poor Gets
Bigger by Mix of General and Specific Views about Government

	All	Steady Critic	Ambivalent Critic	Ambivalent Supporter	Steady Supporter
All gain	17%	30%	15%	13%	14%
Gap between rich and poor gets bigger	76	60	81	77	82
Qualified response	2	2	1	2	1
Don't know	6	8	3	8	3
	100%	100%	100%	100%	100%

[Q.26]

spread in political circles that appeals to class are an effective way of making the case for or against government in some arenas. The question here is whether class bears on ambivalence about government.

When asked "which of the following best describes your situation," 59 percent say they are part of the middle class. Twenty-nine percent identify with the working class. Seven percent describe their situation as lower class, and 3 percent consider themselves upper class.

Class identity turns out to have no substantial bearing on the mix of general and specific views people have about government. Steady Critics are only slightly more likely than Ambivalent Critics to think of themselves as middle class, and there is virtually no difference among supporters of government on the matter of class identification (table 5.5).

One reason that class may have so little to do with views about government is that people from so many walks of life are brought together under the terms "middle class" or "working class." Consider income: more people in households with incomes under $30,000 consider themselves part of the middle class (44 percent) than part of the working class or any other group. Or consider occupation: both professionals and white collar workers tend to think of themselves as middle class. While those in blue-collar occupations are more likely to look upon themselves as part of the working class, 39 percent use "middle class" to describe their situation. Sixty-two percent of respondents in households with a member of a labor union think of themselves as part of the "middle class" (see table A.18 in appendix A).

In short, social class cuts so wide a swath across American society that it tells us little about why some are ambivalent in their thinking about government.

Table 5.5

Percent Identifying with a Class by Mix of General
and Specific Views about Government

	All	Steady Critic	Ambivalent Critic	Ambivalent Supporter	Steady Supporter
Upper class	3%	4%	4%	3%	2%
Middle class	59	66	59	58	58
Working class	29	24	27	32	30
Lower class	7	4	7	4	9
Not sure/refuse	2	2	3	3	1
	100%	100%	100%	100%	100%

[Q.66]

EDUCATION, KNOWLEDGE ABOUT GOVERNMENT, AND INTEREST IN NEWS

Pollsters have been challenged to prove that the opinions they report represent more than top-of-the-head comments from people who may not know or may not have thought much about the topics about which they are being asked. Evidence usually marshalled in support of this critique is that respondents give what seem to be patently inconsistent answers to survey questions.

Skeptics will point out that the opinions people express on an issue often conflict with the broader principles they say guide their thinking on the matter at hand. Or skeptics will be frustrated when people's views on one topic cannot be predicted from their views on a related topic.

The field of opinion research has taken these challenges seriously. A substantial body of empirical work has evolved over the years and, along with it, assurances that the answers respondents give to interviewers warrant respectful attention.[9]

The important inference from this earlier work for purposes of this inquiry is that ambivalence in thinking about government should represent more than people giving superficial answers to questions asked of them. If ambiva-

---

[9] See Donald R. Kinder, "Diversity and Complexity in American Public Opinion," in Ada W. Finifter, ed., *Political Science: The State of the Discipline* (Washington, D.C.: American Political Science Association, 1983), 389–425; Benjamin I. Page and Robert Y. Shapiro, *The Rational Public: Fifty Years of Trends in Americans' Policy Preferences* (Chicago, Ill.: University of Chicago Press, 1992); and Albert H. Cantril and Susan Davis Cantril, "Polls Portray a Considered and Stable Public Opinion," *Public Perspective* 7 (June/July 1996): 23–26.

lence is integral to public opinion about government, we should find it expressed by people regardless of such things as formal education or knowledge about how government works.

This is not to say that education and knowledge about government are unimportant influences on public opinion. Clearly they expose people to perspectives different from their own and may alert them to some of the implications of the opinions they hold. But it may be going too far to suggest that education and knowledge alone would resolve matters to the point where people would no longer hold ambivalent views about something so multifaceted as government. If ambivalence is important to our understanding of American public opinion, it should represent more than differing levels of information people bring to bear as they size up issues facing the country.

We tested this line of argument in several ways. The first question to answer is what effect education and knowledge about government have on the ease with which people express opinions. The issue then becomes whether those with more education and information about government seem to be less ambivalent about government. If so, it would suggest that education and knowledge do indeed help people think things through, thereby reducing their ambivalence about government. If not, it would suggest that ambivalence about government reflects something deeper in American public opinion that goes beyond education and knowledge.

The Expression of Opinion

Earlier research shows more informed people are more likely to express opinions on issues about which they are asked.[10] This is not to say their opinions are "better," just that more informed people offer more opinions about more topics.

Evidence in this survey provides modest confirmation along these lines. We looked at answers to forty-four questions in the survey and counted the number on which respondents expressed an opinion. The questions asked for opinions on a wide range of issues. Not included in the forty-four were questions about kinds of political activity (such as voting or party preference), experience with government, or the respondent's social or demographic characteristics.

The average (mean) number of questions to which the sample as a whole gave answers was 41.6. Thus respondents on balance answered "don't know" to slightly more than two of the forty-four questions.

---

[10] See Michael X. Delli Carpini and Scott Keeter, *What Americans Know about Politics and Why It Matters* (New Haven, Conn.: Yale University Press, 1996), 230–38.

By this measure formal education is seen to have only a slight bearing on the number of opinions expressed. College graduates express opinions on 42.1 questions on average compared to 41.6 questions for those with some college, 41.7 among high school graduates, and 40.9 among those with less than a high school education.

Knowledge about how government works has a similar relationship to the expression of opinion. Our measure of level of information about government is based on correct answers to questions regarding the party having most members in the Congress; the number of votes needed to override a presidential veto; which branch of government determines the constitutionality of a law; and whether Franklin Roosevelt was a Democrat or a Republican.[11]

Again, referring to the forty-four questions, the most informed express opinions on an average of 42.2 questions. This compares to 41.8 for those who are moderately well-informed, 41.9 among those who are less informed and 40.8 among the least informed.

When this yardstick is applied to the matter of ambivalence in thinking about government, the following results emerge:

	Mean number of opinions
Steady Critics	41.7
Ambivalent Critics	42.2
Ambivalent Supporters	41.6
Steady Supporters	42.2
Neither critic nor supporter	38.4

The striking finding here is that there is nothing about being ambivalent, either as a critic or supporter of government, that has to with reticence in voicing an opinion on a wide variety of issues.

Education, Knowledge about Government, and Ambivalence

We still do not know whether education and awareness reduce or, in some cases, increase the amount of ambivalence expressed about government. Those with more education and knowledge about government might be expected to express opinions about specific activities of government that are more likely to reflect their general views about government. Following this line of argument, those with less education and knowledge might be more likely to hold general and specific opinions about government that are at odds with one another.

---

[11] For more information, see appendix C.

Table 5.6

Education and Knowledge about Government by Mix of General
and Specific Views about Government

	All	Steady Critic	Ambivalent Critic	Ambivalent Supporter	Steady Supporter	Neither Critic nor Supporter
Education						
Less than high school	17%	11%	16%	20%	15%	29%
High school graduate	37	38	40	40	37	32
Some college	23	26	24	18	23	25
College and beyond	23	25	20	22	25	14
	100%	100%	100%	100%	100%	100%
Knowledge about government						
Low	28%	14%	29%	30%	29%	40%
Moderately low	24	21	22	25	25	25
Moderately high	26	28	29	26	23	25
High	23	37	20	18	23	11
	101%	100%	100%	99%	100%	101%

[Q.51–54;67]

Data from the survey indicate that there is no significant connection between education and ambivalence in thinking about government. On the one hand, Ambivalent Critics and Steady Critics are quite similar when it comes to their level of education. That the same is true among supporters leads us to conclude that the amount of formal education does not explain why some are ambivalent about government while others are not (table 5.6).

Where education has an effect is whether a person's general views about government can be described as "mostly critical" or "mostly supportive" in the first place. If we look at those whose views cannot be characterized one way or the other, we find a higher proportion of respondents with less than a high school education than among those who are critics or supporters. Thus the effect of education is to bring people far enough into political matters that their general views fall into an overall pattern of being critical or supportive. Once above that threshold, education does not seem to affect whether people are ambivalent in their thinking about government.

Compared to education, knowledge about government appears to have a more direct bearing on ambivalence among government's critics. As measured by the information questions described earlier, there is a 17 percentage point difference between the 37 percent of Steady Critics with "high" knowledge and the 20 percent of Ambivalent Critics (table 5.6).

This is an instance in which cause and effect are difficult to sort out. On the one hand, the higher level of knowledge of Steady Critics may lead to both general and specific doubts about government. On the other hand, it is probably true that many Steady Critics pick up a good deal of information from complaints about government they hear from others or the media, such as talk radio. Knowledge about government has no comparable bearing on the ambivalence of supporters of government (table 5.6).

While not directly related to ambivalence, it is interesting to look at the effect of education and knowledge on the degree to which opinions people hold about government correspond to the way they describe their views on political matters. We noted in chapter 2 that a person's self-described political outlook is often not a good indication of what they actually think about government. For example, one-third (34 percent) of those calling themselves "very conservative" in political matters are supporters of government.

The picture changes, however, when education or knowledge about government are taken into account. There is much greater correspondence between self-described political point of view and opinions about government among the more educated and more knowledgeable (see table A.19 in appendix A).

Interest in News

When it comes to determining how much a person's views on various issues converge around "conservative" or "liberal" positions, it is more important to know about their interest in what is going on in the political arena than about how far they have gone in school. That is, opinions of people most attentive to current developments are more likely to point in a common direction than the opinions of people who are most educated.[12] But is the same true regarding the congruence between general and specific views about government?

We get three insights into this question from the survey. First, ambivalence about government appears to have little to do with where people turn for news. When asked about five sources of news, there are no significant differences across the board in the percent who say they rely on a source "almost every day"—with one exception. The one break from the pattern is that Steady Critics tune into talk radio twice as often as others. But the main finding here

---

[12] This was shown in analyses of the National Election Studies from 1956 through 1972. See Norman H. Nie, Sidney Verba, and John R. Petrocik, *The Changing American Voter* (Cambridge, Mass.: Harvard University Press, 1976), 145–55.

Table 5.7

Sources of News Relied on Almost Every Day and
How Closely Follow Government and Public Affairs
by Mix of General and Specific Views about Government

	All	Steady Critic	Ambivalent Critic	Ambivalent Supporter	Steady Supporter
Rely on almost every day					
Network TV news	59%	56%	61%	54%	60%
Newspaper	51	55	51	52	51
Radio news	44	49	45	42	41
News on CNN or C-SPAN	24	24	20	26	28
Talk radio	15	24	12	10	13
Summary index of amount of news consumed					
Low	37%	40%	37%	37%	36%
Moderate	35	30	31	39	37
High	28	30	32	24	26
	100%	100%	100%	100%	100%
How closely follow what's going on in government and public affairs					
Most of the time	37%	56%	36%	39%	31%
Some of the time	36	27	41	33	39
Only now and then	19	12	18	16	21
Hardly at all	8	5	5	12	9
	100%	100%	100%	100%	100%

[Q.1a–e;46]

is the absence of other differences in the sources people rely on for news (table 5.7).

Second, the overall amount of news people take in does not vary by the presence or absence of ambivalence in their thinking about government. A summary measure of use of the five news sources shows virtually no difference between Steady Critics and Ambivalent Critics or between Ambivalent Supporters and Steady Supporters (table 5.7).[13]

Third, to complement questions about news sources, we asked a more general question about how closely people follow "what's going on in government and public affairs." The results indicate that Steady Critics follow developments much more closely than others. Well over half (56 percent) of Steady

---

[13] See appendix C regarding the makeup of this index.

Critics say they keep abreast of events most of the time compared to a much smaller proportion (36 percent) among Ambivalent Critics. There are no comparable differences among supporters (table 5.7).

To the extent there are differences in these measures of exposure to politics and public affairs, they appear mostly among critics of government. In an effort to pull these findings together and relate them to ambivalence about government, an analysis looked at them simultaneously as possible explanations for ambivalence. It shows that ambivalence among critics is explained as much by close attention to current events as by knowledge about government. Education and the amount of news consumed have less to say about how ambivalent critics are in their thinking.[14]

Below is a brief summary of the impact of education, knowledge, and news interest on ambivalence about government:

- Education, at least in the formal sense, does not have much to do with ambivalence about government. Holding what seem to be ambivalent views appears to be perfectly compatible with higher levels of education.

- Education and knowledge about government appear to provide a grounding on which people form general views of government that come together as being "mostly critical" or "mostly supportive." It is those who cannot be described as either "critics" or "supporters" of government who have least education and knowledge about government.

- Interest in news about government and public affairs and, to a lesser extent, knowledge about government are areas where Steady Critics are in closer touch with things than Ambivalent Critics.

- There are no notable differences among government's supporters when it comes to levels of education, knowledge about government, or interest in what is going on in the news.

EXPERIENCE WITH GOVERNMENT

Another possible explanation for views about government could be self-interest—how much people think government affects their everyday lives. If people think they are being helped by some activity, chances are they will look more favorably upon it. Or, they might be less supportive of an activity that does not seem to be clearly in their own interest. We explored this possibility in several ways.

---

[14] For a description of this multivariate analysis, see appendix D, especially table D.3.

Table 5.8

Percent Who Support Each Specific Activity of Government
by Whether or Not Personally Affected by It

	Percent who support an activity among those who are	
	Affected by it	Not affected by it
Medical research	95%	92%
Job training for low-income people	93	91
Teachers' salaries in poor school districts	90	85
Safe working conditions	91	85
Head Start	91	84
Financing college education	94	82
Medicaid	85	78
Housing assistance for low-income families	82	73
Clean air standards	91	72
Consumer product safety	87	71

[Q.4a–j;5a–j]

We asked people how direct a bearing they thought each of the ten activities of the federal government covered in chapter 2 had on them personally.[15] Replies range from more than three-fourths (78 percent) who say enforcement of clean air standards affects them very or somewhat directly to less than one-third (31 percent) who say the same of housing assistance to low-income families (see table A.20 in appendix A).

What is striking is that support for most activities remains high even among those not personally affected by them. Consider six activities: medical research, job training for low-income people, assistance to poor school districts in paying teachers, monitoring of workplace safety, Head Start, and help in financing college education. More than eight in ten of those who are not directly affected by these activities still think the activities should be continued or expanded[16] (table 5.8).

---

[15] Since the sequence in which questions are asked can influence the results, the order was rotated to avoid possible bias.

[16] This finding is consistent with earlier studies that have shown that the preferences people express in political matters result less from narrowly conceived pocketbook interests than from opinions about how things are going in the national economy. See Donald R. Kinder and D. Roderick Kiewiet, "Economic Discontent and Political Behavior: The Role of Personal Grievances and Collective Economic Judgments in Congressional Voting," *American Journal of Political Science* 23 (August 1979): 495–527; and Donald R. Kinder and D. Roderick Kiewiet, "Sociotropic Politics: The American Case," *British Journal of Political Science* 11 (1981): 129–61.

Table 5.9

Percent Who Say Specific Activities of Government Bear
"Very or Somewhat Directly" on Them Personally
by Mix of General and Specific Views about Government

	All	Steady Critic	Ambivalent Critic	Ambivalent Supporter	Steady Supporter
Percent each of 10 activities bears "very" or "somewhat" directly on respondent					
Clean air standards	78%	66%	81%	79%	82%
Medical research	72	70	71	69	73
Consumer product safety	71	58	76	69	76
Financing college education	60	49	64	54	63
Safe working conditions	52	47	54	47	53
Teachers' salaries in poor school districts	44	40	46	45	44
Medicaid	43	37	46	43	43
Job training for low-income people	38	32	38	36	40
Head Start	32	25	32	35	33
Housing assistance for low-income families	31	23	32	33	32
Summary of activities bearing "very" or "somewhat" directly on respondent					
8 to 10 activities	22%	16%	23%	22%	23%
6 or 7 activities	20	17	20	18	21
4 or 5 activities	29	23	34	29	31
3 or fewer activities	29	44	23	31	25
	100%	100%	100%	100%	100%

[Q.5a–j]

If the ten activities are taken together in an overall measure, we see that Ambivalent Critics are affected more often by government than Steady Critics. In fact, Ambivalent Critics are similar to Ambivalent Supporters and Steady Supporters in the extent to which they feel government has a bearing on their lives. In contrast, more than four in ten (44 percent) of Steady Critics say no more than three of the ten activities have a direct bearing on them (table 5.9).

Government may also bear on people's lives if they are employed by it or receive some benefit or payment from it. We asked about both of these circumstances and found no differences between those who are ambivalent in

Table 5.10

Government Employment and Receipt of Government Benefits
by Mix of General and Specific Views about Government

	All	Steady Critic	Ambivalent Critic	Ambivalent Supporter	Steady Supporter
Member of household employed by government?					
By any level of government	19%	18%	17%	20%	19%
By federal government	7	6	6	6	6
By state government	7	6	6	8	7
By local government[a]	7	7	6	7	7
Member of household receiving government payments or benefits?					
One payment/benefit	17%	17%	19%	18%	14%
Two payments/benefits	12	13	12	10	12
Three or more	6	6	5	6	7
Total: one or more benefits	35	36	37	34	33
Kind of payments or benefits received from government					
Social Security or Medicare	26%	26%	24%	30%	23%
Government/military pension	8	11	12	3	8
Disability, Medicaid, or welfare	8	4	9	6	11

[a]Includes employees of local schools.

[Q.72;74]

their thinking and others who are not. Nineteen percent of those questioned live in a household where someone is employed by government at some level. This proportion is pretty much the same regardless of views about government (table 5.10).

Similarly, 35 percent of respondents report someone in their household receives some kind of payment or benefit from government. These payments or benefits could range from Social Security or Medicare to a government pension or some form of income support. As with government employment, the proportion reporting government payments or benefits does not vary significantly with differences in thinking about government.

The principal conclusions of these analyses are that: (a) support for most specific activities of government is strong even among those not personally affected by them; but that (b) Steady Critics are less likely than others to see what government does as bearing upon them directly.

SENSE OF INTERDEPENDENCE

Early in the twentieth century the horizons of life for most Americans were becoming increasingly national in scope through new means of communications, an expanding transportation network, and the effects of ever larger concentrations of economic power.

Early in the twenty-first century Americans will face an information society in an increasingly global economy. While the setting may have changed, one question is the same: do people have a sense they are living in an interdependent world? Many people support activities of government from which they do not benefit directly. Is this because they see their fortunes linked to others or is something else at work?

Our approach to this question was to identify several issues that some localities face but that others do not. The idea was to see how much people think they may be affected in some way by matters not impinging directly on the part of the country where they live.

Questions asked about five kinds of situations. For each, people were asked whether they saw it "as mostly a local problem, not having much to do with the rest of the country" or "as more than a local problem because the country as a whole is likely to be affected in some way."

In four of the five situations the majority view is that the matter is more than local:

Decisions about how to handle toxic waste from nuclear plants:

Mostly local	10%
More than local	88
Not sure	2
	100%

Areas that have an especially high number of people living in poverty:

Mostly local	24%
More than local	74
Not sure	2
	100%

Schools in areas where the dropout rate is especially high:

Mostly local	33%
More than local	65
Not sure	2
	100%

Decisions about whether to open up a wilderness area to development:

Mostly local	32%
More than local	63
Not sure	5
	100%

Rural areas that are cut off from air and rail transportation:

Mostly local	53%
More than local	42
Not sure	5
	100%

For an overall measure of a sense of interdependence we tallied how many of the five matters were seen as "more than local."[17] By this yardstick ambivalence is linked to a sense of interdependence for both critics and supporters of government but in different ways.

Among government's detractors, those who are ambivalent are *more* likely to see issues as national than are Steady Critics. Just over half (51 percent) of Ambivalent Critics think four or five of the matters are more than local compared to only one-third (33 percent) of Steady Critics. In fact, almost half (45 percent) of Steady Critics think only two or fewer of the issues are more than local (table 5.11).

Among government's supporters, the ambivalent are *less* inclined to a sense of interdependence. More than half (56 percent) of Steady Supporters see four or five of the problems as more than local compared to a smaller proportion (46 percent) of Ambivalent Supporters.

An interesting feature of these differing outlooks is that they do not result from people having more or less information about the world of government and politics. If levels of education or knowledge about government are taken into account, there are no notable differences in the number of matters that are seen as more than local (table 5.12).

A sense of interdependence is apparently *not* much affected by exposure to the larger political world. It appears instead to be an intrinsic part of the framework within which people view developments taking place around them.

At a time when politicians of the right and left are talking about the challenges of an interconnected twenty-first century, it is striking that formal education or knowledge about government do not appear to heighten a sense

---

[17] See appendix C for a description of this index.

Table 5.11
Number of Matters Seen as "More than Local" by Mix of General and Specific Views about Government

	All		Steady Critic		Ambivalent Critic		Ambivalent Supporter		Steady Supporter	
Five	19%	} 48%	8%	} 33%	19%	} 51%	22%	} 46%	23%	} 56%
Four	29		25		32		24		33	
Three	26		22		26		28		25	
Two	17	} 26	27	} 45	18	} 23	18	} 25	13	} 19
None/one	9		18		5		7		6	
	100%		100%		100%		99%		100%	

[Q.6a–e]

Table 5.12
Number of Problems Seen as "More than Local" by Education and Knowledge about Government

		By education			
	All	Less than high school	High school graduate	Some college	College and beyond
Five	19%	19%	19%	21%	19%
Four	29	24	29	32	30
Three	26	28	25	23	28
Two or less	26	29	27	24	23
	100%	100%	100%	100%	100%

		By knowledge about government			
	All	Low	Moderately low	Moderately high	High
Five	19%	20%	21%	20%	16%
Four	29	27	29	30	30
Three	26	27	28	24	24
Two or less	26	25	21	26	30
	100%	99%	99%	100%	100%

[Q.6a–e;51–54;67]

that what happens locally may affect or be affected by what is taking place at a distance.

INTENSITY OF RELIGIOUS BELIEFS AND PRACTICES

Matters of religious faith have long injected themselves into our politics. But in recent years they have done so with unprecedented force as issues of conscience have merged with grassroots political organization and state-of-the-art communications.

As we saw in the last chapter, ambivalence in views about government is distinctly related to opinions about conservative Christian organizations active in politics and some of the issues of particular concern to them. The link is most pronounced among critics of government. We learned that Steady Critics are significantly more likely than Ambivalent Critics to think conservative Christian groups are good for the country, to think that homosexuality is a threat to the American family, and that sex education should stress abstinence until marriage.

Unanswered is the question of whether differences on these issues have to do with the prominence of religion in the lives of Americans. Or, do differences of opinion on issues such as homosexuality, divorce, and sex education exist regardless of varying levels of intensity in religious beliefs and practices?

Do Deeply Religious Christians Speak with One Voice?

A first step in sorting matters out is to determine how much unanimity exists among deeply religious Christians on these issues. We characterized respondents in terms of the place of formal religion in their own experience. We did so by combining their responses to questions about the frequency of attendance at religious services and the importance they personally attach to religion.[18]

Just over one-third (34 percent) of respondents might be described as "deeply religious" in that they report attending religious services at least once a week and see religion as "very important" in their lives. Included in this total are those of all religions, Christian, Jewish, Muslim, as well as other faiths.

By limiting our focus to deeply religious Christians (31 percent of the overall sample), we can compare the views of those who consider themselves part of the conservative Christian movement and others who are deeply religious Christians but not part of the movement.

---

[18] See appendix C for a discussion of this measure.

Deeply religious Christians are united in their concern that greater effort is needed in teaching young people the values of moral character and personal responsibility. But that does not mean they are of one mind on other issues.

Compared to those who identify with the conservative Christian movement, other deeply religious Christians are less persuaded of the movement's positions on matters such as homosexuality and sex education. They are also not sure that political activity by conservative Christian organizations is good for the country. In fact, 44 percent of these Christians either worry about the church-state implications of political activism or do not yet have an opinion on the movement (table 5.13).

There are also differences of political perspective between deeply religious Christians identifying with the movement and others. More than two-thirds (69 percent) of those considering themselves part of the movement describe their political views as conservative as opposed to less than half (45 percent) of deeply religious Christians who are not part of the movement. An equal disparity is evident regarding party support.

Clearly more is at work than the intensity of religious beliefs and practices when it comes to explaining why deeply religious Christians support or reject positions put forward by conservative Christian organizations.

The kinds of influences on political views seen among the public at large are also found among deeply religious Christians. For example, consider household income. Limiting the analysis to those Christians who call themselves "born-again," Evangelical, Fundamentalist, Pentecostal, or Charismatic, results show that party preferences vary dramatically by their income. Those in households with incomes in excess of $50,000 divide 41 percent to 24 percent, Republican over Democrat, while those in households with incomes under $30,000 lean to the Democratic Party over the Republican Party by 39 percent to 30 percent.

Just because people share a sense of the importance of religion in their lives it does not mean they share a wide range of views on political matters. The deeply religious in America are too diverse a population for many broad generalizations about their thinking on political issues.

The Deeply Religious and Ambivalence about Government

The social and attitudinal diversity within the population of deeply religious Americans is further reflected in the limited strength of the link between intensity of religious beliefs and views about government.

The intensity of religious beliefs and practices has only a modest bearing on ambivalence among critics of government and virtually no bearing on am-

Table 5.13

Comparison of Views of "Deeply Religious" Christians by Whether or Not They Consider Themselves Part of the Conservative Christian Movement

	Among deeply religious Christians who	
	Consider themselves part of movement (n=148)	Do *not* consider themselves part of movement (n=449)
Views on teaching young people the values of personal responsibility and moral character		
One of very most important things for the country	92%	84%
Nation is losing ground	63	54
Agreement with positions taken by conservative Christian organizations		
Homosexuality threatens the values of the American family	85%[a]	61%[a]
Sex education should aim at getting young people to abstain until marriage	64[a]	50[a]
Divorce should be granted only for adultery, abuse, or desertion	50	41
View of conservative Christian organizations		
Good for country: make sure government is run by Christian principles	88%[a]	56%[a]
Not good for country: religion should be kept out of government	12[a]	34[a]
Not sure	1	10
	101%	100%
Views on political matters (self-described)		
Conservative	69%[a]	45%[a]
Middle of the road	15[a]	42[a]
Liberal	12	11
Not sure	4	3
	100%	101%
Party support		
Republican Party	58%[a]	35%[a]
Democratic Party	20	33
Other party	2	1
Not support a party	20[a]	32[a]
	100%	101%

[a]Designates a statistically significant difference between those considering themselves part of the conservative Christian movement and those who do not.

[Q.7a–f;21;24a,b;41;44;47–50;56–60]

Table 5.14

Intensity of Religious Beliefs and Practices by Mix of General
and Specific Views about Government

	All	Steady Critic	Ambivalent Critic	Ambivalent Supporter	Steady Supporter
Attend religious services					
At least once a week	37%	47%	39%	30%	34%
Once or twice a month	17	11	15	19	18
A few times a year	28	25	29	28	30
Never	18	17	17	22	18
No answer	*a	*	*	1	*
	100%	100%	100%	100%	100%
Importance of religion in own life					
Very important	60%	63%	62%	58%	57%
Fairly important	24	19	24	24	27
Not very important	15	17	14	18	14
Not sure/no answer	1	1	*	*	1
	100%	100%	100%	100%	99%
Summary: intensity of religious beliefs and practices					
Deeply religious	34%	43%	36%	28%	30%
Fairly religious	32	26	29	34	34
Less religious	34	31	34	38	36
	100%	100%	100%	100%	100%

aDesignates less than half a percent.

[Q.58;59]

bivalence among supporters. Forty-three percent of Steady Critics can be described as "deeply religious" compared to 36 percent of Ambivalent Critics. There is no difference on this score between Steady Supporters and Ambivalent Supporters (table 5.14).

The difference between Steady Critics and Ambivalent Critics in the prominence given to religion is not as great as differences between them on matters of concern to conservative Christians. Further evidence along these lines is found in an analysis that looked at the prominence of religion as an explanation of ambivalence while also taking into account opinions on three issues: when divorce should be granted, what sex education should stress, and whether homosexuality is a threat to the family.

A mixed picture emerges:[19]

• The more prominent religion is, the less the ambivalence about government; the less prominent religion is, the more the ambivalence. Even so, the intensity of religious beliefs and practices makes only a small contribution in explaining why some of government's detractors are more ambivalent than others.

• The issue of sex education has a much stronger relationship to ambivalence about government than any other consideration. The more the support for giving young people the information they may need, the more ambivalent the critic. The more the emphasis on abstinence until marriage, the less ambivalent the critic.

• Much less important in explaining ambivalence among critics are opinions about homosexuality. The less the perceived threat, the more the ambivalence. The greater the threat, the less the ambivalence.

• Views on the issue of divorce have no significant bearing on ambivalence.

Thus two concerns of conservative Christian groups (sex education and homosexuality) are more decisive than the prominence of formal religion in tilting the balance between "steady" or "ambivalent" views among critics of government. That the intensity of religious beliefs and practices does not have a stronger relationship to views about government is again evidence of the immense social and demographic diversity of the population when it comes to matters of faith.[20]

PERSONAL SITUATION AND AMBIVALENCE ABOUT GOVERNMENT: A RECAP

We have seen here that some of the differing situations in which people find themselves bear on the way people think about government, while other aspects of their lives appear to have little influence.

Among those Critical of Government

Many facets of respondents' personal situations, the concern of this chapter, are related to ambivalence among those who are "mostly critical" of gov-

---

[19] For a description of this multivariate analysis, see table D.4 and the accompanying discussion in appendix D. As will be seen in chapter 6, views on these issues recede in importance in understanding ambivalence when the analyses bring in other considerations.

[20] See table A.21 in appendix A.

ernment in general terms (table 5.15). Eight considerations are especially noteworthy:

- Ambivalent Critics are much more likely than Steady Critics to think that when the economy grows the gap between rich and poor gets bigger.
- Ambivalent Critics do not follow what goes on in the news as closely as Steady Critics.
- Ambivalent Critics are much more likely than Steady Critics to have a sense they are living in an interdependent world.
- Ambivalent Critics report that more activities of government bear on them directly than do Steady Critics.
- Ambivalent Critics are less informed about the workings of government than are Steady Critics.
- Ambivalent Critics tend to be more optimistic than Steady Critics about what the future holds for them personally. This reflects the combined effect of two earlier findings: younger people tend to be more upbeat about their prospects than others; critics of government who are younger are more likely to be ambivalent in their thinking than critics who are older.
- Ambivalent Critics feel less secure financially than Steady Critics. They are also much more worried that Social Security may not be able to pay the benefits people count on.

Among those Supportive of Government

Compared to the differences found among government's critics, there are few areas in which we learn much by comparing the personal situations of Ambivalent Supporters and Steady Supporters. Statistically significant differences appear in only three areas:

- Ambivalent Supporters are somewhat less optimistic about their personal future than are Steady Supporters.
- Ambivalent Supporters tend to follow what is going on in government and public affairs more closely than Steady Supporters.
- Ambivalent Supporters are slightly less inclined than Steady Supporters to see challenges facing localities as "more than local."

The findings reported in this chapter say more about the ambivalence of government's critics than about the ambivalence of its supporters. Differences

Table 5.15
Summary of Differences Regarding Personal Situation Between Steady and Ambivalent Critics and Between Steady and Ambivalent Supporters

	Size of difference between Steady Critics and Ambivalent Critics	Size of difference between Steady Supporters and Ambivalent Supporters
Sense of personal well-being		
Personal ladder ratings:		
Shift from past to present	Medium[a]	n.s.
Shift from present to future	Medium	Small
Financial security and perceived equities		
Personal financial security	Medium	n.s.
Perceived equities and inequities		
Amount of attention government pays to low-income people	Large	Large
Amount of attention government pays to middle-income people	n.s.	n.s.
Amount of attention government pays to upper-income people	n.s.	n.s.
Amount of attention government pays to people like you	n.s.	n.s.
Growth in economy means:		
All gain	Medium	n.s.
Gap between rich and poor gets bigger	Large	n.s.
Description of own situation:		
Middle class	Small	n.s.
Working class	n.s.	n.s.
Lower class	n.s.	n.s.
Knowledge about government and interest in news		
Knowledge about government	Medium	n.s.
News consumption	n.s.	n.s.
How closely follow government and public affairs	Large	Small
Experience with government		
Activities of government seen as bearing directly on respondent	Medium	n.s.
Government employment of someone in household: at any level of government	n.s.	n.s.
Payments or benefits from government: one or more received	n.s.	n.s.
Sense of interdependence		
Problems seen as more than local	Large	Small
Intensity of religious beliefs/practices		
Summary index	Small	n.s.

Note: This display is based on data reported in tables 5.1, 5.3–5.7, 5.9–5.10, 5.14, and A.14. For a summary of those data and the differences between groups, see table A.22 in appendix A.

[a]Differences of 16 percentage points or more are considered "large"; differences from 11 to 15 points are "medium"; and differences less than 10 points are "small" if they are statistically significant. Differences that are not statistically significant are designated "n.s."

in the personal situations of Steady Critics and Ambivalent Critics are seen more often and are more pronounced than differences between Ambivalent Supporters and Steady Supporters.

Of particular importance are two characteristics that distinguish Ambivalent Critics from Steady Critics. First, they are *much more* likely than Steady Critics to think the nation as a whole has an interest in problems that are unevenly dispersed across the country. Second, Ambivalent Critics are *much less* likely than Steady Critics to follow what is going on in government and politics.

SIX

What Lies Behind Ambivalence
about Government?

E HAVE EXPLORED MANY AVENUES IN SEARCH OF AN UNDER-
standing of the mixed signals Americans send about government. First, we looked at whether characteristics such as sex,
age, or household income could tell us something about who
was ambivalent and who was not. Next the issue was whether the job government is seen to be doing contributes to ambivalence. Then we turned to opinions on a range of issues that might have some bearing on how the American
people see their government. And, in chapter 5, we explored ways an individual's personal situation might lead to ambivalent feelings about government.

We have encountered striking differences in opinion between Steady Critics and Ambivalent Critics, on the one hand, and between Steady Supporters
and Ambivalent Supporters, on the other. All of these differences may help explain ambivalence.

But what is the relative importance of these alternative explanations? It is
possible to weigh the unique influence each aspect of opinion may have on ambivalence about government through analyses that take the several aspects into
account at the same time.[1]

In preceding chapters we have been focusing on differences between those
who are "steady" and "ambivalent" in their thinking about government. We
have been juxtaposing the "general views" people hold about government's
scope and power with their opinions about specific activities of government
such as job training for low-income people, enforcement of clean-air standards, Medicaid, and standards for safety in the workplace.

---

[1] For example, in order to conclude that consideration A tells us more about ambivalence
than considerations B, C, or D, we would need to show that the strength of its relationship to
ambivalence holds up even when B, C, and D are included in the analysis.

•	*Among critics of government.* Respondents who are generally critical of government have been divided into two groups: those who back eight or fewer activities (Steady Critics) and those who back nine or all ten specific activities even as they criticize government (Ambivalent Critics).

•	*Among supporters of government.* Respondents who are generally supportive of government have been divided into two groups: those who back nine or all ten activities (Steady Supporters) and those who back eight or fewer activities even as they support government (Ambivalent Supporters).

At this juncture, rather than distinguish between "steady" and "ambivalent" respondents, we can get most out of the analysis if we conceive of ambivalence as a continuum. This permits us to look at shades of ambivalence:

•	*Among critics of government.* At one end of the continuum are those who are critical of government in general terms and back none of the ten activities. These people are expressing the least ambivalence in their criticism. At the other end of the continuum are those who want to see all ten specific activities continued, even as they are generally critical of government. These people express the greatest amount of ambivalence.

•	*Among supporters of government.* Here the continuum starts with the least ambivalent people, those who support government in general terms and want all ten activities continued or expanded. At the other end are those wanting few of the activities continued, even as they are generally supportive of government. These people are most ambivalent.

The first thing that becomes clear when ambivalence is looked at in this manner is that there are more degrees of ambivalence among critics than there are among supporters. That is, those who are most ambivalent as critics actually back all ten specific activities in spite of their concern about the scope and power of government. On the other hand, the most ambivalent supporters of government want no more than four activities cut back or ended. Thus there are eleven shades of ambivalence among critics (0 to 10) but only six shades among supporters (5 to 10) (figure 6.1).

There is, in short, more variation in ambivalence to account for among critics of government than there is among supporters. Chances are that with more variation there will be more pieces to the puzzle of ambivalence among critics. In contrast, fewer explanations are likely to lie behind the ambivalence

Figure 6.1

Degrees of Ambivalence in the Thinking of Critics and Supporters of Government

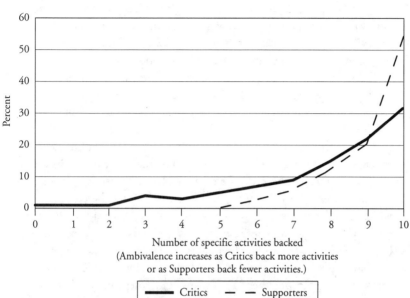

Number of specific activities backed
(Ambivalence increases as Critics back more activities
or as Supporters back fewer activities.)

———— Critics   — — Supporters

of supporters. We have already seen evidence along these lines. Steady Critics and Ambivalent Critics have differed on many important issues. By comparison, Steady Supporters and Ambivalent Supporters do not diverge as often in their opinions.

Since we are trying to explain two kinds of ambivalence about government, we need to separate the analyses of reasons for ambivalence among government's critics from analyses of reasons for ambivalence among supporters. Different factors may be at work.

AMBIVALENCE AMONG CRITICS OF GOVERNMENT

Turning first to ambivalence among critics of government, ten aspects of opinion contribute significantly to our understanding. While some give us more insight than others, when all ten are taken together, they tell us a considerable amount about why critics vary in the number of specific activities of government they think should be continued or expanded.[2]

---

[2] See appendix D, especially tables D.5 and D.6.

Two aspects of opinion are especially noteworthy:

• *Government attention to low-income people.* Central to explaining
ambivalence among critics is how much attention government is seen
as paying to the concerns of the poor. Critics who think there is too
little attention are more ambivalent. Critics who view government's
attention as excessive are less ambivalent. Sentiment on this issue
has the strongest relationship with ambivalence of any of the alternative reasons for ambivalence when taking all others into account
(table 6.1).

• *Sense of interdependence.* Next in importance in explaining how
much ambivalence critics may express is how they view problems that
are unevenly dispersed across the country, that is, whether they are
seen as concerns for the country as a whole or just for the area in
which they occur. Critics who see issues as more national than local
tend to be more ambivalent. Critics who see issues as more local are
less ambivalent. This finding highlights the fact that a major part of
the way critics view the political world is how interdependent they
think it is. As measured here, the "sense of interdependence" covers a
range of issues from the environment to education, transportation, and
poverty. Further, as we saw earlier, it is not simply a proxy for political
awareness: the degree to which matters are viewed as "more than local"
is not accounted for by a person's education or knowledge about the
governmental system.

Next in importance as explanations of ambivalence among critics of government are four other elements of opinion:

• *Confidence in federal agencies.* Critics who carry their antipathy toward government from general opposition to rejection of specific activities are inclined to take a dim view of federal agencies. In contrast,
those who tend to be more ambivalent in their criticism of government
have more confidence in the quality of work done in federal agencies.

• *Dealing with the issue of race.* The issue of race also tells us a lot
about the ambivalence found among critics of government. Critics
who think the nation does not need to push so hard on the matter
tend to be less ambivalent in their criticism of government. On the
other hand, those who think now is no time to let up working for
racial equality are more ambivalent—they criticize government but still
back many of its activities.

Table 6.1

Relative Importance of Aspects of Opinion in Explaining Ambivalence among Critics of Government

	Aspects of Opinion That Help Account for Ambivalence	Views Associated with Ambivalence	Views Associated with Lack of Ambivalence
Most Important Aspects of Opinion	When it comes to the concerns of low-income people . . . Problems different parts of the country face are . . .	Government is paying too little attention to low-income people Often more than local because whole country may be affected	Government is paying too much attention to low-income people Mostly local not having much to do with the rest of the country
Other Important Aspects of Opinion	Confidence in the quality of work done by workers in federal agencies . . . When it comes to the issue of race . . . Age When it comes to getting ahead in the United States . . .	A great deal or fair amount of confidence We still have a long way to go and now is no time to let up in working hard for true equality Younger people Hard work is often not enough to overcome barriers	Not very much confidence or none at all We do not need to push quite so hard now as in the past in light of how far we've come Older people Anyone can get ahead if they are willing to work hard enough
Notable but Less Important Aspects Of Opinion	Follow what's going on in government and public affairs Conservative Christian groups that are active in politics are . . . Personal financial situation Teaching young people values of personal responsibility and moral character	Only now and then or hardly at all Not good for the country because of the need to keep church and state separate Feel insecure The country is making progress	Most or some of the time Good for the country to make sure government is run by Christian principles Feel secure The country is losing ground

• *Age.* The younger the critics of government, the more ambivalent they are in their criticism. The older the critic, the less the ambivalence. It should be noted that age is the only demographic characteristic that is linked to ambivalence.

• *Getting ahead in the United States.* Another reason for ambivalence is the feeling that there are times when barriers stand in the way and even hard work may not be enough for someone to get ahead. Those who think that getting ahead is mostly a matter of hard work are less ambivalent. Those who think barriers may stand in the way tend to be more ambivalent.

Notable but less important are four additional reasons for ambivalence among critics. These do not contribute as much to our understanding as those above. Nonetheless they do have a relationship to ambivalence among critics, which is strong enough that it did not occur by chance:

• *Interest in government and political matters.* The amount of attention critics pay to government and the political world bears on the amount of ambivalence they express. Those following things more closely are less ambivalent; those paying less attention are more ambivalent.

• *Opinion about conservative Christian organizations.* Ambivalence among government's critics is also associated with concern that conservative Christian groups active in politics may not be good for the country. By contrast, those who view these organizations as good for the country are less ambivalent. While opinions about the activities of conservative Christian organizations are related to ambivalence, the same cannot be said regarding support for the issues of concern to those organizations. Opinions on matters such as homosexuality, sex education, or divorce have no significant bearing on whether or not critics are ambivalent in their thinking.

• *Personal financial situation.* While household income appears unimportant as a reason for ambivalence among critics, respondents' views of their own personal financial situation do matter. The greater the uncertainty in finances, the more critics tend to be ambivalent.

• *The values of personal responsibility and moral character.* A further consideration regarding ambivalence among critics is how well people think the country is doing in teaching the values of personal responsibility and moral character. The more likely critics are to sense the country is making progress, the more they are ambivalent. The more people see the country losing ground, the less ambivalent they are.

The importance of these analyses is that they take many possible reasons for ambivalence into account at the same time. In addition to indicating aspects of opinion that are key to explaining ambivalence, these analyses also alert us to aspects that do *not* add much to our understanding. That is, when possible explanations for ambivalence were considered one at a time in preceding chapters, significant differences appeared between Steady and Ambivalent Critics. When looked at as part of a larger mix of possible explanations, however, some of these elements of opinion do not have a strong enough relationship with ambivalence to continue to stand out given the cumulative contribution to our understanding made by the other items.

Among such considerations that do not hold up in these analyses as important explanations of ambivalence are the following:

- *Education or knowledge about government.* Once the aspects of opinion that relate most directly to ambivalence among critics are taken into account (table 6.2), neither education nor knowledge gives much additional insight into why some critics are ambivalent and others are not.
- *Being affected by government.* Ambivalence among critics of government is not influenced by how directly they feel government bears on their lives. Most who support specific activities of government do so whether or not those activities affect them personally. Ambivalence is also unaffected by whether a household receives any government benefits or payments or includes someone who is employed by government at any level.
- *Perception of the gap between rich and poor.* There is a widely shared opinion that the economic deck is stacked in favor of the affluent. Even with a strong economy, growth is seen as passing many Americans by and only expanding the gap between rich and poor. This view is so pervasive that differences are not found between those who are more and less ambivalent in their thinking about government.
- *Dealing with crime.* The survey included two questions regarding crime. Neither had a strong enough relationship with ambivalence to

be significant when the ten key dimensions were taken into account. It is true that those who favor more effort to prevent juvenile crime tend to be more ambivalent in their criticism of government. Conversely, those who advocate getting tougher with juvenile offenders are less ambivalent. Nonetheless, this is an issue whose link to ambivalence is not strong enough to offset the influence of any of the key elements in explaining ambivalence. Also unimportant in explaining ambivalence about government is the matter of police searches without a warrant from the court. In this case, however, the absence of any connection to ambivalence is explained by the fact that critics of government across the board do not like the idea of searches without a warrant.

• *Religious beliefs and practices.* One of the principal aspects of opinion linked to ambivalence is whether political activities of conservative Christian organizations are good for the country. The same does not hold, however, when it comes to the intensity of religious beliefs or practices. There is nothing inherent in the depth of religious commitment that explains variation among critics in the ambivalence of their views about government.

• *Concerns of conservative Christian organizations.* In a similar vein, views on issues central to the advocacy of conservative Christian groups appear to operate somewhat independently of overall impressions of whether or not their activities are good for the country. Even though critics of government are divided on some of these issues, none of the differences of opinion is important enough to explain why some critics are more ambivalent than others. Once the above key elements of opinion are considered, no additional insight is gained by knowing a person's views on sex education, homosexuality, or divorce.

• *Self-control versus self-expression.* We saw earlier that Steady Critics feel there is declining respect these days for the value of self-discipline while Ambivalent Critics place a higher premium on the value of self-expression. The matter does not retain its importance as a reason for ambivalence, however, when other aspects of opinion are taken into account.

AMBIVALENCE AMONG SUPPORTERS OF GOVERNMENT

It is much easier to account for ambivalence in the thinking of those generally supportive of government than those generally critical. There is less variation among supporters that needs to be explained.

The upshot is that there are fewer aspects of opinion that contribute to the relatively small amount of ambivalence expressed among supporters.[3] Three have approximately equal, albeit modest, influence:

- *Dealing with the issue of race.* The more people believe we need not push so hard on the issue of race, the more ambivalent they are as supporters. The more people think this is not the time to let up pushing for equality, the less ambivalent they are.
  - *Changes in the way government works.* The less chance people see for changes in the way government works, the more ambivalent they are. The more the chance of change, the less their ambivalence.
  - *Government attention to low-income people.* The view that government pays too much attention contributes to feelings of ambivalence. Thinking government pays too little attention to the poor is linked to less ambivalence (table 6.2).

Even though these three aspects of opinion contribute to ambivalence in the thinking of supporters of government, we cannot make too much of what they tell us. Their collective effect in understanding ambivalence is quite small.

Opinions on the key issues of poverty and race do have a bearing on ambivalence among supporters. But the link is not very strong. Moreover, as reported earlier, the prevailing views among supporters—whether more or less ambivalent—are that the government is paying too little attention to the concerns of low-income households and that now is no time to let up working for racial equality.

These additional analyses shed little light on why some supporters of government are more ambivalent than others. This is because of the two characteristics of supporters reported earlier: they do not differ much in their opinions on most issues, and, on the matter of ambivalence itself, the distance between the most and least ambivalent supporter is not all that great.

Finding that ambivalence among government's supporters is of limited scope or complexity only heightens the importance of understanding the ambivalence that exists among critics of government. Not only are critics more likely to be of mixed minds about government, the roots of their ambivalence reach deeply into some of the larger issues in the national public discussion.

---

[3] For an account of these analyses, see tables D.6 and D.7 and the accompanying discussion in appendix D.

Table 6.2

Relative Importance of Aspects of Opinion in Explaining Ambivalence among Supporters of Government

	Aspects of Opinion That Help Account for Ambivalence	Views Associated with Ambivalence	Views Associated with Lack of Ambivalence
Modestly Important Aspects Of Opinion	When it comes to the issue of race . . .	We do not need to push quite so hard now as in the past in light of how far we've come	We still have a long way to go and now is no time to let up in working hard for true equality
	When it comes to how much can be done to make government work better . . .	Less chance for change	More chance for change
	When it comes to the concerns of low-income people . . .	Government is paying too much attention	Government it paying too little attention

Consider the salience of the four most influential considerations that account for how much ambivalence is expressed among critics:

- How much attention government should pay to the needs of those who have fallen on hard times;
- Whether problems that are particularly pronounced in one part of the country affect the country as a whole;
- Whether the executive agencies of the federal government warrant public confidence; and
- How much urgency should be attached to continuing efforts to achieve equality among the races.

SEVEN

Some Political Consequences of Ambivalence about Government

U P TO THIS POINT WE HAVE BEEN GAUGING THE PUBLIC'S AMBIVA-
lence about government and trying to understand what may lie
behind it. We have found many people of mixed minds about
government and have gained some appreciation of why they hold
the views they do.

Now we ask what difference ambivalence about government may make in
how people approach politics and in their choices as voters. Is there reason to
believe ambivalence might affect the way people assess the state of the nation? If
people are of mixed minds about government, does that mean they are more reluctant participants in the political process as voters or between elections? When
they vote, are they more likely than others to split their ticket between candidates of different parties? Are those who are ambivalent less likely to support a
political party or more likely to think of themselves as political independents?

PERCEIVED STATE OF THE NATION

A n initial indication of the political importance of ambivalence about government is that it colors the way people see the state of the nation. Evidence in this regard comes from ratings people give the past, present, and future of the United States on the same ladder scale as used earlier to gauge the
sense of personal well-being. Respondents were asked to imagine that the top
of the ladder "stands for the best possible situation for the United States; the
bottom the worst possible situation." They were then asked where the country
stands today, stood five years ago, and is likely to stand five years from now.[1]

---

[1] Trends in these ratings extend back to 1959. The scale was used as a means of exploring
public perceptions of the national well-being of countries at different stages of political and

117

Table 7.1

National Ladder Ratings and Shifts by Mix of General and
Specific Views about Government

	All	Steady Critic	Ambivalent Critic	Ambivalent Supporter	Steady Supporter
Average (mean) ratings					
Past	5.7	5.7	5.7	6.1	5.5
Present	5.5	4.9	5.4	5.9	5.9
Future	5.7	4.7	5.5	5.5	6.3
Rating shifts					
Past to Present	–0.2	–0.8	–0.3	–0.2	+0.4
Present to Future	+0.2	–0.2	+0.1	–0.4	+0.4
Overall: Past to Future	0.0	–1.0	–0.2	–0.6	+0.8

[Q.3a–c]

Looking first at the way critics of government see things, both Steady Critics and Ambivalent Critics start from the same point with respect to where the country stood five years ago. They part company, however, in what they think has happened since then. In the judgment of Steady Critics, the country has lost considerable ground in the last five years. The average (mean) ladder ratings declined from 5.7 (past) to 4.9 (present). Ambivalent Critics see slippage from five years ago, but not of the magnitude seen by Steady Critics (5.7 for the past down to 5.4 for the present) (table 7.1).

Neither Steady nor Ambivalent Critics are very optimistic about where the country will be five years down the road. Both give almost the same ratings for the future as the present.

All in all, Steady Critics see the country losing ground from five years ago and not recovering in the next five years. That is, there is an overall decline of a full step on the ladder (5.7 for the past down to 4.7 for the future). The per-

---

economic development. See Hadley Cantril, *Pattern of Human Concerns*. It stimulated the idea of an annual audit of the public's sense of the "state of the nation." See Albert H. Cantril and Charles W. Roll Jr., *Hopes and Fears of the American People* (New York: Universe Books, 1971); William Watts and Lloyd A. Free, eds., *State of the Nation* (New York: Universe Books, 1973); William Watts and Lloyd A. Free, *State of the Nation, 1974* (Washington, D.C.: Potomac Associates, 1974); and William Watts and Lloyd A. Free, *State of the Nation III* (Lexington, Mass.: Lexington Books, 1978). The scale has since been used widely by numerous polling organizations around the world.

spective of Ambivalent Critics is somewhat different. While they do not see a negative trend over the ten year period, they think the country's situation in five years will be about where it was five years ago.

Turning to supporters of government, differences between Steady Supporters and Ambivalent Supporters are more striking. In this case, both Steady and Ambivalent Supporters see the country at the same point at the present (5.9 on the ladder). The difference is in how it got there: for Ambivalent Supporters, there was a slight decline from five years ago; and for Steady Supporters there was modest progress.

More noteworthy is the divergence regarding the prognosis for the future. Ambivalent Supporters see a decline of almost half of a step on the ladder over the next five years (5.9 down to 5.5). Steady Supporters see just the opposite taking place: progress being made that carries the country forward from 5.9 to 6.3 on the ladder.

Seen in the ten-year time frame, the disparity in these perspectives comes into sharper focus. Ambivalent Supporters see the country on a downward path: past to present and present to future that amounts to an overall drop of over a half of a step on the ladder. In contrast, Steady Supporters view the country as consistently moving forward from past to future: the nation's situation improving by almost a full step over the ten years.

Many considerations no doubt come to mind when people are asked about the well-being of the country. There are also variations among social and demographic subgroups in how things seem to be going in the country (see table A.23 in appendix A).

The question here is whether feelings of ambivalence about government play a significant role in these differing appraisals of the state of the nation. To gauge this possibility, analyses were conducted that placed ambivalence along side other factors likely to influence the direction in which people think the country is headed.[2]

Three kinds of possible explanations were considered. Basic characteristics about respondents included their age, education, and sense of financial security. Government performance was gauged by public confidence in the agencies of the federal government and the U.S. Congress. We also included views on issues in the news that might bear on how people think the country is doing: the teaching of personal responsibility; having leadership with new ideas; dealing with the issue of race; balancing self-restraint and self-expression; and who gains when the economy grows.

---

[2] For details on these multivariate analyses, see tables D.8 and D.9 and accompanying discussion in appendix D.

These analyses confirm that ambivalence about government has a relationship to the national ladder ratings that is strong enough to hold up even when other considerations are taken into account:

• Among critics, ambivalence has more of an influence on the sense the nation has gained ground over the last five years than any other consideration entered into the analysis. The greater the ambivalence, the greater progress the country is seen to have made. The less the ambivalence, the less the progress over the last five years.

• Among critics, ambivalence does not have the same influence on expectations regarding progress the country will make in the future.

• Among supporters, ambivalence has a modest amount of influence over the sense of movement from past to present for the country. Yet its contribution to understanding the ladder shift from five years ago is not as great as are views about how the country is doing in teaching personal responsibility or having leaders with bold ideas. Nor is it as important as a person's education.

• Among supporters, ambivalence is more important than any other consideration in accounting for shifts in national ladder ratings from present to future. The more the ambivalence, the less the optimism about the future. The less the ambivalence, the more the optimism.

In short, ambivalence about government has a different effect on the perceived state of the nation, depending on whether one is a critic or supporter of government. Ambivalence among critics is reflected mostly in a feeling that the country has made progress over the past five years. Ambivalence among supporters is reflected mostly in doubts about how well the country will do over the next five years.

POLITICAL ACTIVITY

One of the most important consequences of ambivalence about government may be its effect on how and when people get involved in political matters. This would have implications for which voices get heard—and which do not.

Are those who are of mixed minds about government less likely to participate in the political process, especially if they also are not following news about government and politics all that closely? Conversely, when general and specific attitudes are in agreement, is there more of an inclination to take part?

In either case, the amount of a person's ambivalence about government may influence the level of their political activity. To explore the several ways ambivalence may affect which voices are heard, we look first at who votes and who opts out of the process.

Likely Voters, Unlikely Voters, and Nonvoters

Just under half (49 percent) of all respondents can be characterized as "likely voters." That is, they are registered, report they voted in the 1996 presidential election, they recall the name of the candidate for whom they voted, and say they always vote in national elections.[3] Just under one-fifth (19 percent) of those polled can be described as "nonvoters." These are people who are not registered and indicate they seldom vote in national elections. In between "likely voters" and "nonvoters" are about one-third (32 percent) of respondents who indicate more interest in elections than nonvoters but still do not reach the threshold where they might be considered likely voters. We refer to these individuals as "unlikely voters."

These levels of voting likelihood highlight two major consequences of ambivalence for the political life of the nation.

- Critics of government who are ambivalent in their thinking are substantially less likely to vote than those who are not ambivalent. In important contrast, two-thirds of Steady Critics show up as likely voters compared to half of Ambivalent Critics (table 7.2).
- Supporters of government who are ambivalent in their thinking are just as likely to vote as those who are not ambivalent. Where the effect of ambivalence is felt among supporters is in the larger number who can be described as "nonvoters." Thirty percent of Ambivalent Supporters are nonvoters compared to 19 percent of Steady Supporters.

The political consequence of these findings becomes clearer if we look at the same results but from a different angle. Up to now we have been asking, for example, how many Steady Critics are likely voters. For a moment, we turn the question around and ask how many likely voters are Steady Critics.

---

[3] 96,273,000 votes were cast for president in 1996, which amounted to 48.9 percent of the voting age population. See U.S. Bureau of the Census, *Statistical Abstract of the United States: 1997* (Washington, D.C.: 1997), table 464. See appendix C of this book for information about the index of likelihood of voting.

Table 7.2

Likelihood of Voting in National Elections and Participation in Activities Other than Voting by Mix of General and Specific Views about Government

	All	Steady Critic	Ambivalent Critic	Ambivalent Supporter	Steady Supporter
Voting likelihood					
Likely voters	49%	66%	50%	43%	46%
Unlikely voters	32	25	33	26	35
Nonvoters	19	9	17	30	19
	100%	100%	100%	99%	100%
Participation in activities other than voting					
Attended public meeting	42%	48%	44%	36%	39%
Called/written member of the state legislature	25	37	24	18	24
Called/written U.S. senator or member of Congress	22	40	17	16	19
Summary: Number of activities other than voting					
Two or three	25%	42%	21%	20%	24%
One	27	21	34	19	25
None	48	37	45	61	51
	100%	100%	100%	100%	100%
Combined: Voting *and* other activities					
Voting and other activities	33%	51%	31%	24%	30%
Voting and no other activities	15	16	15	20	13
Other activities and no voting	19	12	24	15	19
Neither voting nor other activities	33	21	30	41	38
	100%	100%	100%	100%	100%

[Q.34–37,43a–c]

Looked at from this vantage point, we find that likely voters are about evenly split between critics and supporters of government. Steady Critics and Ambivalent Critics constitute 45 percent of the electorate; Steady Supporters and Ambivalent Supporters represent 46 percent of the electorate. The views of the remaining 9 percent are neither critical nor supportive (figure 7.1).

This symmetry between critics and supporters among "likely voters" stands in sharp contrast to the division of opinion among those not likely to vote. Limiting the focus to "unlikely" and "nonvoters," more than half

Figure 7.1

Composition of Likely Voters and Unlikely/Nonvoters

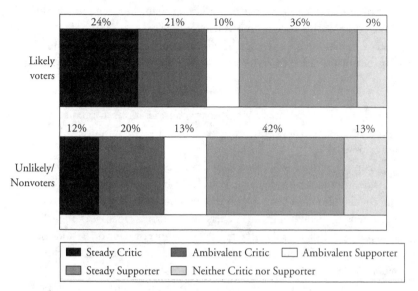

(55 percent) of those who do not show up to vote election day are supporters of government while about one-third (32 percent) are its critics.

The political portrait of "likely voters" is thus very different from that of "unlikely" and "nonvoters." Steady Critics make up 24 percent of likely voters but only 12 percent of unlikely and nonvoters, while Steady Supporters are 36 percent of likely voters but their numbers grow to 42 percent among the unlikely and nonvoters.

Just under one-third (31 percent) of all likely voters are ambivalent in their thinking about government (either as Ambivalent Critics or Ambivalent Supporters). Since these voters are of mixed minds about government, they can tip the balance in how elections turn out and in the way coalitions come together around issues.

To approximate the electoral consequences of these proportions, we project them to the number of potential voters in a presidential election. Starting with the base of the 96,273,000 votes cast for president in 1996, we estimate that:

- 22.8 million voters are Steady Critics;
- 19.9 million voters are Ambivalent Critics;
- 10.0 million voters are Ambivalent Supporters;
- 35.0 million voters are Steady Supporters; and,
- 8.5 million voters are neither critics nor supporters of government.

Ambivalence about government is clearly linked to reduced levels of voting. But how important is it as an explanation for lower turnout when set against other considerations that might also explain the likelihood of voting?

We addressed this question by analyses that weighed ambivalence against a variety of other factors such as age, education, confidence in government, or feeling personally affected by what government does.[4] These analyses show that:

- Age and education are the primary considerations in predicting whether a person is likely to vote, be they a critic or supporter of government.[5]
- Among critics, after age and education, the next most influential consideration is ambivalence. Ambivalence has more to do with reducing the likelihood of voting than the amount of news a person takes in, the intensity of their religious beliefs and practices, their sex, how much they feel personally affected by what government does, and the level of their confidence in the U.S. Congress or the agencies of the federal government.
- Among supporters, after age and education, the next most important factor affecting voting likelihood is the amount of news a person takes in. Ambivalence about government tells little about why supporters vote or stay home. This finding is not surprising given the two points made earlier in chapter 6: there are not as many shades of ambivalence among supporters as critics, and there are few important differences of opinion on issues between Steady Supporters and Ambivalent Supporters.

Participation Other than Voting

Does the effect of ambivalence extend beyond likelihood of voting to other forms of participation between elections? To measure this we focused on three things people may have done "in the last year or so": attended a public meeting in the community; called or written a member of the state legislature; or called or written a U.S. Senator or member of Congress.

---

[4] See table D.10 and the discussion in appendix D.

[5] This finding is consistent with earlier research. Stephen Earl Bennett has shown that education is more important that many other considerations in predicting the level of an individual's political involvement. See Bennett's *Apathy in America, 1960–1984: Causes and Consequences of Citizen Political Influence* (Dobbs Ferry, N.Y.: Transnational Publishers, Inc., 1986), 50–59.

As far as attendance at public meetings is concerned, there is no significant difference between Steady Critics and Ambivalent Critics. Nor are there differences between Ambivalent Supporters and Steady Supporters. But on the matter of writing or calling a state or federal legislator, Steady Critics are much more active than all others. Such contacts are dramatically less frequent among Ambivalent Critics, Ambivalent Supporters, and Steady Supporters (table 7.2).

Taken together as an overall measure of participation, the three kinds of activity highlight the degree to which ambivalence is linked to less political involvement.[6] Steady Critics are twice as likely to have engaged in two or three of the above activities as are Ambivalent Critics.

Among supporters, Ambivalent Supporters are less likely than Steady Supporters to have participated in any of the activities. It should be noted that over half of Steady Supporters (51 percent) and Ambivalent Supporters (61 percent) have not taken part in *any* of the three kinds of political activity.

With ambivalence being so closely linked to these kinds of participation, the question arises of how strong an influence it is when other factors are taken into account. An analysis along these lines shows that ambivalence does contribute to diminished levels of participation among critics of government:[7]

- It is the second most influential consideration, after the amount of news consumed, in accounting for less political involvement.
- It is more important even than such things as education, the intensity of an individual's religious beliefs and practices, confidence in either federal agencies or the Congress, or the sense that what government does has a direct bearing on one's life.

Among supporters of government the picture is quite different. Ambivalence is not a factor in determining how politically involved people may be between elections. Education, and, to a lesser extent, the amount of news a person takes in are what make a difference.

We have been looking at two kinds of involvement: voting and other activities between elections. If we combine these two measures of involvement, we find the principal consequence of ambivalence is a decrease in *both* voting and other kinds of involvement among critics of government. Fifty-one percent of Steady Critics are likely voters *and* participate in some way between elections. Among Ambivalent Critics, the proportion is only 31 percent. Ambivalence has no such effect among supporters with respect to the proportion who both vote and participate in some fashion between elections (table 7.2).

---

[6] See appendix C for a description of this index.
[7] See table D.11 and discussion in appendix D.

The prominent finding regarding levels of political activity is how different Steady Critics are from others in the frequency with which they vote and
participate in other ways. Their influence in the electorate and the political
process as a whole is clearly greater than their actual numbers in the country.

EFFECT OF AMBIVALENCE ON SUPPORT FOR THE
POLITICAL PARTIES

Much of the nation's political business gets done through the two major
political parties. Thus any impact ambivalence may have on attachment
to either party has potential political consequence. People who are of mixed
minds about government may have second thoughts about the party they identify with or may be less likely to support a party at all. Moreover, they may be
more inclined than others to think of themselves as a political "independent."
Equally significant, however, would be any indication that those who are ambivalent about government are more likely to split their ballots election day between candidates of different parties.

Support for a political party has many elements to it. Three are particularly important for purposes of this study. First, it is helpful to think of support for a political party in terms of levels of commitment. These can range
from highly motivated partisanship to casual preference to total detachment
from the party system.

Second, people can be saying many things if they call themselves a political "independent." Some may not be at home with any political party. Others
may support a party but *also* think of themselves as an independent. In short,
we cannot assume that independents are on a continuum between Republicans
and Democrats.

Third, we need to know the direction of political loyalty of those expressing even limited support for a party: Republican, Democrat, or something else.[8]

With these considerations in mind, a sequence of questions asked first: "In
your own mind, do you think of yourself as a supporter of one of the political
parties or not?" Note that respondents were given the explicit option of saying
they do not support a party. Those supporting a party were then asked which
party and how strongly. Those not supporting a party were asked if they feel

---

[8] For a discussion of the many elements of partisanship, see Bruce E. Keith, David B. Ma-
gleby, Candice J. Nelson, Elizabeth Orr, Mark C. Westlye, and Raymond E. Wolfinger, *The
Myth of the Independent Voter* (Berkeley: University of California Press, 1992); and Martin P.
Wattenberg, *The Decline of American Political Parties, 1952–1994* (Cambridge, Mass.: Harvard
University Press, 1996).

closer to one party or the other. Finally, whether they supported a party or not, all respondents were asked if they ever think of themselves as "a political independent."[9]

In most of the analyses that follow, we have narrowed the focus to those most likely to vote.

Support for the Parties

Fifty-two percent of likely voters say they think of themselves as "a supporter of one of the political parties," 30 percent being strong supporters and 22 percent not so strong. An additional 22 percent do not think of themselves as a party supporter but, in answer to a follow-up question, indicate they feel "closer to one of the two major political parties." About the same number (23 percent) say they neither support a party nor feel closer to one of the parties. The remaining 3 percent either support some other party or refuse to say what their preference is (table 7.3).

The point here is not to determine whether party support among likely voters stands at 52 percent (party supporters) or 74 percent (party supporters plus those feeling closer to one of the parties). Instead the purpose is to use the sequence of questions to measure levels of commitment to a political party. These levels range from those whose backing of a party is "strong" or "not very strong," to those who do not back a party but feel closer to one party than another, and finally to those who are neither party supporters nor feel close to a party.

By this yardstick ambivalence about government tends to reduce the intensity with which likely voters back either of the major parties. Fewer "strong" partisans are found among Ambivalent Critics (26 percent) than among Steady Critics (35 percent). Similarly, fewer Ambivalent Supporters (21 percent) are "strong" party backers than Steady Supporters (31 percent) (table 7.3).

Ambivalence has an added consequence when it comes to supporters of government: more than one-third (35 percent) of Ambivalent Supporters turn away from *both* parties. They neither back a party nor think of themselves as closer to one of the parties. This block of likely voters would be more noticeable if Ambivalent Supporters were not outnumbered by Steady Supporters by more than three to one.

In terms of the balance of loyalties between the two parties, ambivalence has a somewhat different influence among critics of government than among

---

[9] This question sequence was adapted from the 1980 National Election Study.

Table 7.3

Levels of Support for the Major Parties by Mix of General and Specific Views about Government

	All	Likely voters	Not likely voters	Among likely voters only			
				Steady Critic (n=249)	Ambivalent Critic (n=196)	Ambivalent Supporter (n=110)	Steady Supporter (n=406)
Strong supporter	22%	30%	16%	35%	26%	21%	31%
Not strong supporter	17	22	13	17	26	19	23
Not supporter but feel closer to one of the parties	24	22	25	28	27	22	19
Neither support nor feel closer to one of the parties	34	23	44	18	18	35	24
	97%[a]	97%	98%	98%	97%	97%	97%

[a] Totals add to less than 100% since they exclude those who support other than a major party or refuse to indicate a party preference.

[Q.47–49]

supporters.[10] Among likely voters who are critics of government, ambivalence is played out in terms of *which* party is preferred. Among likely voters who are more favorably disposed to government, ambivalence has more to do with *whether* a party is supported at all (table 7.4).

Again among likely voters, critics of government are predominantly Republican. Nonetheless, backing for the GOP is 13 percentage points lower among Ambivalent Critics (54 percent) than it is among Steady Critics (67 percent). What makes this finding significant is that the lower support for the Republican Party among Ambivalent Critics is matched by higher support for the Democratic Party, which is backed by 25 percent of Ambivalent Critics compared to 13 percent of Steady Critics.

What is more, Ambivalent Critics support the Republican Party with less intensity than Steady Critics. Steady Critics divide more than two to one between "strong" (31 percent) and "not very strong" (13 percent) Republicans. This is not so for Ambivalent Critics who divide about evenly in terms of the intensity of their support for the Republican Party: 17 percent are strong partisans and 19 percent not so strong.

The effect of ambivalence on views about the parties is quite different among likely voters who are basically supportive of government. They are more likely to be Democrats regardless of ambivalence. Even so, ambivalence is linked to substantially less backing for the Democratic Party among Ambivalent Supporters (35 percent) than is found among Steady Supporters (53 percent). What makes this disparity different from that among critics is that the drop in backing for the Democrats is *not* countered by a corresponding gain for the Republican Party. Instead there is an increase in the proportion who look to neither party (35 percent among Ambivalent Supporters versus 24 percent among Steady Supporters).

In sum, attitudes toward the political parties are anchored in part in the amount of ambivalence people express in their views about government. Among critics, ambivalence is accompanied by a reduction in the Republican margin over the Democrats. Among supporters, ambivalence is linked to diminished enthusiasm for either party.

---

[10] While this analysis concentrates on likely voters, it should be noted that the public at large splits 33 percent to 30 percent in favor of the Democrats. Among likely voters, Republicans enjoy a 39 percent to 35 percent advantage. Democrats have a ten-point margin over Republicans (32 percent to 22 percent) among those not likely to vote, although the largest proportion (44 percent) neither supports a party nor feels closer to one (table 7.4).

Table 7.4

Party Supported by Mix of General and Specific Views about Government

	All	Likely voters	Not likely voters	Among likely voters only			
				Steady Critic (n=249)	Ambivalent Critic (n=196)	Ambivalent Supporter (n=110)	Steady Supporter (n=406)
Republican	30%	39%	22%	67%	54%	27%	20%
Strong supporter	10	15	6	31	17	8	7
Not strong supporter	9	12	6	13	19	9	8
Not supporter but closer to	11	12	10	23	18	10	5
Democrat	33	35	32	13	25	35	53
Strong supporter	12	15	10	4	9	13	24
Not strong supporter	8	10	6	4	7	10	15
Not supporter but closer to	13	10	16	5	9	12	14
Other party	1	1	1	*a	2	0	*
Neither support nor feel closer to one of the parties	34	23	44	18	18	35	24
Refuse/no answer	2	2	1	2	1	2	3
	100%	100%	100%	100%	100%	99%	100%

*Designates less than half a percent.

[a]Designates less than half a percent.

[Q.47–49]

Calling Self an "Independent"

It is often assumed that people who think of themselves as "independents" fall somewhere between Republicans and Democrats in their thinking on political matters. But this conception can misconstrue what people may be saying when they call themselves independents.

Some people describe themselves as independents and still support one of the political parties. As early as 1980, for example, it was shown that many people who call themselves an independent are not doing so as a rejection of the political parties.[11] Independents may want to present themselves as people who look at things on the merits rather than merely accept a package of political ideas.[12]

Other independents are "free agents" in the sense of having no genuine preference for one party or the other. These independents can, in turn, be saying either of two things. Some stand apart from the parties because they do not feel either party is adequately expressing their views. For others, being an independent reflects a disinterest in political matters altogether.[13]

Therefore, one needs to look behind the label "independent" in order to understand what sentiment is being conveyed. Only then is it possible to determine where independent status fits into the mosaic of public opinion and to estimate its political significance.

Just as all respondents were asked initially if they think of themselves as supporters of one of the parties, all were asked if they ever think of themselves as "a political independent"—whether or not they support a party.[14] Taking responses to these questions into account, we can differentiate four political perspectives:

- *Nonpartisan independents* describe themselves as independents and do not support a party;
- *Partisan independents* call themselves independents while they also support a party;

---

[11] Keith, et al., *Myth of the Independent Voter*, 187–96.

[12] This point is made by Jack Dennis in "Political Independence in America, Part I: On Being an Independent Partisan Supporter," *British Journal of Political Science* 18 (January 1988): 87, as cited by Keith, et al., *Myth of the Independent Voter.*

[13] See Arthur H. Miller and Martin Wattenberg, "Measuring Party Identification: Independent or No Partisan Preference?" *American Journal of Political Science* 27 (February 1983): 106–21.

[14] For purposes of this analysis, party supporters are only those who answered affirmatively the general question about thinking of themselves "as a supporter of one of the political parties." Respondents who said "no" to the general question but subsequently said they sometimes feel closer to one of the parties were not considered party supporters in this analysis.

- *Partisan and not independent* respondents back a party and do not think of themselves as independents; and,
  - *Nonpartisan and not independent* respondents neither support a party nor describe themselves as independents.

In light of the effect ambivalence about government has on likelihood of voting and party support, we need to see if it has a comparable effect on whether people call themselves independents and what they may mean by the label. Again we limit the analysis to likely voters.

When it comes to being an independent, likely voters who are critics of government have virtually the same profile regardless of how ambivalent they may be. There is no significant difference between Steady Critics and Ambivalent Critics in the proportion calling themselves an independent or in the balance between nonpartisan and partisan independents (table 7.5).

The picture changes, however, among supporters of government. Here there is a significant difference between Ambivalent Supporters (54 percent) and Steady Supporters (42 percent) who call themselves an independent. There is also a difference in the balance between nonpartisan and partisan independents. Ambivalent Supporters are much more likely to be nonpartisan independents (38 percent) than partisan independents (16 percent). In contrast, Steady Supporters are about evenly divided between being nonpartisan independents (24 percent) and partisan independents (18 percent).

In other words, Ambivalent Supporters who think of themselves as independents tend to be saying they support neither party. On the other hand, to be an "independent" as a Steady Supporter is not so clear a rejection of both parties.

These findings highlight the importance of what was learned earlier about the relevance of ambivalence to party support. We saw that ambivalence among government's critics is related to which of the parties are preferred. But among supporters of government ambivalence is often expressed in terms of detachment from the parties altogether.

Learning whether or not people consider themselves independents adds little to our understanding of the effect of ambivalence on attitudes toward the parties. Among both critics and supporters of government, ambivalence is more likely to express itself in terms of their views of the parties than in terms of their calling themselves "independent."

- Among government's critics, ambivalence affects the balance of loyalty between the two major parties, not whether a party is backed in the first place. There is nothing about also being an "independent" that alters that conclusion.

Table 7.5

Political Independents and Party Support by Mix of General and Specific Views about Government

	All	Likely voters	Not likely voters	Among likely voters only			
				Steady Critic (n=249)	Ambivalent Critic (n=196)	Ambivalent Supporter (n=110)	Steady Supporter (n=406)
Consider self independent	40%	45%	34%	49%	47%	54%	42%
Nonpartisan independent	26	26	25	28	25	38	24
Partisan independent	14	19	9	21	22	16	18
Not consider self independent	59	52	65	49	52	44	55
Partisan and not independent	27	33	21	31	32	24	37
Nonpartisan and not independent	32	19	44	17	20	20	18
	99%[a]	97%[b]	99%	98%	99%	98%	97%

[a]Totals add to less than 100 percent since they exclude those who refuse to indicate a party preference. Those supporting a party other than the Republican or Democratic party are counted as a "partisan independent" or a "partisan and not independent" depending on whether they consider themselves an independent.

[b]This percent includes likely voters who are neither critics nor supporters of government (nor shown).

[Q.47–50]

• Among supporters of government, the consequence of ambivalence is to cast doubt on whether either party should be supported.
There is nothing about also being an independent that warrants modi-
fying that conclusion.

Ticket-Splitting

Since ambivalence about government has a lot to do with how attached voters
are to a political party, it may also make a difference in how much voters stay
with candidates of one party or split their ticket in elections. Voters of mixed
minds about government may also be voters with mixed party preferences at
the polls.

We looked at two kinds of ticket-splitting among likely voters. We asked
first about elections where there are candidates for several offices on the ballot
"such as president, member of Congress, senator, or governor." We then asked
respondents to think back to earlier elections for president and asked whether
they "usually voted for candidates of the same party or voted for the candidate
of one party in one year and the candidate of another party in another year?"

Retrospective questions such as these have their limits as definitive measures of past voting, and it is always difficult to gauge voter intentions. These
challenges are especially exacting when interviews, such as those for this survey, are not conducted immediately after an election or in anticipation of an
upcoming election.

Consequently, more information than was elicited by these two ticket-
splitting questions was needed to come up with a reasonable estimate of probable ticket-splitting. For example, an estimate of probable ticket-splitting needs
to take into account the fact that those who say they are strong backers of a
party are less likely to split their ballot than those with weak party preferences.

Thus taking into account answers to several questions in the survey, respondents were considered likely ticket-splitters if:

• They are a likely voter; *and*
• They report they usually vote for candidates of different parties
when several offices are on the ballot; *and*
• They report they have voted for presidential candidates of differ-
ent parties over the years; *and*
• They are not a "strong" supporter of a political party; *and*
• In the event they support a political party, but not "strongly,"
they also call themselves a political independent.[15]

---

[15] See appendix C for further discussion.

On this basis, we estimate that 33 percent of all likely voters are probable ticket-splitters. The remaining two-thirds of likely voters will be inclined to stay with candidates of one party in a typical presidential election.

Again among likely voters, ambivalence about government appears to have more of an effect on ticket-splitting among critics of government than supporters. Thirty-nine percent of Ambivalent Critics can be expected to vote for candidates of different parties. By contrast, only 26 percent of Steady Critics are likely to split their ballots. The difference between Ambivalent Supporters (36 percent) and Steady Supporters (32 percent) is not large enough to overcome considerations of sample size.

To get a sense of the potential clout of these voters, we need only project their numbers within the electorate. Based on the number of votes cast for president in 1996:

- Probable ticket-splitting by 39 percent of Ambivalent Critics who are likely voters translates into about 7.8 million voters.
- Probable ticket-splitting by 36 percent of Ambivalent Supporters who are likely voters translates into about 3.6 million voters.

The political implications of these numbers are far-reaching. The combined strength of this block of ambivalent voters amounts to approximatey 11.4 million voters—more than the size of Bill Clinton's margin over Bob Dole in 1996.[16]

AMBIVALENCE ABOUT GOVERNMENT AND AMERICAN POLITICS

As we conclude this inquiry, we come away with increased appreciation of what lies behind ambivalence and how fundamental it is to understanding American public opinion on political matters.

Ambivalence as Integral to American Public Opinion about Government

We now know that ambivalence in thinking about government cannot be dismissed simply as a matter of people being out of touch with political issues. Ambivalence about government is explained by many things. One thing it is *not* explained by, however, is a lack of education or knowledge about government. Nor is it found solely among those who turn less frequently to newspapers or to radio

---

[16] Clinton's support of 47.4 million votes exceeded Dole's 39.2 million by 8.2 million. See *Congressional Quarterly, Inc., America at the Polls, 1920–1996* (Washington, D.C.: Congressional Quarterly, Inc., 1997).

and television news. As shown in findings reported here, ambivalence about government is perfectly compatible with being an informed, involved citizen.

Ambivalence is also *not* merely another way in which people resist expressing firm opinions on issues. As was seen earlier, those who are ambivalent about government are just as likely as others to voice opinions on a wide range of matters. In fact, they express those opinions with the same intensity as people who are not ambivalent in their thinking.

The strongest evidence that ambivalence about government is basic to an understanding of the political thinking of Americans are the many, persistent and plausible relationships it has with opinions on a host of matters. Ambivalence about how much government people want comes up again and again as American public opinion is looked at from different angles.

The concept of ambivalence also tells us more about what people think government should be doing than how they describe their own political views. We have seen that the labels people identify with are not always reliable guides to the direction of their thinking. For example, 40 percent of those who call themselves "conservatives" think the federal government has about the right amount of power or not enough. One-third think the federal government has struck the right balance in what it does or should do more. Conversely, more than one-third of self-described "liberals" think government does too many things people could do better for themselves; and more than one-fourth think it has too much power.

The ambivalence of many about government also highlights the difficulties of drawing conclusions about what "the public" thinks on an issue. As we have seen here, to speak of "the public" being pro *or* con on government is to slight—or possibly miss entirely—the fact that some are pro *and* con if both their general and specific views about government are taken into account.

Since ambivalence is so integral to public opinion about government, it is all the more important to consider it as part of the backdrop against which differing conceptions of government compete for public support.

Ambivalence and Competing Visions of Government

Just under one-third of Americans are ambivalent in their thinking about government. As such, they are at the heart of the battle between competing visions of government when it comes to marshalling majority support on issues before the country or putting together winning electoral coalitions.

At the same time, those who are sending mixed signals about government are not a monolithic "center" of American politics that can be appealed to in some generic way. Some, whom we have called Ambivalent Critics, start from a vantage point that worries about government's scope and power, yet they support much of what government does. Others, the Ambivalent Supporters, start from the general premise that there is an important place for government, yet have doubts about some of its activities.

On balance, however, the truly competitive arena is among Ambivalent Critics. There are two reasons for this. First, Ambivalent Critics (20 percent of those responding) outnumber Ambivalent Supporters (12 percent). They are also more likely to be politically active between elections such as by contacting a member of Congress or a member of their state legislature and more likely to keep up with what is going on in the news. In addition there is a greater chance they will vote. In fact, there are twice as many Ambivalent Critics (21 percent) among likely voters as Ambivalent Supporters (10 percent). Further, once in the voting booth, Ambivalent Critics are more likely to split their tickets than other likely voters.

Second, sizeable divisions of opinion exist among critics of government on a broad array of issues. Of the fifty aspects of opinion summarized earlier (tables 4.10 and 5.15), half involved substantial differences between Ambivalent Critics and Steady Critics (in excess of 10 percentage points). The difference was even larger (at least 15 percentage points) on a quarter of the fifty issues. In stark contrast, there were only a half dozen issues on which differences between Ambivalent Supporters and Steady Supporters exceeded 10 percentage points.

Ambivalent Critics are pulled in different directions in their thinking about government as they listen to the give-and-take of national politics. Thus, in reaching out to Ambivalent Critics, those who believe government does too many things strike a responsive chord when they stay at the general, symbolic level. They meet resistance, however, when they seek to cut back in areas that Ambivalent Critics see as worthwhile.

Conversely, those who think there is an important role for government strike a responsive chord with Ambivalent Critics when they speak of the value of the specific things government does or should do. They run into trouble when the debate about what they stand for turns on the issue of "government" rather than the larger issues government may be helping to address.

A related point is that the case for specific activities need not rest on appeals to self-interest. It will be recalled that many critics of government back continuation of activities that have no direct bearing on them personally.

Issues also come into play as those with a stake in the debate try to appeal to Ambivalent Critics. Of the ten principal aspects of opinion that help explain ambivalence in thinking among critics, seven have to do with issues prominent in public discussion. Since these issues have a significant influence on the thinking of government's critics, they stand out as more important than other matters when speaking to the concerns of Ambivalent Critics. The seven issues are:

- The amount of attention government pays to low-income people;
- The extent to which the country as a whole is seen as affected by problems that are particularly acute in one locality but not in another;
- The amount of confidence in the quality of work done by the departments and agencies of the federal government;
- Whether now is no time to let up working hard for equality or whether the country need not push so hard in dealing with the matter of race;
- Whether anyone can get ahead if they work hard enough or whether hard work is often not enough to overcome the barriers some face;
- Whether political activities of conservative Christian groups are good for the country or not; and,
- Whether the country is making progress or losing ground when it comes to teaching the values of personal responsibility and moral character.

It should also be noted that the differences of view between Ambivalent Critics and Steady Critics on all but one of these issues exceed the difference between Ambivalent Critics and either Ambivalent or Steady Supporters.

We have seen here an American public whose opinions about government reflect a tension deeply imbedded in our political tradition. About three in five Americans come down clearly on one side of the political divide or the other:

- Nearly one out of five express a general concern that government has grown too big and want to scale back on many of the specific things it is doing.
- Just under two in five are more favorably disposed to government as a general matter and think much of what it does should be continued or expanded.

A politically important one-third of the public, however, are ambivalent in their thinking about government. Their general views about government are often at odds with what they think government should actually be doing. These are people whose views on issues are nuanced and cannot be easily pigeonholed. Ambivalence about government appears to be integral to the way they see the political world. The evidence here suggests that those who send mixed signals about government will continue to hold the balance of power in American politics.

Appendix A
Supplementary Tables

Table A.1
The "Ideological" Spectrum and the "Operational" Spectrum

Ideological Spectrum

This composite measure was constructed by classifying answers to the following questions. Respondents agreeing with all five statements were classified as "completely conservative" and agreeing with four of the five as "predominantly conservative." Respondents disagreeing with all five statements were "completely liberal" and disagreeing with four of the five were "predominantly liberal." All others fell in the "middle-of-the-road" category.

Question: Generally speaking, any able-bodied person who really wants to work in this country can find a job and earn a living.

Agree	76%
Disagree	21
Don't know	3

Question: The federal government is interfering too much in state and local matters.

Agree	40%
Disagree	47
Don't know	13

Question: The government has gone too far in regulating business and interfering with the free enterprise system.

Agree	42%
Disagree	39
Don't know	19

Question: We should rely more on individual initiative and ability and not so much on governmental welfare programs.

Agree	79%
Disagree	12
Don't know	9

Question: Social problems here in this country could be solved more effectively if the government would only keep its hands off and let people in local communities handle their own problems in their own ways.

Agree	49%
Disagree	38
Don't know	13

Continued on next page

Table A.1   Continued

Operational Spectrum

This composite measure was constructed by classifying answers to the following questions. Respondents answering all five questions in the affirmative were counted "completely liberal" and four of the five as "predominantly liberal." Those answering all five in the negative were "completely conservative" and four of the five negatively were "predominantly conservative." All others were "middle of the road."

Question: A broad general program of federal aid to education is under consideration, which would include federal grants to help pay teachers' salaries. Would you be for or against such a program?

For	62%
Against	28
Don't know	10

Question: Congress has been considering a compulsory medical insurance program covering hospital and nursing home care for the elderly. This Medicare program would be financed out of increased social security taxes. In general, do you approve or disapprove of this program?

Approve	63%
Disapprove	30
Don't know	7

Question: Under the federal housing program, the federal government is making grants to help build low-rent public housing. Do you think government spending for this purpose should be kept at least at the present level, or reduced, or ended altogether?

At least at present level	63%
Reduced	12
Ended altogether	10
Don't know	15

Question: Under the urban renewal program, the federal government is making grants to help rebuild run-down sections of our cities. Do you think government spending for this purpose should be kept at least at the present level, or reduced, or ended altogether?

At least at present level	67%
Reduced	10
Ended altogether	11
Don't know	12

Question: The federal government has a responsibility to try to reduce unemployment.

Agree	75%
Disagree	18
Don't know	7

Source: Lloyd A. Free and Hadley Cantril, *The Political Beliefs of Americans* (New Brunswick, N.J.: Rutgers University Press, 1967), 9–33.

Table A.2

Trend in View of Government Power, 1964–1992

	1964	1966	1968	1970	1972	1976	1978	1980	1984	1988	1992
Too powerful[a]	30%	39%	40%	31%	41%	49%	43%	49%	32%	33%	40%
Not too strong	36	27	30	33	27	20	14	15	22	19	17
No opinion	34	34	29	36	32	31	43	36	46	47	43
	100%	100%	99%	100%	100%	100%	100%	100%	100%	99%	100%

[a]*Question:* Some people are afraid the government in Washington is getting too powerful for the good of the country and the individual person. Others feel that the government in Washington is not getting too strong. Do you have an opinion on this or not? IF "YES": What is your feeling? (Slight variation in wording for 1964–72: Have you been interested enough in this to favor one side over the other? IF "YES": What is your feeling?)

Source: American National Election Studies, 1964–1992.

Table A.3

Mix of General and Specific Views about Government by Age within Sex

	Steady Critic	Ambivalent Critic	Ambivalent Supporter	Steady Supporter	Not Critic or Supporter	Total
All Respondents	18%	20%	12%	39%	11%	100%
Men						
18 to 29	15	23	17	41	4	100
30 to 39	16	19	14	40	11	100
40 to 59	28	22	8	35	7	100
60 and over	28	21	8	34	8	99
Women						
18 to 29	4	23	5	61	8	101
30 to 39	13	16	13	43	15	100
40 to 59	14	18	15	39	15	101
60 and over	21	22	15	25	17	100

Note: This table should be read across. Thus 15 percent of men between 18 and 29 are Steady Critics.

Table A.4

Liberal-Conservative Self-Identification, 1972–1996

	Liberal	Middle of the road	Conservative	Haven't thought much about it; don't know
1972	18%	27%	26%	28%
1974	21	26	26	27
1976	16	25	25	33
1978	20	27	27	27
1980	17	20	28	36
1982	15	22	27	36
1984	18	23	29	30
1986	18	28	30	25
1988	17	22	32	30
1990	16	24	26	33
1992	20	23	31	27
1994	14	26	36	24
1996	18	24	33	25

Question: We hear a lot of talk these days about liberals and conservatives. Here is a 7-point scale on which the political views that people might hold are arranged from extremely liberal to extremely conservative. [CARD SHOWN RESPONDENT] Where would you place yourself on this scale, or haven't you thought much about this?

Note: Scale values 1 to 3 are counted as "liberal"; 4 is "middle of the road"; and 5 to 7 are "conservative."

Source: American National Election Studies, 1972–1996.

Table A.5

Number of Levels of Government for Which Favorable Ratings Are Given by Mix of General and Specific Views about Government

	Steady Critic		Ambivalent Critic		Ambivalent Supporter		Steady Supporter	
All three levels[a]	17%	49%	26%	61%	38%	67%	35%	68%
Two levels	32		35		29		33	
One level	29	51	23	38	17	33	20	32
None of the levels	22		15		16		12	
	100%		99%		100%		100%	

[a]Federal, state, and local.

Table A.6
Ratings of and Confidence in Government by Party Supported

	All	Republican Party	Democratic Party	Not party supporter
Rating of job[a]				
Federal government	53%	39%	67%	51%
State government	62	69	59	58
Local government	60	68	56	56
Confidence[b]				
Federal agencies	55	51	59	55
U.S. Congress	35	37	35	33
State agencies	62	64	63	61
State legislature	50	57	47	47

[a]Excellent or pretty good.

[b]A great deal or fair amount.

Table A.7
Rating of Federal Government and Views on Improving the Way Government Works by Political Party Supported

	By Party Supported		
	Republican	Democratic	Do not support a party
Job rating of federal government			
Excellent and pretty good	39%	67%	51%
Not so good and very poor	59	32	44
Don't know	2	1	5
	100%	100%	100%
Amount of progress toward improving way government works			
Making progress	13%	27%	19%
Standing still	43	41	44
Losing ground	41	28	30
Don't know	3	5	7
	100%	101%	100%
Chances to make government work better			
Major changes possible	40%	42%	36%
Minor changes possible	46	46	45
Not much chance for change	13	9	15
Qualified/don't know	1	3	4
	100%	100%	100%

Table A.8

Views of Opportunity and the Marketplace by Household Income

	Under $30,000	$30,000 to $49,999	$50,000 to $74,999	$75,000 and over
Individual initiative				
Anyone can get ahead with hard work	53%	53%	53%	64%
Hard work often not enough	43	45	45	32
Qualified/don't know	3	2	2	4
	100%	100%	100%	100%
The larger marketplace				
Government keep eye on things; step in if needed	51%	47%	57%	50%
Government should stay out; let the market decide	37	43	38	42
Qualified/don't know	12	10	6	8
	100%	100%	101%	100%
Combined:				
Anyone can get ahead *and* Government should keep an eye on things; step in if needed	26%	21%	23%	26%
Government should stay out; let the market decide	22	27	26	32
Hard work often not enough *and* Government should keep an eye on things; step in if needed	24	25	33	22
Government should stay out; let the market decide	14	15	10	11
Qualified/don't know	14	11	7	10
	100%	99%	99%	100%

Table A.9
Views on Dealing with Race and Immigration by Key Subgroups

	Issue of race			Immigrants to United States		
	No need to push so hard	No time to let up	Qualified/ don't know	Should try to fit in	Live by own traditions	Qualified/ don't know
ALL	20%	75%	5%	54%	38%	8%
By age						
18 to 29	19	78	3	42	50	8
30 to 39	17	77	6	47	46	8
40 to 59	20	76	4	53	38	10
60 and over	23	71	6	73	20	7
By race						
White	22	73	5	55	38	7
Black	7	91	2	49	41	10
By ethnicity						
Latino/Hispanic	24	70	6	55	36	9
By region						
Northeast/Mid-Atlantic	18	78	4	55	38	7
South	24	72	4	56	36	7
Midwest	18	77	5	51	39	10
Southwest/Mountain	25	71	4	56	37	7
Far west	17	76	6	48	44	8

Continued on next page

Table A.9 Continued

	Issue of race			Immigrants to United States		
	No need to push so hard	No time to let up	Qualified/ don't know	Should try to fit in	Live by own traditions	Qualified/ don't know
By education						
Less than high school	19	76	5	61	33	6
High school graduate	19	77	4	61	32	7
Some college	21	72	7	48	43	9
College and up	22	74	4	41	49	10
By income						
Under $30,000	20	76	4	58	34	8
$30,000–$49,999	18	78	4	51	42	7
$50,000–$74,999	22	72	6	54	38	8
$75,000 and over	21	73	6	44	48	8
By union member in household	14	81	5	48	45	7
By party						
Republican	31	63	7	60	32	8
Democrat	14	82	4	51	41	8
Not supporter	17	79	4	50	41	8
By views on political matters (self-described)						
Conservative	29	66	5	60	32	8
Middle of the road	15	81	4	52	41	7
Liberal	11	86	3	44	50	6

Table A.10

Teaching Personal Responsibility and Moral Character: Percent Who Think One of "Very Most Important" Things for Good of the Country and Percent Who Think Country Is Losing Ground by Key Subgroups

	One of most important	Losing ground	One of the most important and losing ground
ALL	79%	54%	45%
By sex			
Men	73	53	43
Women	80	55	46
By age			
18 to 29	70	54	40
30 to 39	80	55	47
40 to 49	81	58	48
50 to 64	81	54	48
65 and over	84	47	43
By race			
White	79	56	46
Black	80	53	45
By ethnicity			
Latino/Hispanic	84	39	33
By region			
Northeast/Mid-Atlantic	77	58	48
South	81	54	46
Midwest	80	51	41
Southwest/Mountain	80	64	53
Far west	76	44	37
By education			
Less than high school	84	48	41
High school graduate	77	52	42
Some college	80	57	49
College and beyond	78	58	48
By income			
Under $30,000	81	49	42
$30,000–$49,999	78	55	45
$50,000–$74,999	77	59	48
$75,000 and over	76	58	45
By union member in household	78	52	43

Table A.11
Views on Issues of Concern to Conservative Christian Organizations by Key Subgroups

	Agree: Homosexuality threatens values of the family	Agree: Consensual homosexual relationship is a private matter	Divorce only for adultery or abuse	Sex education to abstain completely	Christian groups good for country	Consider self part of Christian movement
ALL	51%	72%	28%	29%	43%	13%
By sex						
Men	56	71	26	27	40	11
Women	46	73	30	31	46	14
By age						
18 to 29	45	83	30	20	40	11
30 to 39	47	78	26	22	43	12
40 to 49	57	72	26	30	48	14
50 to 64	50	71	26	29	40	10
65 and over	58	53	32	49	46	17
By race						
White	52	71	29	31	44	12
Black	56	75	25	26	56	23
By ethnicity						
Latino/Hispanic	39	73	25	13	36	16

By region						
Northeast/Mid-Atlantic	43	82	23	24	35	7
South	58	63	34	31	53	18
Midwest	55	69	33	33	48	14
Southwest/Mountain	56	68	27	34	49	14
Far west	38	80	19	22	27	9
By locality size						
Large city	45	77	25	23	38	13
Suburb	45	81	23	32	37	8
Town	53	71	29	28	46	13
Rural area	59	62	35	32	50	16
By education						
Less than high school	56	58	33	34	58	17
High school graduate	52	71	28	28	43	14
Some college	54	79	27	27	41	12
College and beyond	41	79	26	29	35	8
By income						
Under $30,000	54	65	31	31	48	17
$30,000–$49,999	53	76	28	28	46	14
$50,000–$74,999	53	74	27	30	42	7
$75,000 and over	38	86	19	23	30	13
By union member in household	41	79	17	20	42	10
By party						
Republican	72	63	37	46	60	20
Democrat	38	80	21	20	32	11
Not support party	45	73	26	23	40	8

Continued on next page

Table A.11 Continued

	Agree: Homosexuality threatens values of the family	Agree: Consensual homosexual relationship is a private matter	Divorce only for adultery or abuse	Sex education to abstain and completely	Christian groups good for country	Consider self part of Christian movement
By views on political matters (self-described)						
Conservative	67	61	35	45	60	20
Middle of the road	42	80	27	19	36	7
Liberal	33	85	14	16	23	10
By views on moral and social matters (self-described)						
Conservative	66	63	37	44	57	18
Middle of the road	40	82	20	13	31	5
Liberal	27	88	15	12	27	11
By self-described "born again" Christian						
Born again[a]	71	59	38	42	64	23
Other Christian	41	77	25	25	35	8

By whether part of Christian movement						
Yes, part of	80	47	43	52	85	100
No, not part of	46	77	25	25	36	0
By general/specific view of government						
Steady Critic	69	61	37	47	55	17
Ambivalent Critic	54	73	33	29	41	13
Ambivalent Supporter	47	68	27	26	38	12
Steady Supporter	41	80	21	22	39	11

[a]Those whose religious preference was Christian were asked if they described themselves as a "born again," Evangelical, Fundamentalist, Pentecostal or Charismatic Christian. Those who said "no" or expressed no opinion were designated as "other Christian."

Table A.12

Summary of Key Differences of Opinion on Issues between Steady Critics and Ambivalent Critics of Government and between Steady Supporters and Ambivalent Supporters

	Among critics			Among supporters		
	Steady Critic	Ambivalent Critic	Difference	Ambivalent Supporter	Steady Supporter	Difference
Performance of government						
Favorable rating of job done by (from table 3.2):						
Federal government	30%	42%	12%[a]	67%	66%	1
State government	58	64	6	62	65	3
Local government	57	66	9[a]	60	60	0
Express confidence in (from table 3.4):						
Quality of work in federal agencies	37	55	18[a]	60	65	5
U.S. Congress serving all	29	29	0	34	41	7
Quality of work in state agencies	50	68	18[a]	63	69	6
State legislature serving all	52	51	1	47	53	6
Improving the way government works (from table 3.6):						
One of very most important matters	71	75	4	55	61	6
Amount of progress (losing ground)	52	39	13	27	23	4
Leaders who go beyond short-term solutions (from table 3.6):						
One of very most important matters	35	48	13[a]	41	45	4
Amount of progress (losing ground)	44	36	8[a]	30	23	7[a]

Marketplace and opportunity

Getting ahead in the United States (from table 4.1):						
Anyone can with work	71	57	14[a]	56	49	7
Hard work often can't overcome barriers	27	40	13[a]	42	49	7
Operation of the market (from table 4.1):						
Government ensure competition	27	44	17[a]	63	60	3
Let market decide	68	47	21[a]	29	31	2

Social problems

Dealing with juvenile crime (from table 4.2):						
Focus mostly on getting tougher	39	21	18[a]	27	18	9[a]
Focus mostly on preventing	31	45	14[a]	43	52	9[a]
Police search of a person's home (from table 4.2):						
Okay if they believe are acting legally	13	13	0	16	8	8[a]
Search warrant should be required	83	84	1	80	90	10[a]
Dealing with issue of race (from table 4.3):						
No need to push so hard	40	21	19[a]	23	12	11[a]
No time to let up	53	76	23[a]	73	85	12[a]
Immigrants coming from other countries (from table 4.3):						
Should try to fit in	62	55	7[a]	56	51	5
Okay to live by their own traditions	29	39	10[a]	38	43	5
Amount of government attention to low-income people (from table 4.4):						
Too much	48	11	37[a]	25	7	18[a]
About right	24	33	9	31	28	3
Too little	26	55	29[a]	41	63	22[a]

Continued on next page

Table A.12 Continued

	Among critics			Among supporters		
	Steady Critic	Ambivalent Critic	Difference	Ambivalent Supporter	Steady Supporter	Difference
Have "a lot" to do with poverty (from table 4.4):						
Lack of job skills	42	48	6	46	59	13[a]
Not trying enough to make it on their own	59	36	23[a]	53	38	15[a]
Poor schools in low-income areas	26	37	11[a]	27	41	14[a]
Unable to work (family circumstances)	13	22	9[a]	23	28	5
Traditions and social norms						
Teaching personal responsibility and moral character (from table 4.6):						
One of very most important problems	84	82	2	76	76	0
Amount of progress (losing ground)	69	60	9[a]	56	45	11[a]
Have "great deal" to do with family problems (from table 4.7):						
Parents working long hours	73	69	4	63	71	8[a]
Too much sex and violence on TV and in the media	66	54	12[a]	51	53	2
Not enough after school activities	30	35	5	35	41	6
Schools not teaching right from wrong	40	33	7[a]	32	31	1
Standards of conduct these days (from table 4.6):						
Not enough respect for self-control	56	45	11[a]	46	42	4
Self-expression even if others may not approve	36	51	15[a]	45	53	8[a]

What children should be learning (from table 4.6):						
To be themselves	50	58	8[a]	52	55	3
To fit in	41	36	5	36	37	1
Concerns of conservative Christian groups						
Agree that homosexuality (from table 4.8):						
Threatens values of the family	69	54	15[a]	47	41	6
Consensual relationship private matter	61	73	12[a]	68	80	12[a]
Divorce should be granted (from table 4.8):						
Only for adultery, abuse, or desertion	37	33	4	27	21	6[a]
For other reasons as well	58	63	5	64	73	9[a]
Sex education should (from table 4.8):						
Encourage abstinence until marriage	47	29	18[a]	26	21	5
Provide information may need to know	45	66	21[a]	67	74	7
Conservative Christian groups are (from table 4.9):						
Good for country	55	41	14[a]	38	39	1
Not good for country	35	49	14[a]	55	55	0
Consider self part of movement (from table 4.9)	17	13	4	12	11	1

[a]Designates a statistically significant difference (at the 95 percent level of confidence) between Steady Critics and Ambivalent Critics or between Steady Supporters and Ambivalent Supporters. These designations take into account the fact that questions about reasons for poverty and family difficulties were asked of half the sample.

Table A.13
Personal Ladder Ratings and Shifts by Key Subgroups

	Past	Present	Future	Shift: past to present	Shift: present to future
ALL	5.6	6.8	8.0	+1.2	+1.2
By sex					
Men	5.5[a]	6.5	7.8	+1.0	+1.3
Women	5.8	6.9	8.2	+1.1	+1.3
By age					
18 to 29	4.9	6.4	8.6	+1.5	+2.2
30 to 39	4.9	6.7	8.5	+1.8	+1.8
40 to 59	5.8	6.8	8.0	+1.0	+1.2
60 and over	6.9	7.1	6.7	+0.2	−0.4
By education					
Less than high school	5.4	6.5	6.7	+1.1	+0.2
High school graduate	5.6	6.6	6.8	+1.0	+0.2
Some college	5.5	6.7	8.3	+1.2	+1.6
College and beyond	6.0	7.2	8.4	+1.2	+1.2
By income					
Under $30,000	5.6	6.3	7.6	+0.7	+1.3
$30,000–$49,999	5.3	6.8	8.1	+1.5	+1.3
$50,000–$74,999	5.6	6.9	8.3	+1.3	+1.4
$75,000 and over	6.3	7.5	8.6	+1.2	+1.1
By union member in household	6.0	6.8	8.0	+0.8	+1.2
By race[b]					
White	5.8	6.9	8.0	+1.1	+1.1
Black	4.8	6.2	8.5	+1.4	+2.3
By ethnicity					
Latino/Hispanic	4.9	6.3	8.2	+1.4	+1.9
By comparison of present rating to where thought would be					
Done better	5.3	7.2	8.5	+1.9	+1.3
Where thought would be	6.0	7.2	8.1	+1.2	+0.9
Done worse	5.7	5.2	7.0	−0.5	+1.8

[a]We can be 95 percent sure that differences of 0.4 or more between ratings among these subgroups are significant, that is, did not occur by chance in the sampling process.

[b]Not enough cases of other races for reliable percentages.

Table A.14

Levels of Personal Security/Insecurity by Key Subgroups

	Very insecure	Moderately insecure	Moderately secure	Very secure	Total
ALL	28%	21%	23%	28%	100%
By sex					
Men	26	21	21	31	99
Women	30	24	21	24	99
By age					
18 to 29	35	20	22	23	100
30 to 39	34	25	22	20	101
40 to 49	28	30	22	20	100
50 to 64	26	18	24	31	99
65 and over	15	20	17	48	100
By race					
White	25	23	23	29	100
Black	36	23	21	21	101
By ethnicity					
Latino/Hispanic	66	13	12	9	100
By education					
Less than high school	45	18	17	20	100
High school graduate	31	24	22	23	100
Some college	22	26	20	31	99
College and beyond	17	22	25	37	101
By income					
Under $30,000	41	22	17	19	99
$30,000–$49,999	28	23	23	26	100
$50,000–$74,999	18	26	24	32	100
$75,000 and over	10	21	26	43	100
By union member in household	31	21	23	25	100
By class[a]					
Middle	21	22	23	34	100
Working	35	27	22	16	100
Lower	60	18	11	11	100
By party					
Republican	20	20	23	37	100
Democrat	32	25	20	23	100
Not support a party	32	24	22	23	101
By self-described political views					
Conservative	25	19	23	33	100
Middle of the road	32	27	19	22	101
Liberal	27	24	23	26	100

Continued on next page

Table A.14   Continued

	Very insecure	Moderately insecure	Moderately secure	Very secure	Total
By mix of general and specific views of government					
Steady Critic	17	18	22	43	100
Ambivalent Critic	31	19	20	29	99
Ambivalent Supporter	29	22	23	25	99
Steady Supporter	29	26	22	23	100

Note: This table should be read across.

[a]Insufficient number of respondents identifying with the "upper" class for reliable percentages.

Table A.15

Amount of Government Attention to Low-Income People by View of
Government Attention to Middle-Income People and "People Like You"

	All	Among those who think government attention to middle-income people is			Among those who think government attention to "people like you" is		
		Too much	About right	Too little	Too much	About right	Too little
Amount of attention to low-income people							
Too much	18%	29%	12%	20%	41%	14%	19%
About right	28	25	40	23	23	39	21
Too little	52	45	46	56	36	45	60
Don't know	2	1	2	1	*[a]	2	1
	100%	100%	100%	100%	100%	100%	101%

[a]Designates less than half a percent.

Table A.16

Amount of Government Attention to
Those with Low and Middle Incomes and to "People Like You" by
Personal Financial Security Taking Household Income into Account

	Under $30,000		$30,000–$49,999		$50,000 and over	
	Insecure (n=383)	Secure (n=241)	Insecure (n=279)	Secure (n=303)	Insecure (n=215)	Secure (n=403)
Attention paid to low-income people						
Too much	9%	15%	19%	22%	22%	23%
About right	19	35	22	31	23	37
Too little	70	46	56	46	53	39
Don't know	1	4	2	1	2	1
	99%	100%	99%	100%	100%	100%
Attention paid to "people like you"						
Too much	3%	4%	4%	6%	5%	11%
About right	26	57	29	45	31	47
Too little	68	35	64	48	62	41
Don't know	3	4	3	1	2	2
	100%	100%	100%	100%	100%	101%
Attention paid to middle-income people						
Too much	6%	8%	3%	4%	5%	6%
About right	22	35	22	31	27	31
Too little	69	49	72	62	68	61
Don't know	3	8	3	3	*a	2
	100%	100%	100%	100%	100%	100%

[a]Designates less than half a percent.

Table A.17

Whether Economic Growth Means All Gain or Gap Gets Bigger as Seen by Those of
Differing Income, Self-Described Situation (Class) and Views on Related Issues

	All gain	Gap gets bigger	Both or qualified	Don't know	Total
ALL	17%	76%	2%	6%	101%
By household income					
Under $30,000	11	82	1	6	100
$30,000–$49,999	16	78	1	5	100
$50,000–$74,999	25	70	1	4	100
$75,000–$99,999	21	74	3	2	100
$100,000 and over	23	70	1	6	100
By personal financial security					
Very secure	23	68	2	7	100
Moderately secure	16	77	2	5	100
Moderately insecure	19	76	1	4	100
Very insecure	8	85	1	6	100
By union member in household	14	84	0	3	101
By description of own situation[a]					
Middle class	21	71	2	7	101
Working class	10	85	1	3	99
Lower class	10	85	*[b]	5	100
By view on getting ahead					
Anyone can get ahead with					
hard work	22	70	1	7	100
Hard work often not enough	10	85	*	5	100
By view on market competition					
Government keep an eye on					
market to ensure competition	14	81	1	4	100
Government stay out and let					
market decide	20	72	*	8	100

Note: This table should be read across. For example, 11 percent of those in households with an
income under $30,000 think all gain.

[a]Too few respondents who identify with the "upper class" for reliable percentages.

[b]Designates less than half a percent.

Table A.18
Percent Identifying with a Class by Different Income and Occupation Groups

	By household income			
	Under $30,000	$30,000–$49,999	$50,000–$74,999	$75,000 and over
Upper class	1%	1%	2%	14%
Middle class	44	58	81	70
Working class	35	37	16	13
Lower class	19	3	0	2
Not sure/refuse	2	*a	1	1
	101%	100%	100%	100%

	By respondent's occupation[b]			By labor union status
	Executive and professional	White collar	Blue collar	Member in household
Upper class	5%	1%	1%	1%
Middle class	70	58	39	62
Working class	21	37	48	31
Lower class	3	4	11	6
Not sure/refuse	1	1	1	1
	100%	101%	100%	101%

[a]Designates less than half a percent.

[b]Among respondents who are employed.

Table A.19

Correspondence Between Political Outlook as Self-Described and
General Views about Government Taking into Account Education and
Knowledge about Government

By education	High school graduate or less	Some college or more	Difference
Self-described "conservatives" who are			
Mostly critical	47%	61%	+14
Mostly supportive	40	31	
Neither critical nor supportive	13	8	
	100%	100%	
Self-described "liberals" who are			
Mostly critical	26%	21%	
Mostly supportive	66	75	+9
Neither critical nor supportive	9	4	
	100%	100%	

By knowledge about government	Less knowledge[a]	More knowledge	Difference
Self-described "conservatives" who are			
Mostly critical	39%	65%	+26
Mostly supportive	46	27	
Neither critical nor supportive	15	8	
	100%	100%	
Self-described "liberals" who are			
Mostly critical	28%	19%	
Mostly supportive	65	75	+10
Neither critical nor supportive	7	5	
	99%	99%	

[a]"Less" are those with correct answers on two or fewer of the knowledge questions; "more" are those with three or four correct responses.

Table A.20

How Directly People Say Specific Activities of
Government Bear on Them Personally

	Very	Only somewhat	Not very	Not at all	Not sure	Total
Clean air standards	45%	33%	10%	11%	1%	100%
Medical research	38	34	12	15	1	100
Consumer product safety	35	36	13	14	1	99
Financing college education	33	27	13	27	1	101
Safe working conditions	26	26	16	32	*a	100
Teachers' salaries in poor school districts	19	25	18	37	2	101
Medicaid	20	23	16	41	1	101
Job training for low-income people	16	22	18	43	*	99
Head Start	14	18	16	51	1	100
Housing assistance for low-income families	12	19	19	49	1	100

Note: This table should be read across.

[a]Designates less than half a percent.

Table A.21
Intensity of Religious Beliefs and Practices by Key Subgroups

	Deeply religious	Fairly religious	Less religious	Total
ALL	34%	32%	34%	100%
By sex				
Men	28	32	40	100
Women	39	31	29	99
By age				
18 to 29	22	32	46	100
30 to 39	26	38	36	100
40 to 49	34	32	33	99
50 to 64	40	28	32	100
65 and over	56	26	18	100
By race				
White	35	30	36	101
Black	37	48	15	100
By ethnicity				
Latino/Hispanic	30	43	28	101
By region				
Northeast/Mid-Atlantic	28	33	39	100
South	44	30	26	100
Midwest	37	32	31	100
Southwest/Mountain	39	26	36	101
Far west	20	37	43	100
By locality size				
Large city	27	36	37	100
Suburb	30	30	40	100
Town	36	34	30	100
Rural area	39	27	34	100
By education				
Less than high school	39	36	25	100
High school graduate	33	32	35	100
Some college	31	31	38	100
College and beyond	36	28	36	100
By income				
Under $30,000	37	31	32	100
$30,000–$49,999	31	36	33	100
$50,000–$74,999	33	30	37	100
$75,000 and over	34	27	39	100

Note: This table should be read across.

Table A.22

Summary of Key Differences Regarding Personal Situation Between Steady Critics and Ambivalent Critics of Government and between Steady Supporters and Ambivalent Supporters

	Among critics			Among supporters		
	Steady Critic	Ambivalent Critic	Difference	Ambivalent Supporter	Steady Supporter	Difference
Sense of personal well-being						
Personal ladder ratings (from table 5.1):						
Shift from past to present						
Large gain	20%	28%	8[a]	32%	28%	4
Moderate gain	32	28	4	31	34	3
No change	37	24	13[a]	21	32	2
Decline	11	21	10[a]	16	15	1
Shift from present to future						
Great optimism	11	25	14[a]	24	24	0
Modest optimism	37	37	0	38	47	9[a]
No change	41	30	11[a]	30	22	8[a]
Pessimism	11	8	3	8	6	2
Financial security and perceived equities						
Personal financial security (from table A.14):						
Feel very secure	43	29	14[a]	25	23	2
Feel very insecure	17	31	14[a]	29	29	0

Continued on next page

Table A.22 Continued

	Among critics			Among supporters		
	Steady Critic	Ambivalent Critic	Difference	Ambivalent Supporter	Steady Supporter	Difference
Perceived equities and inequities (from table 5.3):						
Amount of attention government pays to low-income people:						
Too much	48	11	37[a]	25	7	18[a]
About right	24	33	9[a]	31	28	3
Too little	26	55	29[a]	41	64	23[a]
Amount of attention government pays to middle-income people: too little	67	66	1	62	62	0
Amount of attention government pays to upper-income people: too much	63	64	1	61	63	2
Amount of attention government pays to people like you: too little	52	54	2	51	50	1
Growth in the economy (from table 5.4):						
Means all gain	30	15	15[a]	13	14	1
Means rich/poor gap gets bigger	60	81	21[a]	77	82	5
Description of own situation (from table 5.5):						
Middle class	66	59	7[a]	58	58	0
Working class	24	27	3	32	30	2
Lower class	4	7	3	4	9	5
Knowledge about government and interest in the news (from tables 5.6 and 5.7)						
Knowledge about government: high	38	20	18[a]	18	23	5

News consumption: high	30	32	2	24	26	2
Follow government and public affairs:						
Most of the time	56	36	20[a]	39	31	8[a]
Some of the time	27	41	14[a]	33	39	6
Experience with government						
Number of government activities bearing directly on respondent (from table 5.9):						
8 of 10	16	23	7[a]	22	23	1
6 or 7	17	20	3	18	21	3
4 or 5	23	34	11[a]	29	31	2
3 or fewer	44	23	21[a]	31	25	6
Government employment of someone in household: any level of government (from table 5.10)	18	17	1	20	19	1
Payments or benefits from government: one or more (from table 5.10)	36	37	1	34	33	1
Sense of interdependence						
Problems seen as more than local (from table 5.11):						
Four or five	33	51	18[a]	46	56	10[a]
Three or fewer	67	49	18[a]	53	44	9[a]
Intensity of religious beliefs/practices						
Summary index (from table 5.14):						
Deeply religious	43	36	7	28	30	2
Fairly religious	26	29	3	34	34	0
Less religious	31	35	4	38	36	2

[a]Designates a statistically significant difference (at the 95 percent level of confidence) between Steady Critics and Ambivalent Critics or between Steady Supporters and Ambivalent Supporters.

Table A.23
National Ladder Ratings and Shifts by Key Subgroups

	Past	Present	Future	Shift: past to present	Shift: present to future
ALL	5.7	5.5	5.7	−0.2	+0.2
By sex					
Men	5.8[a]	5.6	5.8	−0.2	+0.2
Women	5.5	5.4	5.6	−0.1	+0.2
By age					
18 to 29	5.6	5.3	5.6	−0.3	+0.3
30 to 39	5.5	5.4	5.7	−0.1	+0.3
40 to 59	5.6	5.6	5.7	0.0	+0.1
60 and over	6.0	5.6	5.7	−0.4	+0.1
By education					
Less than high school	6.0	5.4	5.7	−0.6	+0.3
High school graduate	5.8	5.5	5.5	−0.3	0.0
Some college	5.4	5.4	5.7	0.0	+0.3
College and beyond	5.5	5.8	5.9	+0.3	+0.1
By income					
Under $30,000	5.7	5.4	5.8	−0.3	+0.4
$30,000–$49,999	5.6	5.4	5.5	−0.2	+0.1
$50,000–$74,999	5.6	5.6	5.7	0.0	+0.1
$75,000 and over	5.7	5.7	5.8	0.0	+0.1
By region					
Northeast/Mid-Atlantic	5.7	5.8	6.0	+0.1	+0.2
South	5.7	5.3	5.4	−0.4	+0.1
Midwest	5.1	5.5	5.7	+0.4	+0.2
Southwest/Mountain	5.8	5.5	5.3	−0.3	−0.2
Far west	5.6	5.6	6.0	0.0	+0.4
By race[b]					
White	5.7	5.5	5.6	−0.2	+0.1
Black	4.9	5.3	5.7	+0.4	+0.4
By ethnicity					
Latino/Hispanic	6.0	6.1	6.4	+0.1	+0.3
By locality size					
Large city	5.6	5.7	5.9	+0.1	+0.2
Suburb of large city	5.6	5.6	5.9	0.0	+0.3
Small city/town	5.7	5.5	5.7	−0.2	+0.2
Rural area	5.7	5.2	5.2	−0.5	0.0
By party support					
Republican	6.0	5.3	5.2	−0.7	−0.1
Democrat	5.4	5.9	6.4	+0.5	+0.5
Not party supporter	5.5	5.3	5.4	−0.2	+0.1

[a]We can be 95 percent sure that differences of 0.4 or more between ratings among these subgroups are significant, that is, did not occur by chance in the sampling process.
[b]Not enough cases of other races for reliable percentages.

Appendix B
Questionnaire and Results

INTRODUCTORY NOTE ABOUT OUR APPROACH

Framing the questions. Two ways of posing issues are common in opinion research: asking whether respondents agree or disagree with a statement; and asking respondents which of two or more alternatives is closest to their view. Each method has its place.

We adopted the balanced-alternative approach for several reasons. We wanted questions to capture the kind of dilemma that exists about most issues in the real world. Most often conflicting values or ideas are at work, even in matters of fundamental beliefs and ideology. The balanced-alternative approach can give respondents more cues as to what a question is really asking.

We also wanted to avoid what is called a "yea-say" bias—the tendency of respondents to agree with statements read to them by interviewers. This is a natural response for some who find themselves in the unique social situation of being asked about their personal views by a professional interviewer who is also a complete stranger. A related concern is that, when presented a series of agree/disagree questions, respondents may get into a kind of rhythm in answering that can make the "yea-say" problem even worse.

An example of what the differing approaches can yield comes from an earlier study. Using a split sample, half a national sample was asked whether they agreed or disagreed that "any able-bodied person can find a job and make ends meet." Sixty-five percent of those polled agreed. The other half of the sample was given the choice between balanced alternatives: whether any able-bodied person can get a job *or* whether "there are times when it is hard to get along and some able-bodied people are not able to find a job." The percent who think anyone can get a job dropped to 43 percent.[1]

---

[1] Albert H. Cantril and Susan Davis Cantril, *Unemployment, Government, and the American People* (Washington, D.C.: Public Research, Inc., 1978).

The difference between the agree/disagree and balanced-alternative approaches has been shown to be most pronounced on matters that are not salient to respondents.[2]

Dealing with "no opinion." One challenge for polling is to write questions that elicit opinions from respondents rather than set up situations where respondents feel they must express an opinion on a topic even when they may not have one. One way of dealing with this is to end a poll question with a phrase such as "or don't you have a view on that?" Too much repetition, however, can interrupt the flow of an interview. We used an alternative approach of letting respondents know at the outset of the interview: "If, as we go through the interview, something comes up that you haven't had a chance to give much thought to, or don't know much about, please do not hesitate to say so." The point was repeated about ten minutes into the interview.

THE QUESTIONNAIRE AND RESULTS

Introduction: Hello, my name is _____ and I am calling from SRBI, the national public opinion research company. We are doing a nationwide study on what people are thinking about important issues facing the country today. The study is being conducted for the Woodrow Wilson Center of the Smithsonian Institution.

I would like to speak with the youngest male/oldest female age 18 or older, who is now at home.

I think you will find these questions interesting. Your answers will be kept completely confidential. They will be used only in combination with answers of other people in the study to give an overall picture of what Americans are thinking.

If, as we go through the interview, something comes up that you haven't had a chance to give much thought to, or don't know much about, please do not hesitate to say so.

1. First, I am going to mention some ways people get information about what is going on in the country.
   a. Thinking about the last couple of weeks, please tell me how often you watched network TV news: almost every day, a few times, only once or twice, or not at all?

Almost every day	59%
A few times	17
Only once or twice	13

---

[2] These points have been demonstrated empirically in Howard Schuman and Stanley Presser, *Questions and Answers in Attitude Surveys* (New York: Academic Press, 1981), 181–87. They also showed that opposing alternatives make a greater difference when it comes to reflecting the views of less-educated respondents.

Not at all	11
Don't know/NA/refused	*3

b. [Form A only] Watched news on CNN (Cable News Network) or C-SPAN?

Almost every day	24%
A few times	18
Only once or twice	18
Not at all	40
Don't know/NA/refused	*

c. Listened to news on the radio?

Almost every day	44%
A few times	15
Only once or twice	15
Not at all	26
Don't know/NA/refused	*

d. [Form A only] Listened to talk radio where people call in to discuss issues?

Almost every day	15%
A few times	10
Only once or twice	15
Not at all	60
Don't know/NA/refused	*

e. Read a newspaper?

Almost every day	51%
A few times	16
Only once or twice	20
Not at all	14
Don't know/NA/refused	0

2. Now, on another subject. Imagine for a moment a ladder that has steps numbered from ten at the *top* down to zero at the *bottom*. Suppose the *top* of the ladder stands for the *best possible* life you could think of for yourself. And suppose the *bottom* of the ladder stands for the *worst possible* life you could think of for yourself.

a. On which step of the ladder do you feel you personally stand *at the present* time? You could be on any step from ten down to zero.

Step	
0	1%
1	*

---

[3] An asterisk (*) designates less than half a percent. Percentages may not add to 100% because of rounding of results to the nearest full percent.

2	1	
3	3	
4	5	
5	18	Mean: 6.8
6	11	
7	21	
8	23	
9	7	
10	8	
Don't know/NA/refused	2	

b. On what number step would you say you stood *five years ago*?

Step		
0	2%	
1	2	
2	5	
3	9	
4	12	
5	22	Mean: 5.6
6	10	
7	11	
8	13	
9	5	
10	7	
Don't know/NA/refused	2	

c. Just your best guess, on what number step do you think you will stand in the future, say about *five years from now*?

Step		
0	1%	
1	1	
2	1	
3	1	
4	1	
5	5	Mean: 8.0
6	5	
7	9	
8	23	
9	19	
10	27	
Don't know/NA/refused	6	

d. You said you thought you were on step [INSERT] on the ladder at the present time. As you look back on things, is this about where you thought you would be now, or have you done better, or have you done worse than you thought you might?

Where thought would be	29%
Have done better	44
Have done worse	21
Don't know/NA/refused	6

3. Thinking of the ladder again, suppose the top stands for the best possible situation for the United States; the bottom the worst possible situation.

a. Please tell me on which step of the ladder you feel the United States is *at the present time?* Again, you can name any step from ten down to zero.

Step		
0	2%	
1	1	
2	3	
3	7	
4	12	
5	24	Mean: 5.5
6	18	
7	18	
8	9	
9	2	
10	2	
Don't know/NA/refused	2	

b. On what number step would you say the United States was about *five years ago?*

Step		
0	1%	
1	1	
2	3	
3	5	
4	13	
5	23	Mean: 5.7
6	20	
7	15	
8	10	
9	3	
10	2	
Don't know/NA/refused	5	

c. Just your best guess, if things go pretty much as you now expect, on what number step do you think the United States will be, let us say, *five years from now?*

Step

0	3%	
1	3	
2	5	
3	9	
4	9	
5	13	Mean: 5.7
6	11	
7	15	
8	15	
9	6	
10	5	
Don't know/NA/refused	7	

4. Next, I am going to mention some things the federal government is doing. For each, please tell me whether you think the amount of money the federal government spends on it should be increased, kept at the present level, decreased, or ended altogether.

First, . . . [INSERT: 4a THROUGH 4j, ROTATED]. Do you think spending should be increased, kept at the present level, decreased, or ended altogether?

a. Enforcing standards for clean air.

Increased	50%
Kept at present level	37
Decreased	8
End altogether	2
Don't know/NA/refused	3

b. Job training for low-income people who want to work and need skills.

Increased	68%
Kept at present level	23
Decreased	4
End altogether	2
Don't know/NA/refused	2

c. Keeping dangerous consumer products off the market.

Increased	45%
Kept at present level	37
Decreased	8

End altogether	5
Don't know/NA/refused	4

d. Health care for low-income families through the Medicaid program.

Increased	40%
Kept at present level	40
Decreased	11
End altogether	4
Don't know/NA/refused	5

e. Head Start, a program for preschool children from low-income families.

Increased	50%
Kept at present level	36
Decreased	5
End altogether	5
Don't know/NA/refused	3

f. Medical research on such things as cancer, AIDS, and heart disease.

Increased	67%
Kept at present level	27
Decreased	3
End altogether	1
Don't know/NA/refused	2

g. Programs to help finance college education.

Increased	59%
Kept at present level	30
Decreased	6
End altogether	3
Don't know/NA/refused	2

h. Helping low-income families afford low-rent apartments.

Increased	34%
Kept at present level	42
Decreased	14
End altogether	5
Don't know/NA/refused	5

i. Financial assistance to help poor school districts pay teachers' salaries.

Increased	61%
Kept at present level	26
Decreased	6
End altogether	4
Don't know/NA//refused	4

j. Making sure working conditions in factories and plants are safe.

Increased	45%
Kept at present level	43

Decreased   6
End altogether   2
Don't know/NA/refused   4

5. Now, I'd like to ask how much each of these activities bears directly on the life you personally are living.

Again, thinking about . . . [INSERT: 5a THROUGH 5j, IN SAME RO-TATED ORDER AS 4a THROUGH 4j]. How directly would you say it bears on your life: very directly, only somewhat directly, not very directly, or not at all?

a. Enforcing standards for clean air.

Very directly	45%
Only somewhat directly	33
Not very directly	10
Not at all	11
Don't know/NA/refused	1

b. Job training for low-income people who want to work and need skills.

Very directly	16%
Only somewhat directly	22
Not very directly	18
Not at all	43
Don't know/NA/refused	*

c. Keeping dangerous consumer products off the market.

Very directly	35%
Only somewhat directly	36
Not very directly	13
Not at all	14
Don't know/NA/refused	1

d. Health care for low-income families through the Medicaid program.

Very directly	20%
Only somewhat directly	23
Not very directly	16
Not at all	41
Don't know/NA/refused	1

e. Head Start, a program for preschool children from low-income families.

Very directly	14%
Only somewhat directly	18
Not very directly	16
Not at all	51
Don't know/NA/refused	1

f. Medical research on such things as cancer, AIDS, and heart disease.

Very directly	38%
Only somewhat directly	34
Not very directly	12
Not at all	15
Don't know/NA/refused	1

g. Programs to help finance college education.

Very directly	33%
Only somewhat directly	27
Not very directly	13
Not at all	27
Don't know/NA/refused	1

h. Helping low-income families afford low-rent apartments.

Very directly	12%
Only somewhat directly	19
Not very directly	19
Not at all	49
Don't know/NA/refused	1

i. Financial assistance to help poor school districts pay teachers' salaries.

Very directly	19%
Only somewhat directly	25
Not very directly	18
Not at all	37
Don't know/NA/refused	2

j. Making sure working conditions in factories and plants are safe.

Very directly	26%
Only somewhat directly	26
Not very directly	16
Not at all	32
Don't know/NA/refused	*

6. Now, I am going to mention some problems different parts of the country sometimes face. For each, please tell me whether you see it as *mostly a local problem*, not having much to do with the rest of the country. Or, whether you see it as *more than a local problem* because the country as a whole is likely to be affected in some way.

a. First, decisions about how to handle toxic waste from nuclear plants. Do you see this as mostly a local problem, or more than a local problem?

Mostly local	10%
More than local	88
Don't know/NA/refused	2

b. Areas that have an especially high number of people living in poverty?

Mostly local	24%
More than local	74
Don't know/NA/refused	2

c. Rural areas that are cut off from air and rail transportation?

Mostly local	53%
More than local	42
Don't know/NA/refused	5

d. Schools in areas where the dropout rate is especially high?

Mostly local	33%
More than local	65
Don't know/NA/refused	2

e. Decisions about whether to open up a wilderness area to development?

Mostly local	32%
More than local	63
Don't know/NA/refused	5

As I mentioned before, if you do not have an opinion on some of the questions I will be asking, please do not hesitate to say so.

7. People have different ideas about what is really important for the good of the country. I am going to mention some things. For each, please tell me how important you personally feel it is.

a. First, teaching young people the values of personal responsibility and moral character? Would you say this is one of the very most important things for the country, quite important, only somewhat important, or not very important?

One of very most important	79%
Quite important	17
Only somewhat important	3
Not very important	1
Don't know/NA/refused	1

b. Pulling together as a nation to get beyond divisions of class, race, and cultural heritage?

One of very most important	57%
Quite important	25
Only somewhat important	13
Not very important	3
Don't know/NA/refused	2

c. [Form B only] Getting through to young people about the dangers of drug abuse?

One of very most important	77%
Quite important	16

Only somewhat important	6
Not very important	1
Don't know/NA/refused	*

d. Having national leaders who go beyond short-term solutions to put bold new ideas before the country?

One of very most important	42%
Quite important	30
Only somewhat important	14
Not very important	5
Don't know/NA/refused	8

e. Improving the way government works?

One of very most important	65%
Quite important	21
Only somewhat important	10
Not very important	1
Don't know/NA/refused	3

f. [Form A only] Providing equal opportunities and pay for women in the workplace?

One of very most important	50%
Quite important	29
Only somewhat important	15
Not very important	3
Don't know/NA/refused	2

8. Now I am going to mention these items again. For each, please tell me how much progress you think the country is making.

a. First, teaching young people the values of personal responsibility and moral character? Do you think the country is making progress, losing ground, or standing still?

Making progress	16%
Losing ground	54
Standing still	28
Don't know/NA/refused	2

b. Pulling together as a nation to get beyond divisions of class, race, and cultural heritage?

Making progress	29%
Losing ground	25
Standing still	45
Don't know/NA/refused	2

c. [Form B only] Getting through to young people about the dangers of drug abuse?

Making progress	37%
Losing ground	28

Standing still   32
Don't know/NA/refused   3

d. Having national leaders who go beyond short-term solutions to put bold
   new ideas before the country?

Making progress   18%
Losing ground   29
Standing still   43
Don't know/NA/refused   9

e. Improving the way government works?

Making progress   20%
Losing ground   32
Standing still   43
Don't know/NA/refused   5

f. [Form A only] Providing equal opportunities and pay for women in the
   workplace?

Making progress   58%
Losing ground   5
Standing still   34
Don't know/NA/refused   3

9. Now I am going to read you some pairs of statements. Each has two different views on an issue. For each pair, please tell me which statement you agree
   with most—the first or second.

   a. First, anyone in the United States can get ahead if they are willing to work
      hard enough; or
      Second, hard work is often not enough to overcome the barriers some
      people face in our society.
      How strongly do you feel about that: very strongly or not too strongly?

Can get ahead with hard work   55%
   Very strongly   48.7
   Not too strongly   6.6
Hard work often not enough   42
   Very strongly   32.9
   Not too strongly   9.1
Depends/qualified [vol]   2
Don't know/NA/refused   1

   b. The next pair of statements is:
      In general, there is too much government regulation of business in this
      country; or
      Government regulation is needed to make sure corporations act
      responsibly.

How strongly do you feel about that: very strongly or not too strongly?

Too much regulation		35%
Very strongly	26.5	
Not too strongly	8.4	
Government regulation needed		56
Very strongly	37.7	
Not too strongly	18.4	
Depends/qualified [vol]		2
Don't know/NA/refused		7

c. The federal government should keep an eye on our free enterprise system and step in if corporations get so powerful they crowd out competition; *or* The federal government should stay out of our free enterprise system and let the market decide who gets ahead.

How strongly do you feel about that: very strongly or not too strongly?

Government keep eye on system		50%
Very strongly	32.6	
Not too strongly	17.3	
Government stay out		40
Very strongly	25.3	
Not too strongly	14.6	
Depends/qualified [vol]		1
Don't know/NA/refused		9

d. In light of how far we have come, we don't need to push quite so hard now as in the past in dealing with the issue of race; *or* We still have a long way to go and now is no time to let up in working hard for true equality.

How strongly do you feel about that: very strongly or not too strongly?

Don't need to push so hard		20%
Very strongly	11.8	
Not too strongly	8.1	
No time to let up		75
Very strongly	63.3	
Not too strongly	11.9	
Depends/qualified [vol]		1
Don't know/NA/refused		4

10. As you know, people from all over the world become U.S. citizens. Which of these statements comes closest to your view:

People who come to the United States from other countries really become "Americans" only if they make an effort to fit into the mainstream of American society; *or*

So long as they support the values of a free society, people coming to the
United States from other countries can be just as "American" if they continue to live by their own traditions.

How strongly do you feel about that: very strongly or not too strongly?

Make effort to fit in		54%
Very strongly	41.1	
Not too strongly	12.5	
Live by own traditions		38
Very strongly	24.7	
Not too strongly	13.7	
Depends/qualified [vol]		2
Don't know/NA/refused		6

11. The next pair of statements is:

   If the police suspect a person is hiding something, they should be able to
   search that person's home without a search warrant from the court if they
   believe they are acting legally; *or*

   A search warrant should be required because it is up to the courts, not just
   the police, to determine if there is a good enough reason to search a person's home.

   How strongly do you feel about that: very strongly or not too strongly?

If police think legal		11%
Very strongly	8.0	
Not too strongly	3.4	
Search warrant should be required		86
Very strongly	77.6	
Not too strongly	8.0	
Depends/qualified [vol]		1
Don't know/NA/refused		2

12. When it comes to the federal government, do you think it does *too many
   things* people could do better for themselves, it *should do more* given the
   problems the country faces, *or* that the government has struck *about the
   right balance* in what it is doing?

Does too many things	45%
Should do more	23
Struck right balance	21
Depends/qualified [vol]	1
Don't know/NA/refused	11

13. Now, some pairs of statements on something different. After I read each,
   please tell me which statement you agree with most—the first, or the second.

a. When you cut through all the talk, most issues facing this country come down to a choice between two fairly clear points of view; *or*
By their nature, issues facing the country have many sides and you usually can't boil things down to two clear-cut choices.
Do you agree with that completely or only somewhat?

Clear choice		17%
Agree completely	7.3	
Agree only somewhat	10.0	
Issues have many sides		78
Agree completely	40.1	
Agree only somewhat	37.5	
Depends/qualified [vol]		*
Don't know/NA/refused		5

b. Too many people are trying to do their own thing these days without showing respect for the values of self-control and discipline that have made this country great; *or*
What has made this country great is that people can act freely and express themselves, even if others may not approve.
Do you agree with that completely or only somewhat?

No respect for self-control and discipline		46%
Agree completely	29.0	
Agree only somewhat	16.6	
People act freely and express themselves		47
Agree completely	26.4	
Agree only somewhat	20.8	
Depends/qualified [vol]		2
Don't know/NA/refused		5

14. On another matter, people have different ideas about what children should learn. Which do you think is more important:
For children to learn to be themselves and not pay too much attention to what other children are doing, even if it means they go it alone later in life; *or*
For children to be encouraged to fit in with what other children are doing because it will help them adjust to life later as an adult.
How strongly do you feel about that: very strongly or not too strongly?

Be themselves		54%
Very strongly	39.8	
Not too strongly	13.8	
Fit in		37
Very strongly	24.2	
Not too strongly	12.8	

Depends/qualified [vol]	3
Don't know/NA/refused	6

15. We all face times when we are not sure which way to turn on an important matter. When it comes to these kinds of situations, would you say you are: *More* the kind of person who feels uneasy if matters aren't resolved one way or the other fairly quickly; *or* *More* the kind of a person who doesn't mind if a decision is left up in the air until things have a chance to sort themselves out? Would you say this is true about you most of the time or only some of the time?

Uneasy if not resolved		57%
True most of the time	45.7	
True only some of the time	10.8	
Don't mind if left up in air		39
True most of the time	24.6	
True only some of the time	14.5	
Neither/depends/qualified [vol]		2
Don't know/NA/refused		2

16. How would you rate the job the *federal* government is doing when it comes to handling the problems facing the country: excellent, pretty good, not so good, or very poor?

Excellent	2%
Pretty good	51
Not so good	35
Very poor	10
Don't know/NA/refused	2

17. How would you rate the job your *state* government is doing when it comes to handling the problems facing the state: excellent, pretty good, not so good, or very poor? [SKIP FOR AREA CODE 202]

Excellent	4%
Pretty good	57
Not so good	27
Very poor	8
Don't know/NA/refused	4

18. How would you rate the job your *local* government is doing when it comes to handling problems: excellent, pretty good, not so good, or very poor?

Excellent	6%
Pretty good	54
Not so good	27
Very poor	10
Don't know/NA/refused	3

19a. [Form A only] All things considered, when it comes to what is best for the country, do you think the *federal* government has about the right amount of power, too much power, or not enough?

19b. [Form B only] All things considered, when it comes to what is best for the country, do you think the *federal* government has too much power, not enough power, or about the right amount?

	Form A (n=1000)	Form B (n=1002)	Both forms (n=2002)
About right amount[4]	42%	50%	46%
Too much	44	41	42
Not enough	9	5	7
Don't know	5	4	5
	100%	100%	100%

20. [Form B only] Now on another topic. Some families and young people face difficult times—sometimes called the "breakdown of the American family." For each thing I mention, please tell me how much you, yourself, feel it has to do with the problems some families are having. First, . . . [INSERT: 20a THROUGH 20d, RANDOMIZED]. How much do you think this has to do with the problems some families are having: a great deal, a fair amount, not very much, or nothing at all?

a. Many parents have to work such long hours that they do not get enough time to spend with their children.

A great deal	70%
A fair amount	23
Not very much	6
Nothing at all	1
Don't know/NA/refused	*

b. Young people see too much sex and violence on television and in the movies. How much do you think this has to do with the problems some families are having: a great deal, a fair amount, not very much, or nothing at all?

A great deal	56%
A fair amount	26
Not very much	15
Nothing at all	2
Don't know/NA/refused	1

---

[4] The main effect of changing the order of alternatives is that if the "too much power" option is offered first, the proportion saying "about right" is slightly higher. This difference is statistically significant at the 95 percent level of confidence.

c. There are not enough after school activities where young people can keep busy and out of trouble. How much do you think this has to do with the problems some families are having: a great deal, a fair amount, not very much, or nothing at all?

A great deal	38%
A fair amount	38
Not very much	18
Nothing at all	5
Don't know/NA/refused	1

d. The public schools don't spend enough time teaching children right from wrong. How much do you think this has to do with the problems some families are having: a great deal, a fair amount, not very much, or nothing at all?

A great deal	33%
A fair amount	34
Not very much	23
Nothing at all	8
Don't know/NA/refused	2

21. On another topic, there has been talk about trying to reduce the number of divorces in the country. Some people think divorce should be allowed only for adultery, abuse, or desertion as a way of getting couples to think more seriously about what marriage involves.

Others think that most couples make serious commitments when they get married but that, if they drift apart, divorce may be the best way to deal with an unhappy situation.

How do you feel? Should divorce be granted only for adultery, abuse, or desertion, *or* should it be allowed for other reasons as well?

Limited to adultery/abuse/desertion	28%
Other reasons as well	66
Depends/qualified [vol]	1
Don't know/NA/refused	5

22. People have different ideas about sex education for young people. Some think it should aim at getting young people to abstain from sex completely until they are married. Others think you have to be realistic and that young people need to know about birth control choices if they are to protect themselves. Which view comes closer to your own?

Abstain completely	29%
Need to know about birth control	65
Depends/qualified [vol]	3
Don't know/NA/refused	2

23a. [Form A only] There is talk about two ways of dealing with juvenile crime. One is to get tougher on young offenders to make clear there is a price to pay for breaking the law. The other is to find ways to help young people stay out of trouble in the first place.

Suppose you had $100 to spend on the problem. How much of the $100 would you spend on getting tougher on young offenders and how much would you spend on helping young people stay out of trouble?

First, how much on getting tougher with young offenders?

Amount on getting tougher

$0	28%
$1–$49	23
$50	26
$51–$99	11
$100	9
Don't know/refused	3

That means you would have about $_____ left for helping young people stay out of trouble. Is that about right?

23b. [Form B only] There is talk about two ways of dealing with juvenile crime. One is to find ways to help young people stay out of trouble in the first place. The other is to get tougher on young offenders to make clear there is a price to pay for breaking the law.

Suppose you had $100 to spend on the problem. How much of the $100 would you spend on helping young people stay out of trouble and how much would you spend on getting tough with young offenders?

First, how much on helping young people stay out of trouble?

Amount on helping young people stay out of trouble

$0	12%
$1–$49	11
$50	31
$51–$99	23
$100	20
Don't know/refused	3

That means you would have about $_____ left for getting tough on offenders. Is that about right?

The combined results for forms A and B:

Amount on getting tougher	Amount on helping young stay out of trouble	
$100	$0	11%
$51–$99	$1–$49	12
$50	$50	29
$1–$49	$51–$99	23
$0	$100	23
	Don't know/refused	2
		100%

24. Now, two statements about homosexuality. For each, please tell me whether you completely agree with it, mostly agree, mostly disagree, or completely disagree with it.

   a. First: Homosexuality threatens the values of the American family. Do you completely agree, mostly agree, mostly disagree, or completely disagree?

Completely agree	33%
Mostly agree	18
Mostly disagree	23
Completely disagree	21
Don't know/NA/refused	5

   b. And second: A homosexual relationship between consenting adults is their own private matter. Do you completely agree, mostly agree, mostly disagree, or completely disagree?

Completely agree	45%
Mostly agree	27
Mostly disagree	9
Completely disagree	15
Don't know/NA/refused	4

25. On another subject, there has been talk about how much attention government pays to the concerns of different kinds of people. For each group I mention, please tell me whether you think the government pays about the right amount of attention to it, too much attention, or too little?

   a. First, what about the concerns of *middle-income* people: would you say the government pays about the right amount of attention to middle-income people, too much attention, or too little?

About right amount	28%
Too much	5
Too little	64
Don't know/NA/refused	3

   b. What about the concerns of *low-income* people?

About right amount	28%
Too much	18
Too little	52
Don't know/NA/refused	2

   c. What about the concerns of *upper-income* people?

About right amount	22%
Too much	63
Too little	11
Don't know/NA/refused	4

d. What about the concerns of *people like you?*

About right amount	38%
Too much	6
Too little	52
Don't know/NA/refused	4

26. When you hear that the U.S. economy has been growing, do you think it is more likely to mean that all Americans are gaining or that the gap between the rich and the poor is getting bigger?

All gaining	17%
Gap betting bigger	76
Both [vol]	1
Depends/qualified [vol]	1
Don't know/NA/refused	6

27. [Form B only] People have different ideas about why we have poverty in this country. As I mention some things, please tell me how much you think each has to do with why some people are poor.

First, . . . [INSERT: 27a THROUGH 27d, RANDOMIZED]. How much do you think this has to do with why some people are poor: a lot to do with it, a fair amount, only a little, or nothing at all to do with being poor?

a. Poor schools in low-income areas.

A lot	35%
A fair amount	38
Only a little	17
Nothing at all	6
Depends/qualified [vol]	*
Don't know/NA/refused	3

b. A lack of skills needed to get a steady job.

A lot	51%
A fair amount	35
Only a little	11
Nothing at all	2
Depends/qualified [vol]	*
Don't know/NA/refused	1

c. Not trying hard enough to make it on their own.

A lot	44%
A fair amount	38
Only a little	13
Nothing at all	4
Depends/qualified [vol]	*
Don't know/NA/refused	1

d. Not being able to hold a job because of family circumstances, such as young children or a dependent parent or spouse.

A lot	24%
A fair amount	43
Only a little	28
Nothing at all	4
Depends/qualified [vol]	0
Don't know/NA/refused	1

28. On something else, how much confidence do you have that members of the United States Congress serve the interests of *all* the people, not just the interests of those with special influence: a great deal, a fair amount, not very much, or none at all?

Great deal	7%
Fair amount	28
Not very much	45
None at all	18
Depends/qualified [vol]	0
Don't know/NA/refused	2

29. How much confidence do you have that members of the legislature in your *state* serve the interests of *all* residents of your state, not just the interests of those with special influence: a great deal, a fair amount, not very much, or none at all? [SKIP FOR AREA CODE 202]

Great deal	5%
Fair amount	45
Not very much	36
None at all	10
Depends/qualified [vol]	*
Don't know/NA/refused	4

30. On balance, how much confidence do you have in the quality of the work done by career workers in the agencies of the *federal* government: a great deal, a fair amount, not very much, or none at all?

Great deal	5%
Fair amount	50
Not very much	31
None at all	6
Depends/qualified [vol]	*
Don't know/NA/refused	8

31. And, how much confidence do you have in the quality of the work done by career workers in the agencies of your *state* government: a great deal, a fair amount, not very much, or none at all? [SKIP FOR AREA CODE 202]

Great deal	5%
Fair amount	58

Not very much	26
None at all	5
Depends/qualified [vol]	*
Don't know/NA/refused	6

32. When it comes to knowing what they stand for, would you say you know more about the views of the people who represent you in your state legislature or the people who represent you in the U.S. Congress, or don't you have a chance to follow it all that closely? [SKIP FOR AREA CODE 202]

State legislature	21%
U.S. Congress	16
About even [vol]	3
Other qualified [vol]	*
Don't follow closely	58
Don't know/NA/refused	2

33. I'm going to mention some things that make some people uneasy when they think about their personal situation. For each, please tell me how much you worry about it, if at all.

a. First, you or someone in your household not having a job or losing a job. Is this something you worry about a great deal, somewhat, not very much, or not at all?

A great deal	30%
Somewhat	23
Not very much	23
Not at all	23
Don't know/NA/refused	*

b. [Form A only] Not having adequate health care or health insurance when you or someone in your family really need it.

A great deal	40%
Somewhat	27
Not very much	16
Not at all	16
Don't know/NA/refused	*

c. Not being able to pay the bills at some point in the next few years.

A great deal	34%
Somewhat	28
Not very much	22
Not at all	16
Don't know/NA/refused	*

d. Not having enough to live on when you are retired.

A great deal	38%
Somewhat	30
Not very much	15

Not at all	16
Don't know/NA/refused	*

e. [Form A only] Social Security not being able to pay the benefits people expect.

A great deal	44%
Somewhat	30
Not very much	13
Not at all	13
Don't know/NA/refused	1

34. Are you registered to vote—that is, is your name currently recorded in the precinct or election district where you are living now?

Yes	79%
No	20
Not sure/NA/refused	1

35. In the presidential election last year, did things come up that kept you from voting, or did you happen to vote?

Voted	69%	[ASK 36]
Did not vote	30	[SKIP TO 37]
Can't recall/NA/refused	*	[SKIP TO 37]

36. Did you vote for Bob Dole, Bill Clinton, or Ross Perot?

Dole	26%
Clinton	31
Perot	5
Other	1
Can't recall/NA/refused	6
Not asked	31

37. How often would you say you vote in national elections, that is for president and Congress—always, almost always, only sometimes, or seldom?

Always	52%	[ASK 38]
Almost always	20	[ASK 38]
Only sometimes	8	[ASK 38]
Seldom	13	I
Not eligible in previous		I [SKIP TO 40, IF FORM B]
elections [vol]	6	I [SKIP TO 41, IF FORM A]
Don't know/NA/refused	1	I

38. In most elections, there are candidates for several offices, such as president, member of Congress, senator, or governor. Do you usually vote for candidates from the same party or do you usually vote for candidates from different parties?

Same party	26%
Different parties	51

Haven't voted before [vol]	*
Depends/qualified [vol]	3
Don't know/NA/refused	*
Not asked	20

39. Thinking back to earlier elections for president, have you usually voted for candidates from the same party or have you voted for the candidate of one party in one year and the candidate of another party in another year?

Same party	37%
Candidates of different parties	39
Haven't voted before [vol]	1
Depends/qualified [vol]	2
Don't know/NA/refused	1
Not asked	20

40. [Form B only] Now some questions about different aspects of education in this country.

   a. First, when it comes to running the schools day-to-day, do you think this should be done mostly at the local or county level, state level, or federal level?

Local or county	59%
State level	27
Federal level	9
More than one level [vol]	1
Don't know/NA/refused	4

   b. What about certifying that teachers are qualified? Do you think that this should be done mostly at the local or county level, state level, or federal level?

Local or county	22%
State level	54
Federal level	20
More than one level [vol]	1
Depends/qualified [vol]	*
Don't know/NA/refused	2

   c. And what about providing financial assistance to schools in low-income areas? Do you think that this should be done mostly at the local or county level, state level, or federal level?

Local or county	16%
State level	47
Federal level	29
More than one level [vol]	4
Depends/qualified [vol]	*
Don't know/NA/refused	3

41. There has been talk about conservative Christian groups that organize in
their communities, taking part in politics, distributing voter guides, and
working to promote Christian values at all levels of government. Some
people think this is good for the country because it is the only way to make
sure government is run by Christian principles. Others feel this is not good
for the country because they believe in the separation of church and state,
and think religion should be kept out of government.
Which view is closest to yours?

Good for country	43%
Not good for country	48
Depends/qualified [vol]	2
Don't yet have a view/NA/refused [vol]	7

[RANDOMIZE ORDER OF 42a AND 42b]

42. Now I'd like to get your feelings toward some groups. Again, thinking of a
ladder with steps from zero to ten, suppose the top of the ladder means that
you feel very favorably about a group and that the bottom means you feel
very unfavorably.

a. Please tell me where you would put people who call themselves conservatives? You can name any step from ten down to zero.

Step		
0	2%	
1	2	
2	2	
3	5	
4	9	
5	29	Mean: 5.7
6	11	
7	12	
8	12	
9	3	
10	6	
Don't know/NA/refused	7	

b. Please tell me where you would put people who call themselves liberals?
You can name any step from ten down to zero.

Step		
0	7%	
1	4	
2	6	
3	8	
4	10	
5	29	Mean: 4.7
6	10	

7	8
8	6
9	1
10	2
Don't know/NA/refused	9

43. [Form A only] Now I am going to mention some things people sometimes do. For each, please tell me whether it is something you have done in the last year or so.

    a. First, attended a public meeting in your community. Is this something you have done in the last year or so?

Yes	42%
No/NA	58
Don't know/refused	0

    b. Have you called or written a member of your *state* legislature in the past year or so? [SKIP FOR AREA CODE 202]

Yes	25%
No	75
Don't know/refused	*

    c. Have you called or written the office of your U.S. senator or representative in Congress in the last year or so?

Yes	22%
No	78
Don't know/refused	*

    d. Have you attended a school meeting in the last year or so?

Yes	42%
No	58
Don't know/refused	0

44a. [Form A only] How would you describe your views on most political matters? In general, do you think of yourself as very conservative, moderately conservative, middle of the road, moderately liberal, or very liberal?

44b. [Form B only] How would you describe your views on most political matters? In general, do you think of yourself as very liberal, moderately liberal, middle of the road, moderately conservative, or very conservative?

	Form A (n=1000)	Form B (n=1002)	Both forms (n=2002)
Very conservative	8%	15%	11%
Moderately conservative	29	28	28
Middle of the road	43	35	39
Moderately liberal	14	15	14
Very liberal	2	3	3
Don't know/NA/refuse	4	4	4
	100%	101%	101%

45a. [Form A only] What about when it comes to moral and social matters? In general, do you think of yourself as very conservative, moderately conservative, middle of the road, moderately liberal, or very liberal?

45b. [Form B only] What about when it comes to moral and social matters? In general, do you think of yourself as very liberal, moderately liberal, middle of the road, moderately conservative, or very conservative?

	Form A (n=1000)	Form B (n=1002)	Both forms (n=2002)
Very conservative	22%	25%	24%
Moderately conservative	27	26	27
Middle of the road	28	25	26
Moderately liberal	14	15	14
Very liberal	6	6	6
Don't know/NA/refuse	3	4	4
	100%	101%	101%

46. Some people seem to follow what's going on in government and public affairs most of the time, whether there's an election or not. Others are too busy or don't have time. Would you say you follow what's going on in government and public affairs most of the time, some of the time, only now and then, or hardly at all?

Most of the time	37%
Some of the time	36
Only now and then	19
Hardly at all	8
Don't know/NA/refused	*

47. In your own mind, do you think of yourself as a supporter of one of the political parties or not?

Yes	43%	[ASK 48]
No	55	[SKIP TO 49]
Don't know/NA/refused	2	[SKIP TO 49]

48. Which political party do you support?

Republican	20%	[ASK 48a]
Democratic	20	[ASK 48b]
Other	1	[SKIP TO 49]
Independent [vol]	*	[SKIP TO 49]
Don't know/NA/refused	2	[SKIP TO 49]

a. Would you call yourself a strong Republican or *not* a very strong Republican?

Strong Republican	10%	[SKIP TO 50]
Not a very strong Republican	9	[SKIP TO 50]
Don't know/NA/refused	*	[SKIP TO 50]

b. Would you call yourself a strong Democrat or *not* a very strong Democrat?

Strong Democrat	12%	[SKIP TO 50]
Not a very strong Democrat	8	[SKIP TO 50]
Don't know/NA/refused	*	[SKIP TO 50]

49. Do you ever think of yourself as closer to one of the two major political parties, or not? [IF "YES," PROMPT: Which one?]

Yes, Republican	11%
Yes, Democratic	13
No	33
Not sure/NA/refused	3
Not asked	40

50. Do you ever think of yourself as a political independent, or not?

Yes	40%
No	54
Depends [vol]	2
Not sure/NA/refused	3

51. Do you happen to know which party now has the most members in the House of Representatives in Washington as a result of the last election in 1996? [IF "YES," PROBE IF NEEDED: Which party?]

Republican	57%
Democratic	10
Don't know/NA/refused	33

52. What is your impression of the number of votes that are required for the U.S. Senate and House to override a presidential veto—a bare majority, two-thirds, or three-fourths?

Bare majority	12%
Two-thirds	56
Three-fourths	16
Don't know/NA/refused	17

53. When it comes to determining if a law is constitutional or not, do you think it is up to the president, the Congress, or the Supreme Court?

President	8%
Congress	18
Supreme Court	66
Don't know/NA/refused	8

54. Do you happen to know whether President Franklin Delano Roosevelt was a Republican or a Democrat? [IF "YES," PROBE IF NEEDED: A Republican or a Democrat?]

Republican	12%
Democrat	57
Don't know/NA/refused	31

55. People have different ideas about how much can be done to make government work better. Some feel it is possible to make major changes that will
really improve things. Others think minor changes are possible but they
won't improve things all that much. Still others think there is not much
chance things can be changed for the better.
What do you think: that major changes are possible, minor changes are possible, or that there is not much chance for change?

Major changes possible	39%
Minor changes possible	46
Not much chance for change	12
Depends/qualified [vol]	1
Don't know/NA/refused	2

56. What is your religious preference? Do you consider yourself Protestant,
Roman Catholic, Mormon, Orthodox (such as Greek or Russian), Jewish,
Muslim, some other religion, or no particular religion?

Protestant (any denomination)	46%	[ASK 57]
Roman Catholic	23	[ASK 57]
Mormon (inc. Latter Day Saints)	2	[ASK 57]
Orthodox	1	[ASK 57]
Christian (unspecified)	6	[ASK 57]
Jewish	1	[SKIP TO 58]
Muslim	*	[SKIP TO 58]
Some other religion	6	[SKIP TO 58]
No particular religion	15	[SKIP TO 58]
Refused, don't know/NA	1	[SKIP TO 58]

57. Would you describe yourself as a "born-again" or Evangelical Christian, or
a Fundamentalist or Pentecostal or Charismatic Christian or not?

Yes, born again	20%
Yes, Evangelical	3
Yes, Fundamentalist	5
Yes, Pentecostal	3
Yes, Charismatic	3
No	32
Don't know/NA/refused	9
Not asked	26

58. Lots of things come up which keep people from attending religious services
even if they want to. Thinking about your life these days, do you go to religious services at least once a week, once or twice a month, a few times a
year, or never?

At least once a week	37%
Once/twice a month	17

A few times a year	28
Never	18
NA/refused	*

59. How important would you say religion is in your own life—very important, fairly important, or not very important?

Very important	60%
Fairly important	24
Not very important	15
Don't know/NA/refused	1

60. Do you think of yourself as part of the conservative Christian movement that is active in politics?

Yes	13%
No	83
Depends/qualified [vol]	*
Don't know/NA/refused	4

And, now I have a few questions for statistical purposes.

61. What is your current marital status? Are you currently married, widowed, divorced, separated, or have you never been married?

Married	62%
Widowed	6
Divorced	9
Separated	2
Never been married	20
Living with partner [vol]	1
Refused/NA	8

62. How many adults eighteen years of age or older, including *yourself*, are living in this household at the present time?

1	14%
2	58
3	18
4	6
5	2
6	1
7	*
9	*
11	*
15	*

63. [Form A only] Are there any children in your household under 6 years of age?

Yes	20%
No	80
Refused	*

64. [Form A only] Are there any children of grade school or high school age?

Yes	32%
No	68
Refused	*

65. [Form A only] Even though they may not be living with you at the present time, do you have parents or other older members of the family whose health or financial situation is of particular concern to you?

Yes	50%
No	50
Refused	*

66. Which of the following do you think best describes your situation: middle class, lower class, working class, or upper class?

Middle class	59%
Lower class	7
Working class	29
Upper class	3
Depends/qualified [vol]	1
Don't know/NA/refused	1

67. What was the last grade you completed in school? [PROBE IF FOREIGN SCHOOLING: What is the American equivalent?]

Grade 4 or less	*
Grades 5–7	1%
Grade 8	2
Some high school (grades 9–11)	14
High school graduate (grade 12)	34
Technical, trade, business school	2
GED	1
Some college (including 2-year)	23
College graduate	14
Graduate training/degree	8
Refusal/no answer	*

68. Which of the following best describes your present work situation? READ

Working full time (35+ hrs/week)	56%	[ASK 69]
Working part time (less than 35/week)	10	[ASK 69]
Temporarily out of work	3	[ASK 69]
Out of work and not looking	1	[SKIP TO 70]
Retired	17	[SKIP TO 70]
Disabled and unable to work	3	[SKIP TO 70]
In school	3	[SKIP TO 70]

A homemaker	6	[SKIP TO 70]
Or, something else	1	[SKIP TO 70]
Refused	*	[SKIP TO 70]

69. What kind of work do you usually do?

Executive/management: senior position in business, government, other organization	3%
Professional: doctor, lawyer, engineer, scientist, teacher/ professor, researcher, registered nurse, social worker, accountant, computer programmer, musician/artist, officer in armed forces, librarian, journalist	16
Paraprofessional: paralegal, dental hygienist, research assistant, cosmetologist, hair-dresser	2
Business/store owner	3
Farm owner/manager	1
Business manager: store manager, sales manager, office manager	4
Technical office worker: computer operator, data entry, typist, bank clerk, medical lab technician, technical work in armed forces other than officer [PROBE IF NEEDED: Does the work involve use of computers or other technical equipment?]	8
Nontechncal office worker: postal clerk, receptionist, nontechnical work in armed forces other than officer [PROBE IF NEEDED: Does the work involve little or no use of computers or other technical equipment?]	2
Sales: clerk in store, door-to-door sales	5
Skilled: electrician, machinist, plumber, baker, linesman, contractor, carpenter, mechanic, printer, tailor (other than runs own business)	9
Semiskilled: assembly line worker, machine operator, truck/bus/ taxi driver	5
Unskilled labor: construction worker, farm laborer, garbage/ hauling	6
Service and protective: police, fire, restaurant, barber, maid, nurse's aid, orderly	5
Other (Specify)	2
Refusal/no answer	*
Not asked	31

70. Is there someone else in your household who works full or part time, or who has been temporarily laid off?

Yes	61%	[ASK 71]
No	39	[SKIP TO 72]
Refused	1	[SKIP TO 72]

71. What kind of work does that person usually do?

Executive/management: senior position in business,
government, other organization   3%

Professional: doctor, lawyer, engineer, scientist, teacher/
professor, researcher, registered nurse, social worker,
accountant, computer programmer, musician/artist,
officer in armed forces, librarian, journalist   14

Paraprofessional: paralegal, dental hygienist, research
assistant, cosmetologist, hair-dresser   2

Business/store owner   2

Farm owner/manager   1

Business manager: store manager, sales manager, office manager   4

Technical office worker: computer operator, data entry,
typist, bank clerk, medical lab technician, technical work
in armed forces other than officer [PROBE IF NEEDED:
Does the work involve use of computers or other technical
equipment?]   6

Nontechnical office worker: postal clerk, receptionist,
nontechnical work in armed forces other than officer
[PROBE IF NEEDED: Does the work involve little
or no use of computers or other technical equipment?]   1

Sales: clerk in store, door-to-door sales   3

Skilled: electrician, machinist, plumber, baker, linesman,
contractor, carpenter, mechanic, printer, tailor (other
than runs own business)   8

Semiskilled: assembly line worker, machine operator, truck/
bus/taxi driver   3

Unskilled labor: construction worker, farm laborer,
garbage/hauling   6

Service and protective: police, fire, restaurant, barber, maid,
nurse's aid, orderly   4

Other (Specify)   2

Refusal/no answer   1

Not asked   39

72. Do you or anyone in your household work for the federal government,
government of your state, or government of your community or county?

Federal government (includes military)   7%

State government   7

County/community government (includes
teacher, police, fire)   7

No	81
Don't know/NA/refused	*
	102[5]

73. [Form B only] Is anyone in this household a member of a labor union?

Yes	17%
No	82
Don't know/refused	2

74. [Form A only] Do you or anyone in this household receive payments or benefits from the government at any level, such as . . . [READ LIST AND RECORD EACH "YES"]

Received one or more payments/benefits		35%
A government or military pension	6%	
Veterans benefits	4	
Social Security	24	
Disability	4	
Medicare	15	
Medicaid	4	
Welfare for families or individuals (includes AFDC, ADC, public aid, general assistance, home relief)	2	
Anything else?	3	
	62[6]	
No payments/benefits		64
Refused		1
		100%

75. Which of the following best describes the place where you now live: a large city, a suburb near a large city, a small city or town, or a rural area?

A large city	18%
Suburb near large city	21
Small city/town	38
Rural area	21
Don't know/refused	1

76. What is your age?

Four categories	
18–29	23%
30–39	22

---

[5] Total adds to more than 100 percent because of multiple government employees in the household.

[6] Adds to more than 35 percent because of multiple payments/benefits.

40–59	32
60 and over	21
Refuse/NA	1
Five categories	
18–29	23%
30–39	22
40–49	19
50–64	18
65 and over	17
Refuse/NA	1
Coded by cohort	
Generation X (18–32)	28%
Baby Boomers (33–51)	39
Vietnam/civil rights (52–64)	14
World War II (65 and older)	18
Refuse/NA	1

77. In 1996, was the total income of your household from all sources, before taxes, under or over $30,000?

Under $30,000	32%	[ASK 77a]
Over $30,000	61	[ASK 77b]
Don't know/NA/refused	7	[SKIP TO 78]

a. Was it under or over $15,000?

Under $15,000	10%
Above $15,000	21
Don't know/NA/refused	1
Not asked	68

b. Was it between $30,000 and $50,000, between $50,000 and $75,000, between $75,000 and $100,000, or was it over $100,000?

Between $30,000 and $50,000	29%
Between $50,000 and $75,000	18
Between $75,000 and $100,000	8
Over $100,000	5
Don't know/NA/refused	2
Not asked	39

Household income: Six categories

Under $15,000	10%
$15,000–$29,999	21
$30,000–$49,999	29
$50,000–$74,999	18
$75,000–$99,999	8

$100,000 and over	5
Don't know/NA/refused	10

78. What race do you consider yourself: [READ LIST]

White	79%
Black or African American	9
Asian or Pacific Islander	3
American Indian or Native	
Alaskan	1
Or, of mixed race?	3
Other [vol]	3
Refused	2

79. Are you of Hispanic or Latino origin or descent?

Yes, Hispanic	6%
No, not Hispanic	93
NA/refused	1

Respondent's sex:

Male	48%
Female	52

Appendix C
Notes on Construction of Indices and the Framing of Selected Questions

S OME OF THE ANALYSES REPORTED IN THIS STUDY ARE BASED ON INDICES. THE purpose of an index is to combine into a single overall measure responses to several questions on different facets of a common topic.

GENERAL VIEWS ABOUT GOVERNMENT

Three questions were used in the index of general views about government:[1]

 • Whether government does too many things or has struck about the right balance [Q.12];
 • The amount of power the federal government is perceived to have [Q.19]; and,
 • Whether regulation of business is excessive or needed [Q.9b].

Two other questions were considered for the index because they were framed in general terms and tapped basic attitudes: whether "anyone can get ahead if they are willing to work hard enough" [Q.9a] and whether government should keep an eye on

---

[1] Research on the relationship of general and specific attitudes reaches back to the 1930s. Perhaps the first formal distinction was by Krueger and Reckless who wrote of "concrete attitudes, which are directed toward specific objects, and generalized attitudes, which are directed toward a class of objects." See E. T. Krueger and W. C. Reckless, *Social Psychology* (New York: Longmans, 1931), 270. The first empirical examination of the relationship of these different levels of attitudes was by Hadley Cantril. See Hadley Cantril, "General and Specific Attitudes," *Psychological Review* (Psychological Monographs Series) 42, no. 5 (1932).

the marketplace to ensure its competitiveness [Q.9c]. These questions were not incorporated in the index because they proved not to have strong relationships with the three that were used, all of which were reasonably correlated with each other (table C.1). In addition, the question about getting ahead did not ask explicitly about government. While the question about government keeping an eye on the marketplace was correlated most strongly with the item about regulation (r=.35), its correlations were much lower with the questions about government power (r=.19) and what government does (also r=.19).

As described in the text, respondents voicing two or three of the three "critical" opinions were classified as "mostly critical." Respondents giving two or three "supportive" answers were classified as "mostly supportive." Eleven percent of respondents were classified as "neither critic nor supporter." Within this "neither" category were 6 percent answering only two questions but expressing diverging opinions; 4 percent answering only one of the three questions; and 1 percent having no opinion on all three questions.

Table C.1

Correlations among Questions That Were Candidates for
Inclusion in the Index of General Views about Government

	Amount government does	Power of federal government	Regulation: too much versus needed	Getting ahead: anyone can versus barriers	Eye on market versus stay out
Amount government does	1.00				
Power of federal government	.32	1.00			
Regulation: too much versus needed	.27	.31	1.00		
Getting ahead: anyone can versus barriers	.13	.12	.18	1.00	
Eye on the market versus stay out	.19	.19	.35	.19	1.00

Note: Correlation coefficients indicate the degree of association between two variables. They do not imply that one variable *causes* the other. Coefficients range from +1.00 (all respondents giving answers to two questions that go in the same direction) through zero (no association) to −1.00 (all respondents giving answers to two questions that go in the opposite direction). All of these coefficients are statistically significant (p=.000).

SPECIFIC VIEWS ABOUT GOVERNMENT

This index counts how many of the ten specific governmental activities a respondent wants to see continued or increased. The index has eleven values since it ranges from zero to ten.

This approach produced an index whose validity is apparent on substantive grounds. Empirically it is also reliable. That is, the interrelationship among its ten items is strong enough that they point fairly precisely to some underlying dimension. Cronbach's alpha for the index is .76.[2]

An alternative would have been to assign weights to response categories: four points for "increase," three for "continue at present level," two for "decrease," and one for "end altogether." Each respondent's score on the index would be the sum of the points for the ten questions and range from zero to forty. Were respondents then divided into groups according to their score, the cutoff points between groups would have been determined arithmetically, not in terms of the content of the response. It would not be possible, therefore, to say exactly how many activities a respondent actually wanted to see increased, continued at the present level, or cut back.

It might be argued that "continue at the present level" was for some respondents a "no opinion." This would suggest limiting support for an activity to only those who said funding for it should be increased. We did not take this tack for two reasons. First, the question format provided four response categories, not three (which might have given some respondents a comfortable middle position through which to express their lack of an opinion). Second, it would have been a greater mistake to exclude someone who wanted an activity continued than to include a handful of respondents who may have been undecided.

COMBINING THE GENERAL AND SPECIFIC INDICES

Combining the general and specific indices yielded two measures of ambivalence: one among those "mostly critical" of government, another among those "mostly supportive." These measures were used in two ways in the analyses.

The first was to look at bivariate relationships between ambivalence and each of many variables to determine which of those variables had a strong enough relationship with ambivalence among critics or supporters to be included in the multivariate analyses.

For this purpose, it would have been unwieldy to use all values on the specific index (zero to ten) to characterize the views of critics and supporters. It was necessary to summarize which respondents were more and less ambivalent (that is, were "am-

---

[2] This statistic reflects how highly correlated items in an index are to one another. A coefficient of .76 is relatively high, suggesting the index is quite reliable. See Lee J. Cronbach, "Coefficient Alpha and the Internal Structure of Tests," *Psychometrika* 16 (1951): 297–334.

bivalent" or "steady" as critics or supporters). Our approach was to use a cutoff of backing for nine or all ten specific activities as opposed to eight or fewer. This seemed reasonable given the distribution of respondents (table 2.3 in the text).

Alternative cutoffs were considered but they yielded too few cases of "ambivalent supporters" for statistically reliable comparisons with "steady supporters" as well as with "ambivalent" or "steady" critics of government (table C.2).

As a check on the effect of alternative cutoffs on differences between "steady" and "ambivalent" respondents, the tabulations summarized in tables A.12 and A.22 were rerun using a dividing line of 8 of ten versus 7 or fewer. The differences between Steady Critics and Ambivalent Critics were very close to those resulting from the 9 or 10 versus 8 or fewer cutoff. Where there were differences they were never in the direction of the relationship, only slightly in degree. Differences between Ambivalent Supporters and Steady Supporters were generally similar to those with the cutoff of 9 or 10, but would be difficult to interpret given the small number of respondents falling into the "ambivalent supporter" category.

The second use of these ambivalence measures was in connection with the multivariate analyses. As spelled out in chapter 6 and appendix D, the ambivalence measures were used without cutoffs so that the full range of values (constrained for outliers) could be taken into account.

A final consideration when combining the general and specific indices was the possibility that one of the questions concerning general views contributed a disproportionate amount to the mix. Table C.3 shows that the number of activities supported is

Table C.2

Effect of Alternative Levels of Backing of
Specific Activities on the Mix of General and Specific Views

	Alternative Cutoffs[a]		
	9 or 10 versus 8 or fewer	8 to 10 versus 7 or fewer	7 to 10 versus 6 or fewer
Steady Critic	18%	12%	8%
Ambivalent Critic	20	26	30
Ambivalent Supporter	12	6	3
Steady Supporter	39	45	48
Neither critic nor supporter	11	11	11
	100%	100%	100%

[a]Number of specific activities on which the amount of money the federal government spends should be increased or kept at the same level.

Table C.3

Number of Specific Activities Backed among

Those Expressing Various Views "Critical" of Government

Number of specific activities backed	Among those who say		
	Federal government does too many things	Federal government has too much power	Too much government regulation of business
10 of 10	34.6%	36.9%	31.5%
9 of 10	22.6	21.9	23.4
8 of 10	14.3	13.4	13.8
7 of 10	9.2	8.1	8.8
6 of 10	6.5	7.3	7.3
5 or fewer	12.8	12.5	15.2
	100.0%	100.1%	100.0%

virtually the same among respondents selecting the "critical" response alternative on each of the three questions.

This shows that none of the three questions about general views has a unique relationship with backing for specific activities. Had responses to one of these been uniquely associated with views on specific activities, it would not have been possible to combine the general and specific indices and retain confidence in the reliability of the combined measure.

GOVERNMENT PERFORMANCE

With respect to the federal government, the job-rating question draws out different aspects of respondents' thinking than the question about confidence in the work of the executive agencies. This point could be missed by merely noting the fact that 53 percent of those polled give an "excellent" or "pretty good" rating to the federal government and that 55 percent express at least a fair amount of confidence in federal agencies.

Without digging further it would not be learned, for example, that 43 percent of those who give the federal government a poor job rating express confidence in the work of the agencies of its executive branch. In other words, it cannot be assumed that respondents will give a favorable evaluation on one question simply because they are favorable on the other.

This discrepancy is relevant when trying to identify reasons people may be of mixed minds about government. Consider the ambivalence among government's critics. The job-rating question elicits a favorable view from 30 percent of Steady Critics and 42 percent of Ambivalent Critics, a difference of 12 percentage points. The question about confidence in executive branch agencies, however, finds an 18 percentage point divergence in opinion: 37 percent among Steady Critics compared to 55 percent among Ambivalent Critics.

Since results show critics are less divided on the job-rating question than the executive-branch question, it can be assumed that the job-rating question is picking up some of the same threads of opinion as are included in the measure of "general views" about government. Corroborating this conclusion is the fact that the correlation between "general views" about government is higher with the job rating of the federal government (r=.34) than the level of confidence in federal agencies (r=.18).[3]

QUESTION REGARDING IDENTIFICATION WITH CONSERVATIVE CHRISTIAN GROUPS

It has been shown that asking people whether they think of themselves "as a member of the religious right movement" without elaboration yields ambiguous results. Sizeable proportions of those responding in the affirmative describe their political views as other than conservative, indicate they are Democrats, and report infrequent church attendance.[4]

It also has been shown that adding "political" to the description is an important qualifier and yields a more precise measure of identification. Moreover, it has been found that many Christian conservatives find the term "religious right" to be pejorative.[5] Accordingly to avoid these pitfalls, we asked: "Do you think of yourself as part of the conservative Christian movement that is active in politics?"

INTENSITY OF OPINIONS ON ISSUES

Is there anything inherent to being "steady" in whatever one's view of government may be that makes one feel more intensely about matters? Conversely, if one is "ambivalent" about government, is there reason to believe opinions are less strongly held?

As a check on these possibilities, we took nine of the issues discussed in chapter 4 on which the intensity of opinion was measured and tallied the number of times respondents indicated they felt strongly about an issue. Virtually no differences appear

---

[3] "General views" of government are based on the index described earlier. As used in this correlation, the index has five values: endorsement of three of three "critical" views, two of three, neither "critic" nor "supporter," two of three "supportive" views, and three of three "supportive."

[4] David W. Moore, "The 'Religious Right': Definition and Measurement," *Public Perspective* (April/May 1995): 11–13.

[5] Cheryl Mercado Arendt, "The Religious Right: Self-Identification and Measurement of Political Groups," paper for delivery at the meeting of the American Association for Public Opinion Research, Salt Lake City, May 16–19, 1996.

by those with varying views about government in the intensity with which views on these nine issues are expressed. There seems to be no reluctance on the part of those who are ambivalent in their thinking about government to express opinions with an intensity equal to those who are not ambivalent (table C.4).

INDEX OF PERSONAL SECURITY

Five questions were included in the survey about things that "make some people uneasy when they think about their personal situation." Given the constraints of questionnaire space, two of the items were asked of only half the sample. These were selected because we thought their exclusion from the full sample would be least likely to affect the quality of the index to be used for all respondents. Neither item was decisive in the reliability of the index.

The index was built on the remaining three items: not having enough for retirement, not being able to pay the bills, and not having a job. Values were assigned to the response categories: four for "a great deal"; three for "somewhat"; two for "not very much"; and one for "not at all." Values for each respondent's answers to the three questions were then added for an overall index score. Cronbach's alpha for the index is .80. This is almost as high as the .85 for the index based on half the sample when all five items were included. We used the three-item index since it permitted tabulations with the full sample. The distribution of scores was divided into four groups ("very secure" to "very insecure") for purposes of some tables.

Table C.4

Intensity of Opinion on Nine Issues by
Mix of General and Specific Views about Government

	All	Steady Critic	Ambivalent Critic	Ambivalent Supporter	Steady Supporter
Of nine issues[a], opinions are expressed "very strongly" on					
8 or 9 issues	16%	17%	15%	15%	17%
6 or 7 issues	42	41	44	43	42
5 or fewer issues	42	42	40	42	42
	100%	100%	99%	100%	101%

[a]The nine issues on which intensity was measured: whether anyone can get ahead; whether government should keep an eye on market competition; dealing with race; immigrants fitting in or living by own traditions; police search without a warrant; respect for the value of self-control; what children should learn; dealing with juvenile crime; and homosexuality as a threat to the American family.

INDEX OF KNOWLEDGE ABOUT GOVERNMENT

In developing this index we have benefitted from the work of Delli Carpini and Keeter who examined three distinct facets of "political knowledge": knowing how government works; basic information about matters in public debate; and being able to identify people in public life. They found that "political knowledge tends to form a single dimension" and can be measured with a relatively few questions.[6]

Accordingly we were less interested in covering a broad range of topics than including items of varying difficulty in order to construct an index that differentiated among respondents' levels of knowledge. We used three of the five items Delli Carpini and Keeter recommend for an index of political knowledge: which party controls the Congress; overriding a presidential veto; and judicial review. We added a fourth question that asked whether Franklin Delano Roosevelt was a Democrat or a Republican.

Respondents were scored by the number of items for which they gave correct answers. The index has an alpha of .51. The distribution of scores was divided into four groups ("high" to "low") for purposes of some tables.

INDEX OF NEWS CONSUMED

The survey asked how frequently respondents relied on each of five news sources. Given the constraints of interview length, questions about two of those sources (CNN or C-SPAN and talk radio) were asked of only half the sample. To get maximum benefit from an index of news consumption in subsequent multivariate analyses involving the full sample, the index did not include these two items. (The three-item index picked up almost as much as the five-item index: the correlation between the two indices within the half sample is .84.)

Values were assigned to the response categories ("almost every day" = 4; "a few times" = 3; etc.). Values for each respondent's answers to the three questions were then added for an overall score. The resulting distribution of index scores (3 through 12) was then divided into three approximately equal groups ("high," "medium," and "low") for some tables.

INDEX OF PERCEIVED INTERDEPENDENCE

Respondents were asked whether five kinds of situations were "mostly a local problem, not having much to do with the rest of the country" or "more than a local problem because the country as a whole is likely to be affected in some way."

One of the situations presented was "areas that have an especially high number of people living in poverty." We were concerned that this item might tap the same di-

---

[6] Delli Carpini and Keeter, *What Americans Know about Politics*, 143, 299–301.

mensions of opinion as four items included in the ambivalence measure that related to poverty. If that were the case, an artificially strong relationship might emerge between interdependence and ambivalence in regressions trying to account for ambivalence.

We examined this possibility by entering into the regressions on ambivalence an interdependence index that excluded the "areas of poverty" item. Compared to regressions using the five-item interdependence index, the four-item index makes little difference in the relative importance of variables included or overall insight gained into ambivalence.

We also found the four-item interdependence index (alpha = .36) is less reliable than the five-item index (alpha = .46). The size of the difference between these coefficients held up when computed among critics and when computed among supporters.

A related issue was whether use of "rural" in the item about areas cut off from transportation biased results in the direction of "mostly local." This might explain why this was the only item of the five measuring interdependence in which a majority selected the "mostly local" response. There are also slight (although statistically significant) differences in the proportion who say the problem is "mostly local" between those living in large cities and rural areas. Even so, this item was important for the reliability of the overall index. Its deletion would have reduced the reliability more than deletion of the items about toxic waste or development of wilderness areas.

Accordingly we retained the five-item index of ambivalence.

INTENSITY OF RELIGIOUS BELIEFS AND PRACTICES

In measuring Americans' religious beliefs, we have benefitted from the work of George Gallup Jr. We adopted his approach to an overall measure of religious beliefs and practices by relying on two questions: all respondents' reports of the frequency of their attendance at religious services and the importance of religion in their lives.[7] The correlation between the two items is high (r=.65).

A twelve-value index emerges when responses to the two questions are combined. Thirty-four percent of the sample (the "deeply religious") had the highest value on the index: they attended religious services at least once a week and said religion was "very important" in their lives. Other respondents were characterized as "fairly" and "less" religious.

LIKELIHOOD OF VOTING

The likelihood-of-voting measure is based on answers to four questions: whether respondents are registered, whether they voted in 1996, for whom they voted (to identify those not recalling their preference, an indication of not having voted), and how often they vote in national elections. Questionnaire space permitting, we would

---

[7] *Gallup Poll Monthly* 353 (February 1995): 21.

have used more questions. Those we did use have been shown to be good predictors of a person's likelihood of voting.[8]

The index was used in different ways. For regressions, all five values of the index were used. For purposes of some cross-tabulations, values on the index were used to define three categories: "likely voters" (49 percent), "unlikely voters" (32 percent), and "nonvoters" (19 percent). Finally, other tabulations differentiate between "likely voters" and the combination of "unlikely" and "nonvoters."

POLITICAL PARTICIPATION OTHER THAN VOTING

Many kinds of participation could have been included in this index. Since this is a study of attitudes toward government, we focused on activities relating directly to government by asking about efforts to contact elected representatives. We also included a measure about attendance at a "public meeting in your community." This three-item index has an alpha of .64.

TICKET SPLITTING

Respondents' reports of what they are likely to do about voting are most reliable just before elections. Reports of how they have voted are always most reliable just after elections.[9]

Since interviews for this survey were conducted a year after a presidential election and a year before a midterm election, we could not simply ask people how they voted in the last election and thought they would vote in the next. Instead we asked whether people usually vote for or have voted for candidates of the same or different parties (a) in elections where there are candidates for several offices on the ballot and (b) in earlier elections for president. Taken together the two questions yielded 40 percent of likely voters who indicated they have voted for candidates of different parties in *both* electoral situations.

We were concerned that this result was somewhat inflated in part because of the desire of respondents to give the socially acceptable response that they considered the candidates on the merits regardless of party. Accordingly we excluded (a) those who report they think of themselves as a *strong* Republican or Democrat and (b) those whose support for a party is not strong but who indicate they are *not* a political independent. This reduced the ticket-splitting percentage and produced a total of 33 percent of likely voters who could well cast ballots for candidates of different parties in a presidential election.

---

[8] See Paul K. Perry, "Certain Problems in Election Survey Methodology," *Public Opinion Quarterly* 43 (Fall 1979): 320–21.

[9] See Irving Crespi, *Pre-Election Polling: Sources of Accuracy and Error* (New York: Russell Sage Foundation, 1988): 163–84.

Appendix D
Notes on Multivariate Analyses

R EFERENCE IS MADE IN THE MAIN BODY OF THE BOOK TO ANALYSES THAT TAKE several considerations into account at the same time. These multivariate analyses relied upon multiple regression.

BRIEF COMMENT ABOUT MULTIPLE REGRESSION

M ultiple regression is a statistical procedure used frequently to determine how much change in one variable (the "independent" or "explanatory" variable) accounts for change in another variable (the "dependent" variable).

Regression analysis is especially useful because it can help sort out the relative importance of competing explanations for variations in the dependent variable. It does so by taking one independent variable at a time and assessing the strength of its relationship with the dependent variable *while all other independent variables are being held constant.*

Regression analysis produces many statistics. Two are used in this book.

• *Beta coefficient:* This indicates the amount of change in the dependent variable resulting from a change in the independent variable. Beta coefficients should be compared in terms of their absolute values.[1]

---

[1] In a regression the amount of change in the dependent variable is often expressed in terms of the standard deviation which is a measure of how widely or narrowly respondents are distributed from high to low values on each variable. Standardization is helpful in comparing the effect of independent variables because variables have different ranges (such as six levels of household income and nine levels of educational attainment). All entries in tables in this appendix are standardized regression coefficients and are estimated with constant terms that are not reported.

- *Adjusted R^2:* This indicates the percent of the variation in the dependent variable that has been explained by the independent variables collectively *when taken together.*[2] It is a good indication of how much our overall understanding has been improved by a particular mix of independent variables.

Since we are dealing with a sample of the public, sampling error must be taken into account when computing beta coefficients. As with percentages in a poll, the beta coefficients have varying degrees of statistical reliability. Only those coefficients that are significant at the 95-percent level of confidence appear in this report.

Most of the tables that follow include variables for which the beta coefficient is not significant (designated by "n.s."). This does not mean that the effect of these variables is not reflected in the other coefficients. It means that the relationship to the dependent variable is not strong enough to be sure it did not occur by chance in the sampling process.

These "n.s." variables have been retained in tables here to indicate that they have been taken into account in the analysis. The fact that they do not have a significant relationship to the dependent variable is itself an important finding.

BEHIND VIEWS ON GOVERNMENT ATTENTION TO LOW-INCOME HOUSEHOLDS

The primary interest in this study is accounting for ambivalence about government. The following analyses do not address that issue but are reported here because they shed light on the somewhat related matter of how people with different general views about government ("mostly critical" versus "mostly supportive") can come to the same conclusion about an issue but for very different reasons.

The question here is to see what lies behind opinions about the amount of attention government is seen as paying to the concerns of low-income Americans. Are the opinions of critics and supporters on this issue based on similar or different understandings of the reasons for poverty?

The first of two analyses was limited to those whose general views about government are "mostly critical." It considered five possible explanations. We drew on the four reasons "why some people are poor" discussed in chapter 4. In addition, to test

---

[2] The "adjusted" refers to the fact the statistic takes into account the number of variables involved. This is important since an R^2 that is not adjusted can increase simply because a new variable has been added to the mix, even if the variable contributes nothing to an explanation of the dependent variable. Use of the Adjusted R^2 provides some protection against specious conclusions about how much has really been explained.

the degree to which the issue of race may lie behind attitudes regarding poverty, we included the question about whether there is no need to push so hard now as in the past or whether now is no time to let up in working hard for true equality.

Most powerful by far in explaining differing views among critics regarding government's attention to the poor are opinions about how to deal with the issue of race. That is, those who think we do not need to push quite so hard in dealing with the issue of race are also most likely to say the government is paying too much attention to the poor. Conversely, those who say this is no time to let up on pushing for equality are most likely to think government pays too little attention to the concerns of low-income people (table D.1).

Almost as powerful in explaining differences of view among critics is the perceived adequacy of schools in lower-income areas. Those attaching particular importance to the quality of schools think government is paying too little attention. Conversely, those minimizing the importance of schools think government is doing too much.

A second analysis focused on that portion of the sample who are "mostly supportive" of government. Again, these individuals are not of one mind about how much attention government is paying to low-income households.

Most powerful in explaining views about government's attention to low-income households is how important people find "not trying hard enough" as a reason for poverty. The more importance attached to not trying hard enough, the more likely is the view that government is paying too much attention. Conversely, those who do not see lack of effort as a reason for poverty tend to think government is not doing enough.

Putting the results of these two analyses together, we find that some critics and some supporters of government agree that government is paying too little attention to the poor, but they do so for different reasons:

- Critics reach that conclusion largely because they think now is no time to let up on the issue of race and that inferior schools are a reason for poverty.
- Supporters will come to the conclusion that government is paying too little attention because they think people may remain poor even though they are trying hard to make it on their own.

We also find that some critics and some supporters of government will agree that government is paying too much attention to the poor, but for different reasons:

- Behind critics' thinking is a sense that the country need not push so hard on the matter of race and that inferior schools are not all that important.
- The route for supporters to the conclusion that government pays too much attention to low-income people is that they are not trying hard enough.

Table D.1

Multiple Regressions of Reasons for Poverty and Issue of Race in Explaining Views about Amount of Government Attention to Low-Income People (Among Those "Mostly Critical" and "Mostly Supportive" of Government)

	View associated with		beta	
	Government paying too much attention to low-income people	Government paying too little attention to low-income people	Among those mostly critical of government	Among those mostly supportive of government
Dealing with issue of race	Do not need to push so hard	Now is no time to let up	.24	.10
Poor schools	Nothing to do with being poor	A lot to do with being poor	.19	.10
People not trying hard enough to make it on their own	A lot to do with being poor	Nothing to do with being poor	n.s.[a]	.22
Family circumstances	Nothing to do with being poor	A lot to do with being poor	n.s.	.13
Lack of job skills	Nothing to do with being poor	A lot to do with being poor	n.s.	n.s.
Adjusted R^2 =			.13	.11
n =			335	494

[a]Indicates beta coefficient is not significant at the 95 percent level of confidence.

Table D.2

Multiple Regressions of Possible Explanations for Shifts in Personal Ladder Ratings
(Among Full Sample)

	Shift from past to present	Shift from present to future
Age	−.27[a]	−.38[c]
Personal financial security	.12	−.07[c]
Household income	n.s.[b]	−.07[c]
Education	n.s.	n.s.
Sex	0.6	n.s.
Rating of federal government	n.s.	n.s.
Adjusted R^2 =	.07	.19
n =	1902	1833

[a] The negative coefficient indicates that the amount of progress (past-to-present shift) decreases as age increases.

[b] Indicates beta coefficient is not significant at the 95 percent level of confidence.

[c] The negative coefficients indicate that the amount of optimism (present-to-future shift) decreases as age increases, as financial security increases, and as household income increases.

SHIFTS IN PERSONAL LADDER RATINGS

The respondent's sense of progress or decline is determined by subtracting the past ladder rating from the present rating. Accordingly the difference can extend from +10 (greatest progress) to −10 (greatest decline). Similarly, optimism or pessimism is determined by subtracting the present ladder rating from the future rating with differences extending from +10 (greatest optimism) to −10 (greatest pessimism).

Age contributes more than other considerations to respondents' sense of progress or decline from the past and optimism or pessimism about the future (table D.2). We should add that this pattern holds when regressions are limited first to critics of government and then to supporters of government.

INFORMATION ABOUT GOVERNMENT, INTEREST IN NEWS, AND AMBIVALENCE

The regression examined degrees of ambivalence among critics of government (as described below in "Ambivalence among Critics of Government"). The regression tested the effects of self-reported interest in "what's going on in government and public affairs," the amount of news consumed, knowledge about the governmental system, and formal education.

Table D.3

Multiple Regression of Knowledge about Government and Attention to
News as Explanations for Ambivalence among Those Critical of Government

How closely follow what's going on in government and public affairs	.20
Knowledge about governmental system	.19
Amount of news consumed	.10
Education	n.s.[a]
Adjusted R^2 =	.10
n =	764

[a]Indicates beta coefficient is not significant at the 95 percent level of confidence.

It shows that ambivalence is associated with less attention to what is going on in government, less knowledge about government, and less consumption of news. Education has no significant relationship to ambivalence when these other considerations are taken into account. The Adjusted R^2 is quite low, suggesting that the cumulative effect of these variables is modest in explaining ambivalence in the thinking of critics of government (table D.3).

INTENSITY OF RELIGIOUS BELIEFS AND PRACTICES

The purpose of the analysis was to determine the relative importance of variables in explaining ambivalence in the thinking of critics of government. Accordingly the regression was based only on those who are "mostly critical" of government. In addition, the regression was limited to respondents who consider themselves Christians: Protestant, Roman Catholic, Mormon, Orthodox, or other unspecified Christian faith. This was in order to gauge the appeal of issues of concern to conservative Christian organizations as well as the importance of religious beliefs and practices. The *more* likely critics are to share positions of Christian organizations, the *less* likely they are to be ambivalent as critics (table D.4).

AMBIVALENCE AMONG CRITICS OF GOVERNMENT

Multiple regressions regarding ambivalence among those "mostly critical" of government are limited to respondents giving the "critical" response to two or three of the three questions about general views of government. However, rather than compare the views of Steady Critics and Ambivalent Critics (as in chapters 2 through 5), *degrees of ambivalence* are examined. Instead of a threshold of support for specific ac-

Table D.4

Multiple Regression of the Intensity of
Religious Beliefs/Practices and Views on Issues of Concern to
Conservative Christian Organizations as Explanations for Ambivalence
(Among Critics of Government Who Are Christians)

Sex education	.22
Homosexuality as threat to family	.12
Intensity of religious beliefs/practices	.10
Divorce	n.s.[a]
Adjusted R^2 =	.06
n =	555

[a]Indicates beta coefficient is not significant at the 95 percent level of confidence.

tivities (nine or ten versus eight or fewer), the actual number of activities supported is used.

Numerous regressions were run to test the strength of competing explanations for ambivalence in thinking about government. Variables selected for inclusion were those where significant differences of view had emerged between Steady Critics and Ambivalent Critics (summarized earlier in tables 4.10 and 5.15).

In the course of these analyses, ten dimensions appeared time and again as contributing significantly to our understanding of ambivalence (table D.5).

These dimensions prove remarkably stable in accounting for ambivalence. That is, the importance of their contribution is not diminished when other plausible explanations are entered into the mix. Thus, for example, if education is added to the mix, its relationship with ambivalence is not strong enough to be statistically significant. The same is true for other factors one might expect would make an important contribution. These are spelled out in the main body of the text.

Most influential in explaining ambivalence are respondents' views about how much attention government is paying to low-income people. Our concern was that the strength of the relationship might result from including in the ambivalence measure support for activities relating to poverty. (Included in the ten specific activities are job training, Medicaid, housing assistance, and support for teachers' salaries in poor school districts.)

As a check on this possibility, we redefined the measure of ambivalence. Rather than counting how many of ten activities the respondent supported, we counted the six not making explicit reference to issues of poverty. We then reran the final regression. It showed that the question about government attention to the low-income pop-

Table D.5

Multiple Regression of Explanations for Ambivalence
(Among Critics of Government)

	View associated with		
	More ambivalence	Less ambivalence	beta
Amount of attention government pays to low-income people	Too little attention	Too much attention	.25
Sense of interdependence	Problems more than local	Problems mostly local	.20
Confidence in the quality of work in federal executive agencies	More	Less	.18
Dealing with the issue of race	Now is no time to let up	Do not need to push so hard	.14
Age	Younger	Older	.13
Getting ahead in the United States	Hard work often not enough	Anyone can with hard work	.12
Follow what's going on in government and public affairs	Hardly at all	Most of the time	.09
Conservative Christian groups active in politics	Not good for the country	Good for the country	.08
Worry about personal financial situation	More worried	Less worried	.08
Teaching young people values of personal responsibility and moral character	Country is making progress	Country is losing ground	.07
Adjusted R^2 =			.37
n =			637

ulation remained important in accounting for degrees of ambivalence among critics of government (see the top of table D.6).

AMBIVALENCE AMONG SUPPORTERS OF GOVERNMENT

Comparable analyses were conducted regarding the portion of the sample classified as "mostly supportive." Similarly, rather than compare the views of Steady Supporters and Ambivalent Supporters (as in chapters 2 through 5), *degrees of ambivalence* are examined here, using the actual number of activities respondents want to see continued or expanded. In these analyses, the greater the number of activities supported,

Table D.6

Multiple Regressions of Explanations for Ambivalence Using Measures of Ambivalence That Include and Exclude Activities of Government Relating to Poverty (Among Critics and Supporters of Government)

	Ambivalence measured as	
	The number of specific activities supported when those relating to poverty are *included*	The number of specific activities supported when those relating to poverty are *excluded*
Possible explanations among critics		
Amount of government attention to low-income people	.25	.20
Sense of interdependence	.20	.22
Confidence in federal executive agencies	.18	.15
Dealing with issue of race	.14	.14
Age	−.13[a]	−.15[a]
Getting ahead in the United States	.12	.11
Follow public affairs	−.09[a]	−.08[a]
Conservative Christian groups	.08	n.s.[b]
Personal financial security	−.08[a]	n.s.
Teaching personal responsibility	.07	n.s.
Adjusted R^2 =	.37	.27
n =	637	637
Possible explanations among supporters		
Amount of government attention to low-income people	.21	.11
Dealing with issue of race	.18	.17
Changes possible re government	.09	.12
Juvenile crime	.09	n.s.
Adjusted R^2 =	.11	.06
n =	964	964

[a] The negative coefficients indicate that ambivalence decreases as age increases, as attention to public affairs increases, or as financial security increases.

[b] Indicates beta coefficient is not significant at the 95 percent level of confidence.

the less the respondent's ambivalence; the fewer the number of activities supported, the greater the respondent's ambivalence.

Our approach was similar to that among critics. Numerous regressions were conducted as we examined the importance of particular facets of opinion in explaining ambivalence. We also paid attention to those items on which there were statistically significant differences between those who were "steady" and "ambivalent."

As in regressions among critics of government, we found several dimensions emerging repeatedly among supporters regardless of the mix of independent variables entered into the regressions. But, whereas it took ten factors to account for ambivalence among critics, only a few were needed regarding ambivalence among supporters. Also, unlike regressions among critics, these analyses did not prove very helpful in explaining ambivalence among supporters. As seen in figure 6.1 in the main text, this is due in part to the fact that there is such little variation among supporters of government in the degree of ambivalence they express.

As in the regressions among critics, we were concerned that the influence of the item about government's attention to the poor might result from inclusion in the ambivalence measure support for four activities relating to poverty. Accordingly we ran the regressions with two measures of ambivalence: one included the poverty activities, the other excluded the poverty-related activities. We found a modest overlap between the government attention item and the ambivalence measure, which included the poverty activities. This regression produced a higher beta (.21) than emerged in the regression on the ambivalence measure excluding the poverty activities (.11) (see the bottom of table D.6).

Accordingly we relied on the ambivalence measure that excluded the four activities of government dealing with poverty. On that basis what little ambivalence is explained in the regression is due to the roughly equal influence of views on dealing with race, possible changes in government, and government's attention to the poor (table D.7).

Dimensions that play no significant role in accounting for ambivalence in the thinking of supporters of government are:

- Education;
- Household income or sense of financial security;
- Knowledge about the governmental system;
- The amount of news consumed;
- The intensity of religious beliefs and practices;
- Views on whether immigrants should try to fit into the American mainstream or live by their own traditions;
- Concern about diminished respect for the value of self-restraint versus affirmation of the importance of self-expression even if others do not approve;
- Views on homosexuality, sex education, and divorce;

Table D.7
Multiple Regression of Possible Explanations for
Ambivalence among Supporters of Government

	View associated with		
	More ambivalence	Less ambivalence	beta
Dealing with the issue of race	Do not need to push so hard	Now is no time to let up	.17
How much can be done to make government work better?	Not much can be done	Major changes are possible	.12
Amount of attention government pays to low-income people	Too much attention	Too little attention	.11
Adjusted R^2 =			.06
n =			964

- How much what government does is seen to bear on people directly;
- Views about juvenile crime and police searches;
- Concern about the gap between rich and poor; and,
- The respondent's sex.

EXPLAINING SHIFTS IN RATINGS OF THE STATE OF THE NATION

Perceived progress or decline for the country was measured by subtracting the past national ladder rating from the present national rating. Accordingly the difference can extend from +10 (greatest progress) to −10 (greatest decline). Similarly, optimism or pessimism is determined by subtracting the present national ladder rating from the future rating with differences extending from +10 (greatest optimism) to −10 (greatest pessimism).

To test the strength of the relationship of ambivalence about government and these ladder-rating shifts, we included in the regressions other possible explanations for the perceived state of the nation. Three sociodemographic characteristics that seemed pertinent were education, age, and financial security. Measures of government performance were also included: confidence in the quality of work of federal agencies and in the U.S. Congress.

Finally, we tested the effect of specific issues some associate with the direction in which the nation is headed: progress or decline in the teaching of personal responsibility; progress or decline in leadership that goes beyond short-term solutions; views on pushing for racial equality; concern about lack of restraint in personal conduct; and whether economic growth means all gain or the gap between rich and poor gets bigger.

The regression shows that ambivalence about government is a factor in explaining the ladder-rating shifts. Among critics, ambivalence contributes to a sense the nation has made progress over the last five years. Among supporters, ambivalence helps account for the feeling things have slipped backward in the last five years and will not get better in the next five (table D.8).

None of these regressions explain much of the variation that occurs in the ladder ratings. This is seen by the low Adjusted R^2 for all four regressions. The important point, however, is that ambivalence about government has a relationship to the shifts in ladder ratings that is strong enough to be statistically significant when other possible explanations for the ladder shifts are also taken into account.

RATINGS OF GOVERNMENT AND
THE CURRENT STATE OF THE NATION

In the course of the analyses of national ladder ratings, we found significantly different results were produced depending upon the approach taken to measure government performance. We found this when looking at possible explanations for ratings respondents gave when asked where the country stands at the present time. The regressions included key sociodemographic characteristics as well as a variety of questions on political matters that might explain present national ladder ratings.

Two regressions yielded quite different results when alternative measures of governmental performance were introduced. The first measured government performance in terms of public confidence in the U.S. Congress and federal agencies. It showed that government performance was one of a number of factors that influenced the national ladder rating. Also included were the two components of our measure of ambivalence: the index of "general attitudes" toward government's scope and power and the index of support for "specific activities" of government.

The alternative measure of government performance was respondents' rating of "the job the federal government is doing." This approach to government performance overwhelmed all other dimensions being taken into account. It diminished the importance of general views about government and assessments of leadership. The rating question also produced a higher Adjusted R^2 than the confidence questions primarily because of the strength of its relationship to the national ladder rating (table D.9).

This finding suggests that asking respondents to rate the performance of the federal government is very close to asking how well the country is doing at the present time.[3] In other words, if two measures are picking up pretty much the same thing, it is difficult to assert that one is causing or explaining the other.

---

[3] In fact, there is a strong relationship between the two questions (r=.44).

Table D.8

Multiple Regressions of Possible Explanations for National Ladder Rating Shifts among Critics and Supporters of Government

	Shift from past to present		Shift from present to future	
	Among critics	Among supporters	Among critics	Among supporters
Key sociodemographic characteristics				
Education	.16	.15	n.s.	n.s.
Age	n.s.[a]	.08	n.s.	n.s.
Financial security	n.s.	n.s.	n.s.	-.08[d]
Performance of government				
Confidence in federal agencies	n.s.	n.s.	n.s.	n.s.
Confidence in U.S. Congress	n.s.	n.s.	n.s.	.10
Concerns regarding direction of the nation				
Teaching personal responsibility: country is making progress versus losing ground	n.s.	.15	n.s.	n.s.
Leaders with new ideas: country is making progress versus losing ground	.14	.12	n.s.	.13
Dealing with issue of race: no time to let up versus not need push so hard	n.s.	n.s.	.15	n.s.
Declining self-restraint versus free expression	-.13[b]	-.07[b]	.11	n.s.
Growth in economy means all gain versus rich/poor gap	n.s.	-.11[c]	n.s.	n.s.
Ambivalence about government	.17	-.08[c]	n.s.	-.13[d]
Adjusted R^2 =	.08	.09	.04	.05
n =	584	772	567	769

[a] Indicates beta coefficient is not significant at the 95 percent level of confidence.

[b] The negative coefficient indicates that feelings of decline are associated with seeing a need for more respect for the value of self-restraint.

[c] The negative coefficient indicates that feelings of decline are associated with the view that all gain when the economy grows and with greater amounts of ambivalence.

[d] The negative coefficient indicates that feelings of pessimism are associated with increased financial security and with increased ambivalence.

Table D.9

Multiple Regressions of Possible Explanations for National Present Ladder Ratings Using Alternative Measures of Government Performance (Among Full Sample)

	Government performance measured as	
	Confidence in U.S. Congress and federal agencies	Rating of the job the federal government is doing
General views of government: more supportive to more critical	.13[a]	.05[a]
Leaders with new ideas: country making progress versus losing ground	.13	.08
Teaching personal responsibility: country making progress versus losing ground	.10	.06
Age	.09	.07
Growth in economy means all gain versus rich/poor gap gets bigger	−.08[b]	−.07[b]
Specific activities of government: support more to support fewer	.08[c]	n.s.
Education	.07	.06
Being affected by government	n.s.[d]	n.s.
Income	.07	.05
Confidence in the U.S. Congress	.08	—[e]
Confidence in federal agencies	.07	—
Rating of the federal government	—[e]	.38
Adjusted R^2 =	.12	.22
n =	1,533	1,617

[a] The positive coefficient indicates performance ratings increase as general views of government become more supportive.

[b] The negative coefficient indicates performance ratings decrease as the view all gain increases.

[c] The positive coefficient indicates performance ratings increase as number of specific activities supported increases.

[d] Beta coefficient not significant at the 95 percent level of confidence.

[e] No coefficient computed since the variable was not included.

LIKELIHOOD OF VOTING

Regressions were conducted separately for critics and supporters of government using a five-value measure of likelihood of voting as the dependent variable (described in appendix C).

Table D.10

Multiple Regressions of Possible Explanations for Likelihood of Voting
(Among Critics and Supporters of Government)

	Among critics	Among supporters
Age	.22	.29
Education	.21	.29
Ambivalence among critics	−.13[a]	—[c]
Amount of news consumed	.11	.14
Intensity of religious beliefs/practices	.10	n.s.
Personal financial security	n.s.[b]	n.s.
Sex	n.s.	n.s.
Being affected by government	n.s.	n.s.
Confidence in the U.S. Congress	n.s.	n.s.
Confidence in federal agencies	n.s.	n.s.
Ambivalence among supporters	—[c]	n.s.
Adjusted R^2 =	.17	.23
n =	692	904

[a] The negative coefficient indicates that voting likelihood decreases as ambivalence increases.

[b] Beta coefficient not significant at the 95 percent level of confidence.

[c] No coefficient computed since the variable was not included.

Among critics of government, ambivalence has a significant influence on voting likelihood. The more ambivalent people are, the less likely they are to show up election day. Conversely, the less ambivalent critics of government are, the more likely they are to vote. No such relationship emerges among supporters (table D.10).

PARTICIPATION BETWEEN ELECTIONS

Findings similar to voting likelihood emerged in regressions regarding other forms of participation between elections. The more ambivalent critics of government are, the less likely they are to get involved. Conversely, less ambivalent critics participate more between elections. No significant relationship along these lines exists among supporters of government. Among supporters, education plays the dominant role in determining how actively engaged people are between elections: those who have more education being more likely to be politically engaged (table D.11).

Table D.11

Multiple Regressions of Possible Explanations for Political Participation Other than
Voting (Among Critics and Supporters of Government)

	Among critics	Among supporters
Amount of news consumed	.26	.15
Ambivalence among critics	−.19[a]	—
Education	.16	.25
Intensity of religious beliefs/practices	.15	n.s.
Confidence in federal agencies	−.11[a]	n.s.
Age	n.s.[b]	n.s.
Being affected by government	n.s.	n.s.
Personal financial security	n.s.	n.s.
Sex	n.s.	n.s.
Confidence in the U.S. Congress	n.s.	n.s.
Ambivalence among supporters	—[c]	n.s.
Adjusted R^2 =	.19	.12
n =	355	426

[a]The negative coefficient indicates that participation decreases as ambivalence increases and as confidence in federal agencies increases.

[b]Indicates beta coefficient is not significant at the 95 percent level of confidence.

[c]No coefficient computed since the variable not included.

Appendix E
Sample Design and Composition

THE SAMPLE DESIGN DEVELOPED BY SCHULMAN, RONCA, AND BUCUVALAS, Inc. (SRBI) and used in this survey was a random digit dialing (RDD) sample of the entire United States. The sample was stratified by census region to control for different response rates among regions. Within each region and designated counties within regions, a simple random sample of banks of working residential telephone numbers was drawn. A bank consists of the area code, exchange, and first two digits of the number. Within each selected bank, the final two digits of the phone number were randomly chosen thereby permitting inclusion of unlisted telephones. The eligibility of each number was checked to ensure it was a residential number in service. The sample was released in replicates.

Up to five calls were made to designated numbers on different days and at different times of day and evening. At the household interviewers asked to speak with the youngest male 18 years or older at home at the time of the call and, if no male was present, to the oldest female. When the quota of men or women for each replicate was reached, interviewers asked to speak to respondents of the opposite sex until that quota was filled. Refusals and respondents who terminated the interview before it was completed were contacted two days later to attempt completion of the interview.

The sample was weighted to compensate for three possible selection biases. First, the number of separate phone lines for each household was taken into account to prevent households with more than one phone number from having an unequal chance of falling into the sample. Since the number of adults in a household affects the probability of a respondent being selected, a second weighting was introduced. Third, since the respondent was selected from household members at home at the time of the call,

Table E.1

Sample Composition

	Weighted percent	Unweighted percent	Number of interviews
Sex			
Male	47.6	48.1	962
Female	52.4	51.9	1,040
Age			
18 to 29	22.9	19.1	382
30 to 39	22.4	21.9	439
40 to 49	19.1	21.2	425
50 to 64	17.7	20.0	400
65 and over	16.7	16.8	333
Refuse/no answer	1.1	1.1	23
Household income			
Under $15,000	9.7	9.4	188
$15,000–$29,999	20.9	21.4	428
$30,000–$49,999	28.7	29.2	584
$50,000–$74,999	18.0	17.4	349
$75,000–$99,999	7.7	7.8	157
$100,000 and over	4.6	5.7	115
Refuse/no answer	10.4	9.0	181
Region: Census			
Northeast	20.1	18.0	360
South	34.5	34.4	689
Midwest	24.5	24.5	490
West	20.9	23.1	463
Region: By tradition[a]			
Northeast/Mid-Atlantic	24.5	22.2	444
South	23.3	23.0	461
Midwest	24.5	24.5	490
Southwest/Mountain	13.4	15.2	304
Far west	14.3	15.1	303
Locality size			
Large city	17.9	18.2	364
Suburb near city	21.4	22.4	449
Small city/town	38.4	37.5	751
Rural area	21.0	20.9	418
Not ascertained	1.4	1.0	20
Education			
Less than high school	16.5	9.7	194
Grade 8 or less	3.0	1.7	34
Some high school	13.5	8.0	160

	Weighted percent	Unweighted percent	Number of interviews
High school/technical/GED	37.3	35.8	716
Some college	23.3	24.4	488
College and beyond	<u>22.6</u>	<u>29.7</u>	<u>595</u>
College graduate	14.2	18.0	360
Graduate school	8.4	11.7	235
Refuse/no answer	0.4	0.4	9
Race			
White	78.8	81.3	1,628
Black	9.0	7.9	158
Asian/Pacific Islander	2.8	2.1	42
Native American/Alaskan	1.1	1.0	21
Of mixed race (volunteered)	3.2	3.0	60
Other (volunteered)	3.5	3.1	63
Refuse/no answer	1.6	1.5	30
Hispanic/Latino origin			
Yes	6.2	5.2	105
No	92.8	93.7	1,876
Refuse/no answer	1.0	1.0	21
Employment status			
Executive/professional	25.2	29.9	599
White collar	17.3	16.6	322
Blue collar	24.7	20.7	415
Retired	16.8	17.1	343
Other nonlabor force	14.0	13.7	274
Refuse/no answer	2.0	1.9	39
Marital status			
Married	62.1	60.0	1,201
Separated/divorced	10.5	13.2	265
Widowed	6.2	7.4	149
Never married	21.3	19.3	387

[a]States included in these regions were as follows:
Northeast/Mid-Atlantic: Conn., D.C., Del., Maine, Md., Mass., N.H., N.J., N.Y., Pa., R.I., Vt.
South: Ala., Ark., Fla., Ga., Ky., La., Miss., N.C., S.C., Tenn., Va., W.Va.
Midwest: Iowa, Ill., Ind., Kans., Mich., Minn., Mo., N.Dak., Nebr., Ohio, S. Dak., Wis.
Southwest/Mountain: Ariz., Colo., Idaho, Mont., N.Mex., Nev., Okla., Tex., Utah, Wyo.
Far west: Alaska, Calif., Hawaii, Oreg., Wash.

some bias may be introduced because of the likelihood of being at home. This was addressed by weighting to reflect how many of the previous three days the respondent was at home at the time of the call.[1]

Finally, to minimize problems with biases of unknown origins, the sample was weighted using U.S. Census Bureau data for 1996 and 1997 to ensure its representativeness within region by sex, age, and education.

A total of 2,002 interviews were conducted between August 22 and September 15, 1997. The overall maximum expected sampling error at the 95 percent level of confidence is ±2.2 percentage points. Sampling tolerances have been taken into account in the analyses reported here with respect to the significance of differences between percentages among subgroups and the significance of coefficients in multiple regressions.

The cooperation rate (defined as the number of completed interviews divided by the number of completed interviews plus refusals and terminations) was 70.8 percent.

---

[1] See Alfred Politz and W.R. Simmons, "An Attempt to Get the 'Not at Homes' into the Sample without Callbacks," *Journal of the American Statistical Association* 44 (March 1949): 9–31; and Alfred Politz and W.R. Simmons, "Note on 'An Attempt to Get the Not at Homes into the Sample without Callbacks,'" *Journal of the American Statistical Association* 45 (March 1950): 136–37.

Bibliography

Allport, Gordon W., "Attitudes," in C.C. Murchison, ed., *A Handbook of Social Psychology*, (Worcester, Mass.: Clark University Press, 1935), chap. 17.

Allport, Gordon W., Philip E. Vernon, and Gardner Lindzey, "A Scale for Measuring the Dominant Interests in Personality," in *A Study of Values*, rev. ed. (Boston: Houghton Mifflin, 1951).

Arendt, Cheryl Mercado, *The Religious Right: Self-Identification and Measurement of Political Groups*, paper prepared for delivery at the American Association for Public Opinion Research, Salt Lake City, May 16–19, 1996.

Aronson, Elliot, "Dissonance Theory: Progress and Problems," in Robert P. Abelson, E. Aronson, W.J. McGuire, T.M. Newcomb, M.J. Rosenberg, and P.H. Tannenbaum, eds., *Theories of Cognitive Consistency: A Sourcebook* (Chicago: Rand McNally, 1968), 5–27.

Beer, Samuel H., "In Search of a New Public Philosophy," in Anthony King, ed., *The New American Political System* (Washington, D.C.: American Enterprise Institute, 1978), 5–44.

———, "Introduction" to Timothy Conlan, *New Federalism: Intergovernmental Reform from Nixon to Reagan* (Washington, D.C.: Brookings Institution Press, 1988).

———, "Ragged Individualism," *Wilson Quarterly* (Summer 1996): 89–91.

———, *To Make a Nation: The Rediscovery of American Federalism* (Cambridge, Mass.: Harvard University Press, 1993).

Bennett, Stephen Earl, *Apathy in America, 1960–1984: Causes and Consequences of Citizen Political Influence* (Dobbs Ferry, N.Y.: Transnational Publishers, Inc., 1986).

Bennett, William, "What to Do About the Children," *Commentary* (March 1995): 23–28.

Bishop, George, "The Effect of Education on Ideological Consistency," *Public Opinion Quarterly* 40 (1976): 337–48.

Cantril, Albert H., ed., *Psychology, Humanism, and Scientific Inquiry: The Selected Essays of Hadley Cantril* (New Brunswick, N.J.: Transaction Books, 1998).

Cantril, Albert H., and Charles W. Roll Jr., *Hopes and Fears of the American People* (New York: Universe Books, 1971).

Cantril, Albert H., and Susan Davis Cantril, "Polls Portray a Considered and Stable Public Opinion," *Public Perspective* (June/July 1996): 23–26.

———, *Unemployment, Government, and the American People* (Washington, D.C.: Public Research, Inc. 1978).

237

Cantril, Hadley, et al., *Gauging Public Opinion* (Princeton, N.J.: Princeton University Press, 1944).

Cantril, Hadley, "General and Specific Attitudes," *Psychological Review* (Psychological Monographs Series) 42, no. 5 (1932).

————, *The Pattern of Human Concerns* (New Brunswick, N.J.: Rutgers University Press, 1965).

Carville, James, *We're Right, They're Wrong: A Handbook for Spirited Progressives* (New York: Random House, 1996).

Chubb, John E., Michael G. Hagen, and Paul M. Sniderman, "Ideological Reasoning," in Paul M. Sniderman, Richard A. Brody, and Philip E. Tetlock, eds., *Reasoning and Choice: Explorations in Political Psychology* (New York: Cambridge University Press, 1991), 140–63.

Clohan, William C., Jr., "Education and Training in the Public Debate," in James Leach and William P. McKenzie, eds., *A Newer World: The Progressive Republican Vision of America* (Lanham, Md.: Madison Books, 1988), 95–111.

Clore, Gerald L., "Why Emotions Require Cognition," in Paul Ekman and Richard J. Davidson, eds., *The Nature of Emotion: Fundamental Questions* (New York: Oxford University Press, 1994).

Conlan, Timothy, *New Federalism: Intergovernmental Reform from Nixon to Reagan* (Washington, D.C.: Brookings Institution Press, 1988).

Conover, Pamela Johnston, and Stanley Feldman, "The Origins and Meaning of Liberal/Conservative Self-Identifications," *American Journal of Political Science* 25 (November 1981): 617–45.

Council on Excellence in Government, *Excellence in Government* (a national survey conducted by Peter D. Hart and Robert Teeter, March 1995).

————, *Findings for a Research Project about Attitudes Toward Government* (a national survey conducted by Peter D. Hart and Robert Teeter, March 1997).

Cox, Harvey, "The Warring Visions of the Religious Right," *Atlantic Monthly* (November 1995): 59–69.

Crespi, Irving, *Pre-Election Polling: Sources of Accuracy and Error* (New York: Russell Sage Foundation, 1988).

Cronbach, Lee J., "Coefficient Alpha and the Internal Structure of Tests," *Psychometrika* 16 (1951): 297–334.

Delli Carpini, Michael X., and Scott Keeter, *What Americans Know about Politics and Why It Matters* (New Haven, Conn.: Yale University Press, 1996).

Dennis, Jack, "Political Independence in America, Part I: On Being an Independent Partisan Supporter," *British Journal of Political Science* 18 (January 1988): 77–109.

Devitt, James, *The Effect of Critical News Coverage on Public Confidence in Institutions*, paper presented at the American Association for Public Opinion Research, Salt Lake City, 1996.

Dionne, E.J., Jr., "The Irony of Democratic History," in Peter B. Kovler, ed., *Democrats and the American Idea* (Washington, D.C.: Center for National Policy Press, 1992), 305–16.

———, *They Only Look Dead: Why Progressives Will Dominate the Next Political Era* (New York: Simon & Schuster, 1996).

———, *Why Americans Hate Politics* (New York: Simon & Schuster, 1991).

Edelman, Peter, "The Worst Thing Bill Clinton Has Done," *Atlantic Monthly* (March 1997).

Faux, Jeff, *The Party's Not Over: A New Vision for the Democrats* (New York: Basic Books, 1996).

Feldman, Stanley, and John Zaller, "The Political Culture of Ambivalence: Ideological Responses to the Welfare State," *American Journal of Political Science* 36 (February 1992): 268–307.

Festinger, Leon, *A Theory of Cognitive Dissonance* (Evanston, Ill.: Row, Peterson, 1957).

Forman, Ira, "Introduction" to Peter B. Kovler, ed., *Democrats and the American Idea* (Washington, D.C.: Center for National Policy Press, 1992), xi–xxvi.

Free, Lloyd A., and Hadley Cantril, *Political Beliefs of Americans* (New Brunswick, N.J.: Rutgers University Press, 1968).

Galston, William, and Elaine Ciulla Kamarck, *The Politics of Evasion: Democrats and the Presidency* (Washington, D.C.: Progressive Policy Institute, September 1989).

Gardner, Howard, *Frames of Mind: The Theory of Multiple Intelligences* (New York: Basic Books, 1983).

Gillon, Steven M., "The Travail of the Democrats: Search for a New Majority," in Peter B. Kovler, ed., *Democrats and the American Idea* (Washington, D.C.: Center for National Policy Press, 1992), 285–303.

Graham, Cole Blease, Jr., Robert W. Oldendick, and Michael W. Link, "Across the Great Divide: Examining Black-White Differences in Political Attitudes," paper presented at the American Association for Public Opinion Research, Salt Lake City, 1996.

Greenberg, Stanley B., *Middle Class Dreams: The Politics of Power and the New American Majority* (New York: Times Books, 1995).

Hamby, Alonzo L., "The Democratic Moment: FDR to LBJ," in Peter B. Kovler, ed., *Democrats and the American Idea* (Washington, D.C.: Center for National Policy Press, 1992), 247–84.

Hamilton, William R., and Robert Teeter, *Public Opinion Toward Entitlements and the Federal Deficit*, A National Voter Survey for The Concord Coalition, June 1995.

Hochschild, Jennifer L., *What's Fair? American Beliefs about Distributive Justice* (Cambridge, Mass.: Harvard University Press, 1981).

Hunter, James Davison, and Carl Bowman, *The State of Disunion: 1996 Survey of American Political Culture* (Ivy, Va.: In Medias Res Educational Foundation, 1996).

Katz, Daniel, "Consistency for What? The Functional Approach," in Robert P. Abelson, E. Aronson, W.J. McGuire, T.M. Newcomb, M.J. Rosenberg, and P.H. Tannenbaum, eds., *Theories of Cognitive Consistency: A Sourcebook* (Chicago: Rand McNally, 1968), 179–200.

Keith, Bruce E., David B. Magleby, Candice J. Nelson, Elizabeth Orr, Mark C. Westlye, and Raymond E. Wolfinger, *The Myth of the Independent Voter* (Berkeley: University of California Press, 1992).

Kerlinger, Fred N., *Liberalism and Conservatism: The Nature and Structure of Social Attitudes* (Hillsdale, N.J.: Erlbaum Associates, 1984).

Kerr, W., "Untangling the Liberalism-Conservatism Continuum," *Journal of Social Psychology* 35 (1952): 111–25.

Kinder, Donald R., "Diversity and Complexity in American Public Opinion," in Ada W. Finifter, ed., *Political Science: The State of the Discipline* (Washington, D.C.: American Political Science Association, 1983), 389–425.

Kinder, Donald R., and D. Roderick Kiewiet, "Economic Discontent and Political Behavior: The Role of Personal Grievances and Collective Economic Judgments in Congressional Voting," *American Journal of Political Science* 23 (August 1979): 495–527.

———, "Sociotropic Politics: The American Case," *British Journal of Political Science* 11 (1981): 129–61.

Kinder, Donald R., and Lynn M. Sanders, *Divided by Color: Racial Politics and Democratic Ideals* (Chicago, Ill.: University of Chicago, 1996).

Kinder, Donald R., and David Sears, "Public Opinion and Political Action," in Gardner Lindzey and E. Aronson, eds., *Handbook of Social Psychology*, 4th ed. (New York: Random House, 1985).

King, David C., "The Polarization of American Parties and Mistrust of Government," in Joseph S. Nye Jr., Philip D. Zelikow, and David C. King, eds., *Why People Don't Trust Government* (Cambridge, Mass.: Harvard University Press, 1997), 155–78.

Klinsky, Steven B., "Untying the Knot: The Economics of Honesty," in James Leach and William P. McKenzie, eds., *A Newer World: The Progressive Republican Vision of America* (Lanham, Md.: Madison Books, 1988), 23–47.

Kristol, William, "The Future of Conservatism in the United States," *The American Enterprise* (July/August 1994).

———, "The Politics of Liberty, the Sociology of Virtue," in Lamar Alexander and Chester E. Finn Jr., eds., *The New Promise of American Life* (Indianapolis: Hudson Institute, 1995).

Krueger, E.T., and W.C. Reckless, *Social Psychology* (New York: Longmans, 1931).

Kuttner, Robert, *Life of the Party: Democratic Prospects in 1988 and Beyond* (New York: Viking, 1987).

Lacey, Michael J., "Federalism and National Planning: The Nineteenth Century Legacy," in Robert Fishman, ed., *The American Planning Tradition: Culture and Policy* (Washington, D.C.: Woodrow Wilson Center Press; Baltimore: Johns Hopkins University Press, forthcoming).

Lane, Robert E., *Political Ideology* (New York: Free Press, 1962).

League of Women Voters, "Alienation Not a Factor in Nonvoting," news release on survey by The Mellman Group and Wirthlin Worldwide, May 30, 1996.

Levitin, Theresa E., and Warren E. Miller, "Ideological Interpretations of Presidential Elections," *American Political Science Review* 73 (1979): 751–71.

Luttbeg, Norman R., "The Structure of Beliefs among Leaders and the Public," *Public Opinion Quarterly* 32 (1968): 398–409.

Mann, Thomas E., "Is the Era of Big Government Over?" *Public Perspective* 9 (February/March 1998): 27–29.

Mayer, William G., *The Changing American Mind: How and Why American Public Opinion Changed Between 1960 and 1988* (Ann Arbor: University of Michigan Press, 1992).

————, *The Divided Democrats: Ideological Unity, Party Reform, and Presidential Elections* (Boulder, Colo.: Westview Press, 1996).

McClosky, Herbert J., "Conservatism and Personality," *American Political Science Review* 52 (1958): 27–45.

McClosky, Herbert J., and Alida Brill, *Dimensions of Tolerance: What Americans Believe about Civil Liberties* (New York: Russell Sage, 1983).

McClosky, Herbert, and John Zaller, *The American Ethos: Public Attitudes Toward Capitalism and Democracy* (Cambridge, Mass.: Harvard University Press, 1984).

McKenzie, William P., "A Statement of Principles," in James Leach and Willliam P. McKenzie, eds., *A Newer World: The Progressive Republican Vision of America* (Lanham, Md.: Madison Books, 1988), 1–9.

Miller, Arthur H., "Comment on 'Where's the Schema?'" *American Political Science Review* 85 (December 1991): 1369–76.

————, "Is Confidence Rebounding?" *Public Opinion* 6 (June/July 1983): 16–20.

————, "Political Issues and Trust in Government: 1964–70," *American Political Science Review* 68 (September 1974): 951–72.

Miller, Arthur H., and Stephen A. Borrelli, "Confidence in Government during the 1980s," *American Politics Quarterly* 19 (April 1991): 147–73.

Miller, Arthur H., and Martin P. Wattenberg, "Measuring Party Identification: Independent or No Partisan Preference?" *American Journal of Political Science* 27 (February 1983): 301–17.

Moore, David W., "The 'Religious Right': Definition and Measurement," *Public Perspective* (April/May 1995): 11–13.

Morin, Richard, and Claudia Deane, "Public Blames Clinton, Gives Record Support," *Washington Post*, February 15, 1999, A-1.

Neuman, W. Russell, *The Paradox of Mass Politics: Knowledge and Opinion in the American Electorate* (Cambridge, Mass.: Harvard University Press, 1986), 64–67.

Newman, Katherine S., *Falling from Grace: The Experience of Downward Mobility in the American Middle Class* (New York: Free Press, 1988).

Nie, Norman H., Sidney Verba, and John R. Petrocik, *The Changing American Voter* (Cambridge, Mass.: Harvard University Press, 1979).

Page, Benjamin I., and Robert Y. Shapiro, *The Rational Public: Fifty Years of Trends in Americans' Policy Preferences* (Chicago: University of Chicago Press, 1992).

Peffley, Mark A., and Jon Hurwitz, "A Hierarchical Model of Attitude Constraint," *American Journal of Political Science* 29 (November 1985): 871–90.

Perry, Paul K., "Certain Problems in Election Survey Methodology," *Public Opinion Quarterly* 43 (Fall 1979): 312–25.

Peterson, Paul E., *The Price of Federalism* (Washington, D.C.: Brookings Institution Press, 1995, A Twentieth Century Fund Book).

Pomper, Gerald, ed., *The Election of 1988* (Chatham, N.J.: Chatham House, 1989).

Richardson, Elliot L., "Making Self-Government Work: Recruiting the Best for Public Service," in James Leach and William P. McKenzie, eds., *A Newer World: The Progressive Republican Vision of America* (Lanham, Md.: Madison Books, 1988), 49–59.

Robertson, Rev. Pat, *Teaching Sheet on Divorce and Marriage* (Virginia Beach, Va.: Christian Broadcasting Network, 1966).

Rokeach, Milton, *The Nature of Human Values* (New York: Free Press, 1973).

Rosenstone, Steven J., Roy L. Behr, and Edward H. Lazarus, *Third Parties in America: Citizen Response to Major Party Failure* (Princeton, N.J.: Princeton University Press, 1984), especially chap. 5.

Sandel, Michael J., "America's Search for a New Public Philosophy," *The Atlantic Monthly* (March 1996): 57–74.

Schambra, William A., "The Roots of the American Public Philosophy," in Robert B. Hawkins Jr., ed., *American Federalism: A New Partnership for the Republic* (San Francisco, Calif.: Institute for Contemporary Studies, 1982), 19–35.

Schechter, Stephen L., "The State of American Federalism," in Robert B. Hawkins Jr., ed., *American Federalism: A New Partnership for America* (San Francisco, Calif.: Institute for Contemporary Studies, 1982), 59–74.

Schlesinger, Arthur M., Jr., "In Defense of Government," *Wall Street Journal*, June 7, 1995.

———, "Afterword," in Peter B. Kovler, ed., *Democrats and the American Idea* (Washington, D.C.: Center for National Policy Press, 1992), 359–69.

Schuman, Howard, Charlotte Steeh, Lawrence Bobo, *Racial Attitudes in America: Trends and Interpretations* (Cambridge, Mass.: Harvard University Press, 1985).

Schuman, Howard, and Stanley Presser, *Questions and Answers in Attitude Surveys* (New York: Academic Press, 1981).

Smith, M. Brewster, "Opinions, Personality, and Political Behavior," *American Political Science Review* 52 (March 1958): 1–26.

Smith, M. Brewster, "Personal Values in the Study of Lives," in Robert W. White, ed., *The Study of Lives: Essays on Personality in Honor of Henry A. Murray* (New York: Atherton Press, 1963), 324–47.

Smith, M. Brewster, Jerome S. Bruner, and Robert W. White, *Opinions and Personality* (New York: John Wiley, 1959), 34–37.

Smith, Tom W., *Factors Relating to Misanthropy in Contemporary American Society*, General Social Survey Topical Report No. 20 (June 1996).

———, "Nonattitudes: A Review and Evaluation," in Charles F. Turner and Elizabeth Martin, eds., *Surveying Subjective Phenomena*, vol. 2 (New York: Russell Sage Foundation, 1984), 215–55.

———, "Public Support for Public Spending, 1973–1994," *Public Perspective* 6 (April/May 1995): 1–3.

Sniderman, Paul M., Richard A. Brody, and Philip E. Tetlock, eds., *Reasoning and Choice: Explorations in Political Psychology* (New York: Cambridge University Press, 1991).

Stewart, John G., *One Last Chance: The Democratic Party, 1974–1976* (New York: Praeger, 1974).

Stimson, James A., "Belief Systems: Constraint, Complexity and the 1972 Election," *American Journal of Political Science* 19 (1975): 393–417.

Sullivan, Kathleen M., "The Contemporary Relevance of *The Federalist*," in Alan Brinkley, Nelson W. Polsby, and Kathleen M. Sullivan, *New Federalist Papers: Essays in Defense of the Constitution* (New York: W.W. Norton, 1997): 7–14.

Sullivan, William M., *Reconstructing Public Philosophy* (Berkeley: University of California Press, 1982).

Teixeira, Ruy A., *The Politics of the High-Wage Path: The Challenge Facing Democrats* (Washington, D.C.: Economic Policy Institute, 1994), 9–10.

Tetlock, Philip E., "A Value Pluralism Model of Ideological Reasoning," *Journal of Personality and Social Psychology* 50 (1986): 819–27.

Tomkins, Silvan S., "Left and Right: A Basic Dimension of Ideology and Personality," in Robert W. White, ed., *Study of Lives*, 388–411.

———, "The Quest for Primary Motives: Biography and Autobiography of an Idea," *Journal of Personality and Social Psychology* 41 (1981): 306–29.

Vernon, Philip E., and Gordon W. Allport, "A Test for Personal Values," *Journal of Abnormal and Social Psychology* 26 (1931): 233–48.

Wattenberg, Martin P., *The Decline of American Political Parties, 1952–1994* (Cambridge, Mass.: Harvard University Press, 1996).

Watts, William, and Lloyd A. Free, eds., *State of the Nation* (New York: Universe Books, 1973).

Watts, William, and Lloyd A. Free, *State of the Nation, 1974* (Washington, D.C.: Potomac Associates, 1974).

———, *State of the Nation III* (Lexington, Mass.: Lexington Books, 1978).

Weaver, R. Kent, Robert Y. Shapiro, and Lawrence R. Jacobs, "Poll Trends: Welfare," *Public Opinion Quarterly* 59 (Winter 1995): 606–27.

Zaller, John R., and Stanley Feldman, "A Simple Theory of the Survey Response: Answering Questions versus Revealing Preferences," *American Journal of Political Science* 36 (1992): 579–80.

Ziegler, M., and T. Atkinson, "Information Level and Dimensionality of Liberalism-Conservatism," *Multivariate Behavioral Research* 8 (1973): 195–213.

Index